Friction and Fantasy

Opening Pandora's Jar

REV 12/17/2021

Friction and Fantasy

Opening Pandora's Jar
REV 12/17/2021

Ramon Piñon Jr

CITIOFBOOKS, INC.
3736 Eubank NE Suite A1
Albuquerque, NM 87111-3579
www.citiofbooks.com

Hotline: 1 (877) 389-2759
Fax: 1 (505) 930-7244

Ordering Information:
Quantity sales. Special discounts are available on quantity purchases by corporations, associations, and others. For details, contact the publisher at the address above.

Printed in the United States of America.

ISBN-13:   Paperback   979-8-89391-020-9
           eBook   979-8-89391-021-6

Library of Congress Control Number: 2024905276

Contents

Dedication

For Kathleen and all our children

Acknowledgements

I want to thank Kathleen, my wife and partner of 60 years for prodding me to start this project, for keeping me on track, and believing that it was worthwhile.

Dear Reader

Sex is composed of friction and fantasy

Helen S. Kaplan, 1974

*The acquisition of learning is much more
dangerous than that of any other food or drink. . . But learning
we cannot at the outset put in any other vessel but our minds;
we swallow it as we buy it, and by the time we leave the market
we are already either infected or improved.*

Michel de Montaigne, Essays

Today the discourse on the entire range of human sexuality in all
its complexities is no longer limited to a few specialists, but has become
a widespread public discussion with hundreds of articles appearing in
newspapers, magazines, and in cyberspace, and in dozens of radio and
television reports. It is not my intent to compete with this voluminous
literature. This is not a "how to" book. Rather, the guiding spirit of
this book has been inquiry and reflection. I have employed a historical
perspective to trace the development of our understanding of our
sexuality. This approach has provided for me a more coherent way of
trying to make sense of one of the most emblematic aspects of our
humanity.

This book is not meant for the experts, but, borrowing a phrase
from Samuel Johnson, for the 'common reader', a person seen by
Virginia Woolf as *"guided by an instinct to create for himself out of
whatever odds and ends he can come by, some kind of whole . . ."*
(Virginia Woolf, 1925, *The Common Reader*). I have sought that "kind
of whole" in writing this book, and I hope it serves that purpose for

you. Think of this book as a primer, a way to get you started on your own journey of self-discovery, a journey that may help you begin to appreciate the mysteries and complexities of our humanity in ways that you may not have done so before. This journey is not always an easy one, but I hope you will find my book interesting and rewarding, and that it provides you with the foundation that will form the basis for your own continuing education.

The Irish poet William B. Yeats expressed an interesting take on sex - *"I am still of opinion that only two topics can be of the least interest to a serious and studious mood - sex and the dead."* I would guess that he is probably wrong about sex. It's not clear why 'a serious or studious mood' necessarily interferes with an interest in sex, for sex is probably for most eternally interesting, always intriguing, fascinating, even mysterious, and also often myth laden, controversial, or problematic. Learning about our sexuality is somewhat like reading an adventure story, exciting, full of the unexpected and mystery. It also means learning about ourselves in a particularly intimate, sometimes disturbing way, because we are forced to confront the often self-defeating, perverse, embarrassing aspects of ourselves. Learning about our sexuality not only may affect our well being as individuals, but also collectively, on our society.

Keep in mind that although we have learned a lot about the nuts and bolts of our sexual tissues, we remain woefully ignorant of the diverse ways in which our sexuality develops. Human sexuality is not simply a matter of biology, but an expansive universe of ideas, myths, received ideas, traditions that have a long historical trajectory. We are still groping our way through the mysteries of our sexual universe, trying to disentangle myth from reality, but too often vociferous and irreconcilable religious and cultural ideas interfere with our progress. The scientific exploration of human sexuality while perhaps not in its infancy is still in an early stage, and uncertainties, controversies and conflicting views abound. Do not let these uncertainties trouble you too much – they are the stuff of science. Keep in mind Francis Bacon's advice: *If we begin with certainties, we will end in doubt, but if we begin with doubts and bear them patiently, we may end in certainty.*

As indicated in the Table of Contents, I have divided my discussion into seven chapters titled: *What is Sex Anyway?, Rumination on Sex and Love, Anatomy of Sex, Our Sexual Theater, Erotic Preference and Gender Diversity, Our Disturbing Sexual Corridors, and Sexual Discontent and its Origins.* The subheadings indicate the questions and issues covered in each chapter, and will give you an idea of the scope and extent of my exploration. I have tried to make each chapter as self-contained as possible, so that referral to other chapters is kept to a minimum. I have ordered the topics in a way that seemed reasonable to me, but you are free to peruse them in the order you wish.

There are undoubtedly different ways of telling this story. Being a history buff, I felt a historical perspective would be important in describing how our knowledge developed. I have also included commentaries and vignettes from those who have influenced and shaped the diverse ways in which we view our sexuality. My hope is that my presentation may help you in your own search for understanding. I have striven for objectivity and fairness, but inevitably my personal interpretations have colored my discussions. I leave it to you to come to your own conclusions, but I hope you will continue to remain open to new perspectives.

The list of citations and a bibliography for additional reading is included at the back of the book.

This book is a companion volume to my other book **Our Human Odyssey** *Becoming Female and Male* that focuses on the biological aspects of human reproduction.

Pablo Picasso, "Splitting of the Cell, 1945" (c2013 Estate of Pablo Picasso/Artists Rights Society (ARS), New York) An intriguing way of picturing cell division (1 cell into 2 cells) and sexual reproduction (2 cells into 1)

Chapter 1

What is Sex Anyway?

One and one equals another one. . . That's how we all got here, daughter. (1, Margaret Atwood, *The Female Body*)

For starters – *What is sex?* Don't feel bad if you have trouble with the question. Evolutionary biologists have been struggling with different aspects of this question for at least a century. They understand that the existence of sex is one of the most profound facts in all of biology. They have struggled with two questions: first, how, when, and why did sex originate, and second, why has it persisted and become so ubiquitous? To appreciate these questions lets try to examine them from the point of view of the evolutionary biologist.

To begin we need to understand a few basic facts about the way in which living organisms reproduce. Consider first the bacteria – microscopic (not visible to the naked eye), unicellular (single-celled) organisms. There are thousands of bacterial species. We harbor millions of one bacterial species, *Escherichia coli,* in our large intestine. *E. coli* like other bacteria reproduces *asexually*, meaning that a single cell divides into two cells. Each of the two daughter cells reproduces exactly like the original mother cell, and so on. Hence, each individual cell has only one parent. This is the trademark of an asexual species.

When we come to animals we find something quite different. Animals and also many plants reproduce *sexually*, meaning that each individual animal or plant is formed by the fusion of two specialized cells – the egg and the sperm in animals, or the ovule and the pollen grain in plants. In animals we call the member of the species that produces the egg the female, and the member of the species that produces the sperm the male, the egg always being much larger than the sperm. Hence, the trademark of sexually reproducing species is that every individual has two parents.

The fusion of the egg with the sperm, or fertilization, really gives us the important insight into the biological meaning of sex. Sex, then, represents the mixing or fusion of genetic information (in molecular terms, DNA molecules) from two different organisms. Each one of us then is a sexual being because we originated from the fusion of DNA produced by our mother (the egg) with the DNA produced by our father (the sperm). This insight may appear trivial, but in fact, it is the root of the problem of sex.

The origin of sex

Sex is the queen of problems in evolutionary biology. Perhaps no other natural phenomenon has aroused so much interest; certainly none has sowed so much confusion. (2, G. Bell *The Masterpiece of Nature*)

What accounts for the origin of sex? The short answer is that we don't know, but biologists have been speculating about it for decades. One conjecture favored by many biologists is that sex may have arisen as a survival mechanism, perhaps as a protection against the harsh conditions of the planet in that remote time. The ability to incorporate fragments of DNA from various sources, from other cells, or from the debris of dead cells in the environment may have been essential for survival in the earliest organisms. Many bacteria today have this ability to take up and incorporate free DNA from their environment. Such extremely primitive forms of sex may have been elaborated over many millions of years to the sexual system we find today.

The sexes

Sexual reproduction requires a distinction between the mating partners. Yeast, for example, can reproduce sexually and asexually. How do yeast cells recognize whether they are of the same or different sex? Very simply it turns out – by communicating with each other. The cells of one sex send out a chemical signal, a *mating hormone,* and the cells of the other sex send out a different hormone. If the cells are in close proximity, each cell responds to the mating hormone of the opposite sex, and the two cells engage in a mating ritual that is the first step in the fusion of the two cells.

We humans engage in our own mating rituals, much more complicated than the yeast rituals. Yet the idea is the same and hinges on the ability to recognize a mating partner. Hence, these very simple and ancient organisms display a very sophisticated form of sexuality. Even more remarkable is that the two yeast mating hormones are molecules that are very similar to the hypothalamic hormone, gonadotropin-releasing hormone (GnRH), which is the master regulator of reproduction in all mammals. The striking fact is that the essential features of our own sexual system are extremely ancient.

Why only two sexes?

A two-sex system, one geneticist has quipped, is the reason why it's so hard to get a date on Saturday night. He was probably paraphrasing one of Woody Allen's jocular statements: *"I am a heterosexual . . . but if I were bisexual my chances of getting a date on Saturday night would double."* Allen was right in principle - if there were several sexes, the choice of possible mating partners would increase substantially. With a two sex system our chance of meeting someone of the opposite sex is about one in two, but if there were four sexes, then our chances would go up to three in four, substantially better.

It is very difficult if not impossible, however, to imagine anything other than two sexes. For one thing, what would the different sexes look like? For another, might we have several types of males and several types of females, or would we have only one type of male and several types of females? Females are really crucial because they are the carriers of the young. So let's say that we have several types of males and several types of females. How could they tell who would be a possible partner? Well, recall the yeasts, or even better consider your pet cat. Even from a short distance it is very difficult to tell if a cat is male or female. Cats, however, have no problem. They rely on olfactory (smell) signals. In fact, most animals' olfactory systems are amazingly acute, and by smelling each other or smelling the urine deposited by another animal they can discern each other's sex and reproductive status. Anyway, we could imagine that the different sexes would send out the proper signals – visual, olfactory, chemical – so that mating partners could be identified.

But you may protest - this exercise in imagining a multi-sex system in humans is pointless - there are no multi-sex systems in animals. But are multi-sex organisms possible? In fact, we know that multi-sex organisms exist. Many fungi (yeasts and mushrooms, for example, belong to the fungal world) are known for their experimenting with different forms of sex. The species that takes the prize is a slime mold known as *Physarum polycephalum* that has 13 sexes, each of which can mate with any other sex except its own.

What we don't know is why multi-sex systems are not found in animals. The female versus male distinction was established perhaps around 600 million years ago with the emergence of multi-cellular organisms. A crucial feature of these organisms was that different members of a species began to specialize in either egg or sperm production. We don't really know if multi-sex animals ever appeared, but if they did, they didn't survive. Evolutionary biologists suspect that multisexuality is somehow incompatible with multi-cellularity, but precisely why remains unknown.

The cost of sex

Thinking about sex has been one of the main occupations of evolutionary biologists for almost half a century. (3, Denis Roze, Disentangling the benefits of sex)

Now let's consider the second question – the persistence and ubiquity of sex. There is no denying its success for it has spread everywhere and a huge number of plant and animal species reproduce sexually. For evolutionary biologists, however, sex is a paradox – it is very expensive. They argue that sex exerts at least three kinds of costs.

First, are the genetic costs. A female who reproduced asexually would transmit 100 percent of her genes to her progeny. In contrast, a female who reproduces sexually will only transmit 50 percent of her genes to each of her progeny. Sexual reproduction, according to this argument, introduces a "cost", or disadvantage of 50 percent, when compared to asexual reproduction. In evolutionary terms the cost is huge.

Second, there is the cost of producing males. Males are an extravagant luxury because although they make up roughly half of the population, in the great majority of species they contribute little to the care of offspring. In other words, a female wastes half of her reproductive potential by having sons.

There are many species that opted for the less expensive alternative and they maintain both a sexual as well as an asexual mode of reproduction. Examples include grasshoppers, locusts, moths, mosquitoes, roaches, fruit flies, and bees. Other species have been more radical and have adopted an asexual mode exclusively and dispensed with males altogether. Some of these are geckoes, whiptail lizards found in Mexico, other lizards found in the Amazon region, and many species of fish. Still such asexual species are in the minority.

Third, sex is expensive also because of the time, energy, and resources expended in the mating ritual – finding a partner, dressing for the partner, driving off other contenders, the courting. Securing a partner requires a substantial investment in what we might call the sexual infrastructure, and this is true not only for us but for most other species as well. Asexual species don't incur this cost because they don't need a mating ritual. They just reproduce.

Is sex good for you?

The obvious evolutionary success of sex indicates that despite its disadvantages compared to asexual reproduction, sex must have some compensatory power. That is, while sex may have started out as a survival mechanism for primitive unicellular organisms in the unimaginable past, maybe it now fulfills some other important function, and this is why it has been maintained. What then could be its function? Reproduction is not it. Asexual species reproduce perfectly well without sex. We, of course, cannot reproduce (at least not yet) without sex, but clearly when we consider the entire living world, reproduction and sex are separable. Is it for pleasure? For us it may be, but there are thousands of very simple species that experience no pleasure in sex.

The function of sex must lie elsewhere. Amazingly, despite a century of study and more than twenty models there is no general consensus among evolutionary biologists that accounts for the widespread occurrence of sex on the one hand, and the retention of asexual potential by many animal and plant species on the other. One old idea first proposed around the turn of the 20th century, is that sex is valuable because it increases diversity in the population. The importance of bringing together the DNAs of two different individuals is that offspring are not identical to the parents. Sex increases genetic diversity, which in turn enhances the ability of the species to adapt to environmental changes. Diversity of offspring will mean more offspring surviving in the long run. Sex may spread the infrequent beneficial mutations and to generate gene combinations that confer survival advantage. This idea has an inherent plausibility, but it has been difficult to substantiate experimentally. There is no doubt that sex increases genetic diversity, but not all evolutionary biologists are convinced that diversity itself is the ultimate "purpose" of sex.

Another idea - sex as rejuvenation – has an ancient history. In Plato's *Symposium*, Diotima, a woman wise in the ways of love, tells Socrates that in procreation the ***"old worn-out mortality" is discarded, "leaving another new and similar existence behind. And in this way, Socrates, the mortal body, or mortal anything, partakes of immortality*** (4, Plato *Symposium*). Perhaps a modern way of rephrasing this old idea is that sex may provide a way of correcting or mitigating the effects of our heavy mutation load (see Appendix 1 of my companion book ***Our Human Odyssey Becoming Female and Male*** for a more complete discussion of mutations). According to human geneticists our mutations load was so heavy that humans should have become extinct long ago. The prominent geneticist James Crow suggests an answer to the question: *Why are we not extinct?* ***"I think the answer lies in the effectiveness of sexual reproduction in reducing the mutation load. . . it permits elimination of harmful mutations in groups. This is not possible with asexual reproduction."*** (5, J.F. Crow, Age and sex effects on the human mutation rates) In the face of a continual barrage of mutations, sex then provides a mechanism for continual rejuvenation

Opening Pandora's Jar

Sex began as a necessary and mechanical process of gene repair. And it forever changed the landscape of the living world. (6, Richard E. Michod, Eros and Evolution)

For most of us all of these arguments about the paradox of sex may seem very esoteric and uninteresting. From an every day human perspective the central mystery is that sex, whose origin we don't understand, has now become central to our lives and continued existence. Sex is still necessary for reproduction, but in the totality of our lives that may be of minor significance. The central truth is that for the huge majority of us, sex means pleasure, not reproduction. How was it that a survival mechanism originating 1.5 billion years ago has been transformed by the human mind into the essentially unbounded expression of our sexuality – the mystery of passion and desire, of the erotic, of the search for completeness, and the limitless ways, both positive and negative, in which we give it expression. For us sex may be likened to a Pandora's jar – opening it has released many spirits – love, fidelity, compassion, disease, sorrow, jealousy, violence, and crime – spirits that complicate our lives immeasurably, but also give it meaning, significance, and value.

Lee Krasner, "Memory of Love, 1966 (c2013 The pollock- Krasner Foundation / Artist Rights Society (ARS), New York)

Chapter 2

Rumination on Sex and Love

Everything to do with Love is a mystery His arrows, his quiver, his torch, and his childhood Exhausting this science is not Something that can be done in a day: So I make no claim to explain everything here (1, Jean de la Fontaine, *L'Amour et la folie*)

Tela Incantata – *reality and illusion*

An old Roman legend tells of a young orphan girl, Geia, befriended by an old woman, Nuntia, who owned an ancient magical loom. Nuntia taught Geia how to use the loom that allowed them to "weave the richest fabrics out of the poorest wools." The two of them prospered for some years, but eventually Nuntia died. Before she died, Nuntia made Geia promise that she would always keep the magical loom. But Geia being young and innocent was tricked into giving away the loom, and without the loom she lost everything and was forced to wander the countryside eking out a meager existence. One day she discovers an old woman with an injured ankle, and Geia nurses her back to health. The old woman, of course, turns out to be her old friend Nuntia. When she reveals herself as Nuntia, the magical loom reappears. "I have returned to recover thy loom," Nuntia tells Geia. For this loom was made by Virgil, after the plan of the Great Loom of his mother. On Her Loom his mother weaveth the tapestry of the world, the warp and woof of reality and illusion, thus creating the world." (2)

"Warp and woof of reality and illusion" is a wonderful metaphor for the way in which the human brain tries to give meaning and purpose to the universe around us, a universe that has been frustratingly silent about its meaning and purpose. As a result human culture in its myriad incarnations is concocted out of a rich stew of observation, science, mythology, religion, morals, and magic.

Sex and love are a parallel universe that we inhabit more or less simultaneously with our everyday universe, that of eating, drinking, working, playing. Sex and the pleasures of the body may occupy an inordinate portion of our mental lives, especially at certain periods of our lives. At the same time an extraordinary and complex mixture of illusion and reality has always been a hallmark of our sexual universe, and our failure to distinguish between illusion and reality of our sexual universe has been the source of probably most of the conflicts that characterize the so-called 'cultural wars' that dominate our national public discourse. Examples include the meanings and implications of sexual preference and gender diversity, ambivalent desires, role of women, the relations between men and women, the future of marriage, sex education, reproductive rights, the new reproductive technologies, and the role of the state in regulating our erotic lives and cybersex. Coming to grips with our sexuality is no easy task, for our attempts to understand ourselves are mired in mythologies of the past, misinformation, moral and religious imperatives, lack of scientific knowledge, and wishful thinking. We have made progress, however. In sex, as in so many other aspects of our lives, our history as a species has been our slow, but consistent, efforts to distinguish between reality – the way things are – and illusion – the way we may wish they were, or the way our religion, society, or the temper of our times dictates that they should be.

Human sexuality is too vast. It resists simple or facile evaluations and no generalization can do justice to the vast inventory of sexual feelings, practices, or behaviors. I enter this arena with much trepidation, but with the hope that my exploration of this complex subject will be informative and useful to you.

An unbounded fabrication

Sex and love are two of the four raw materials (the other two being adventure and war) that are the basis for all human storytelling and literature. Infinitely fascinating and mysterious, sex and love are 'deep' subjects, and many talented men and women throughout our history have tried to understand them. The literature on sex and love is vast, ranging from ancient love poetry, to the novels and short stories written today, to an extensive scientific literature, and to the proliferation of articles in our popular magazines, reports on radio and television. There appears to be no end to this outpouring of information.

One of the more unique and unusual of these writings is *The Anatomy of Melancholy* by Robert Burton, first published in 1621. Burton catalogs and describes the symptoms of all manner of sicknesses and ailments that afflict humans. Whatever value this rambling, eccentric, and often difficult to understand text offers to us today is due to its humor and psychological insight into many of humanity's afflictions. Burton could be thought of as the predecessor of the many advice columnists that we regularly turn to. Burton explains the causes and origins of our ailments, which he says can result in 'melancholy' (literally, "black choler", or a peevish or irascible temperament), and which in turn leads to the 'anguish of the mind'.

Burton devotes almost a third of his massive work to Love and its afflictions – *Love Melancholy* – as he calls it, and explains ***"its causes, enticements, symptoms, allurements, and remedies, lawful and unlawful loves, and the destructive passions of lust itself."*** (3) Burton didn't have the benefits of 21st century science, but it probably would not have helped him very much in understanding Love Melancholy. Despite enormous progress in our understanding of the biology of sex, that is, the nuts and bolts of our sexual apparatus, we still do not understand how the complex interaction of nerve cells and hormones in different parts of our bodies yield and lead to what we experience as sexual thoughts and feelings. The impressive discoveries in brain chemistry and neurophysiology unfortunately tell us very little about what matters most to us – how to understand the mystery and complexity of our sexuality.

The noted sex researcher and scholar William Simon once proposed that human sexuality is an *illusion*. At first thought, most of us would probably have a hard time accepting that point of view. Certainly it doesn't seem to be an illusion. After all, sex is very real, even messy not only literally, but figuratively as well. So, in what way is it reasonable to think of sex as an illusion?

For William Simon sex is an illusion because its meaning and significance go beyond our sexual organs. Perhaps it might be better to say that human sexuality is a fabrication, a concoction, like human culture itself – unfathomable, unbounded, idiosyncratic, multi-dimensional, fashioned mysteriously by the human mind. For us sex has incredible transformative powers. Consider the act of sexual intercourse itself: viewed objectively, putting a penis into a vagina or an anus, is an atrocious, outrageous, maybe even grotesque act. Marcus Aurelius, the Roman emperor and philosopher, regarded intercourse dismissively: *"an internal rubbing with spasmodic spurting of slime"* (4). James Joyce defines it in his own unique way:

"Of a bodily and mental male organism specially adapted for the superincumbent posture of energetic human copulation and energetic piston and cylinder movement necessary for the complete satisfaction of a constant but not acute concupiscence resident in a bodily and mental female organism, passive but not obtuse." (5)

And yet, this arbitrary, objectively meaningless act has been transformed into not only a source of joy, wonderment, emotional release, and happiness, but also of frustration, revenge, intimidation, and deadly power. It is part of the incredible assembly of feelings, conflicting drives and behaviors all of which together form our sexual universe, and in diverse ways tries to give meaning to our existence. The incongruity and mystery of sex is that it *"has taught us to love the meaningless and thereby turn it into the meaningful."* (6)

In ways that we do not understand yet (and maybe never will) our biological inheritance and our life story determine the expanse and details of our sexuality. The combination of all of these factors almost defies comprehension, but it is this mix that makes sex so fascinating and compelling, often so difficult to comprehend, and also the source of so many of our problems.

We begin our ruminations on sex and love by considering first one universal and mysterious quality of our sexuality – *sexual fantasy* – and, second, two questions that perhaps all of us have thought about at one time or another – *Why we have sex, and Does sex have meaning?*

Sexual Fantasy – our secret inner life

A man's life contains hidden depths and large secret areas (7, Pliny the Younger)

The questions

The noted psychotherapist and sexologist Helen Kaplan's pithy 1974 remark that **"*sex is composed of friction and fantasy*"** (8) is probably the briefest and most incisive description of our sexuality. No one would quarrel with the 'friction' aspect, but fantasy, especially erotic or sexual fantasy, has had a more troubled history. We all daydream and fantasize, and these projections of our inner lives are unlimited in subject matter or scope. Who has not fantasized about winning the lottery or becoming famous.

In contrast, fantasies involving sexual activity, although we may find them pleasurable may also be a source of anxiety, shame, guilt, or confusion. Before Kaplan's time sexual fantasies, especially women's fantasies, were considered a taboo subject, and were the province of psychoanalysts who generally followed Sigmund Freud's view that sexual fantasies represented a sexual deficiency or pathology. Freud developed his view from his analysis of a few of his women patients. In 1895 he described the case of Frau P. J., a young singer and newly wed who came to see him about her problem. Frau P. J. had enjoyed sex with her husband during their honeymoon, but afterwards she was left alone because her husband, a traveling salesman, was often away. Frau P. J. came to see Freud because she had an orgasm every time she sang the *Seguidille* aria from the opera *Carmen*. Freud concluded that because of her husband's absence, Frau P. J. was sexually unfulfilled, and the fantasy was a means of satisfying a frustrated wish. Other cases suggested to Freud that sexual fantasies represent primitive, unbearable wishes. The fantasy somehow protects the individual from disturbing and uncomfortable thoughts. In his inimitable way, and leaving no room for doubt, Freud declared that **"a happy person never phantisizes (sic), only an unsatisfied one."** (9)

Probably no mental health professional holds that view today. Research findings over the last 40 to 50 years have shown that sexual fantasies are not only ubiquitous, but are an integral, perhaps even necessary, part of everyone's daily life. The tables have been turned on Freud – *not having*, rather than having sexual fantasies is now considered a sign of pathology. In fact, infrequent sexual fantasy is one of the defining criteria for the disorder 'inhibited sexual desire'.

The world of sexual fantasy entered the public discourse in the United States in 1973 with the publication of Nancy Friday's *My Secret Garden*, based on a compilation of interviews of women who volunteered to discuss their sexual lives and fantasies. *My Secret Garden* had the force and audaciousness of a confessional - real people revealing something important about their sexuality. *My Secret Garden* as well as others that followed (*Forbidden Flowers, Men in Love*) were highly erotic in content, but they were quite different from the type of erotic literature that had existed for decades before - fictionalized soft– and hard-core pornographic writings written by and for men. Perhaps the one major exception to this maledominated genre was the erotic fiction written by the Spanish writer, Anäis Nin, which appeared in the 1930s. Most of this literature, however, was not widely distributed, and hence not available to the general public. In contrast, *My Secret Garden* was available to everyone, and its publication coming during the tumultuous sexual liberation and sexual revolution movements that were rocking the country found a large receptive audience. It is interesting to note that only a couple of years before *My Secret Garden* was published, the psychiatrist Allen Fromme, writing in the then somewhat risqué *Cosmopolitan* magazine: " . . . *women do not have sexual fantasies. How do we know? Ask a woman, and she will usually reply NO. The reason for this is obvious: women haven't been brought to enjoy sex. . . Women are by and large destitute of sexual fantasy*". (10, p3) But only a few years later, in 1975, another New York psychiatrist writing as a monthly-advice columnist, for the same magazine stated *" . . . all women have sexual fantasies, though sometimes they won't admit it to themselves. Fantasies are make-believe states used to enhance reality."* (10, p4) Well, so much for the experts.

As might have been expected, given the temper of the times, Friday's book became a best seller. The revelations of women's sexual appetites, desires, and fantasies regarding masturbation, group sex, incestuous sex, oral sex, anal sex – none of which was mentioned in polite society - scandalized, but also titillated, the many who read it. Of course, all of this helped its sales. Its graphic descriptions of women's fantasies was greatly disturbing to many because it revealed an aspect of women that contrasted greatly with the traditional non-sexual image of the female as demure mothers and 'ladies'.

Consider just two examples:

First, an excerpt of one fantasy in which the woman imagines herself with four men:

"I imagine that one man kneels between my legs, kissing my slit, which is hairless, by the way; another kneels beside the bed kissing my mouth; and the two others kneel on the bed each side of me, sitting on their heels, and leaning forward to suck my nipples, while I stretch out my hand and take hold of their penises to masturbate them. From there, the fantasy progresses. I tip my head back over the side of the bed, and man inserts his penis in my mouth. The man between my legs inserts is penis into my vagina, and with my mouth, hands and vagina I make all of them come at once." (11, p25)

Second, a masturbatory fantasy:

"When I masturbate, I have a recurring 'day dream' of a salesman approaching a lovely white cottage on a beach and finding the door partly open. He calls, and getting no answer, wanders through all the rooms looking for some sign of occupancy. Finally, he comes to a closed door and hears water running within. Opening the door he finds a woman showering and he proceeds to undress, climb into the shower to make love the woman. By this time I usually have my climax." (11, p95)

Unintended or not, Friday's books probably had a significant beneficial therapeutic effect: the revelations of women's inner sexual lives permitted readers to accept their own sexuality and relieve their anxiety and guilt about their own sexual impulses and fantasies. As Jonathan Ames, the American novelist and comic memoirist, put it: *"I guess we all like to know other people's secrets so that we can live with our own."* (12) Fantasies, in a word, were not pathological, nor weird, but healthy and natural. The books also had another important consequence – they gave the public a more profound and complete picture of what it is to be a woman. Henry Miller, whose novels *Tropic of Cancer, Black Spring, Tropic of Capricorn* were banned in the U.S. in the 1930s on the grounds of obscenity, captured this important insight when he wrote to Nancy Friday commenting on her book *Forbidden Flowers:*

"I've always suspected that women had richer, wilder fantasies than men. From my limited experience with women I must also add that I have found them more capable of abandoning themselves completely in intercourse with men. In a good healthy sense I would say to use an old-fashioned word, that they are more "shameless" than men. Men are only beginning to perceive the true nature of women's being. They have created a false image of her. If she is no longer an enigma she is an everlasting source of wonder and rich in unexplored possibilities in every domain of life." (10, p8)

Whether the full ramifications of this insight will be completely realized is difficult to predict, for its acceptance frightens many, perhaps men especially, and is considered by many societies and groups to be threatening to the stability of the 'traditional' family structure. Still, Friday's books revealing as they were, could be said to represent only the tip of the fantasy iceberg. Many questions about the nature of sexual fantasies, their origin, meaning, and function persisted. The British psychoanalyst Brett Kahr in his compelling narrative, *Who's Been Sleeping in Your Head. The Secret World of Sexual Fantasies* (2008), lists a number of questions that have been raised by the many people whom he has interviewed. They are also questions that at one time or another we may have asked ourselves. (13, p21)

- *What is a sexual fantasy?*

- *What constitutes a "normal" sexual fantasy?*

- *Why do we have sexual fantasies in the first place?*

- *What purpose or purposes do our sexual fantasies serve?*

- *Does everybody have sexual fantasies?*

- *Should we be worried if we have no fantasies at all?*

- *Should we ever share our fantasies with our partners or our friends?*

- *Can our fantasies ever be damaging or dangerous?*

- *If we fantasize about 'ordinary" sex, does this mean that we must be boring?*

- *If we have very outlandish fantasies, does this mean that we must be mentally unbalanced?*

- *If we fantasize about someone other than our partners during sex or masturbation, does that mean that our relationship might be in trouble?*

- *If we fantasize about something "illegal", does this mean that we may be a risk for acting it out?*

- *Do our fantasies represent just a bit of private fun, or do they have more profound implications for how we lead our lives?*

- *How can we explain the range of fantasies experienced by human beings? In other words, why do some people prefer to be kissed and cradled while others enjoy the infliction of often agonizing physical pain?*

- *Can we ever change our fantasies?*

Do we control our fantasies, or do our fantasies control us?

How do we go about answering these questions? Unfortunately, we don't really have objective ways of studying sexual fantasies. We have to rely on self-reports, and hence, what we know has come primarily from questionnaires, and reports from in-depth interviews conducted by psychoanalysts or psychiatrists. Kahr's book, for example, provides excerpts of several hundred in-depth interviews that he has conducted over many years. The questionnaire data cannot be considered in any real sense representative in an inclusive sense, since the respondents have been mainly young adults from English speaking countries. We have little information about sexual fantasies in other societies or cultures. Still, despite these limitations, these studies have given us a reasonably consistent picture of important attributes of the fantasies from these sample populations, and to some extent they do provide partial answers to Kahr's questions. We summarize some of the major findings in what follows.

A brief view of our sexual fantasy world

- A sexual fantasy, as the term is normally used, is not simply a brief romantic daydream or sexual thought, but is any mental activity that in many cases ends in orgasm. The story line can be very simple or highly elaborate, and generally will be pleasurable to the fantasist, but not always.

- Sexual fantasies are almost universal: some 95% of men and women report having sexual fantasies either during sexual activity with a partner, or while masturbating, or both. The fantasies can be triggered by many different stimuli – images of people or places, events or experiences from the past - and in some cases by a fetish object. Consider the following example:

All my fantasies start with footwear. I'll see a woman out wearing high heels or knee boots and that will start me off. Don't ask me why, but ever since I was a little boy, I found leather really stimulating, and now that I'm a grownup, I can't get enough of it." (13, p177)

- Although the partners in the fantasy may include past, present, or imaginary lovers, and sometimes more than one. Fantasies are generally not shared with the partner, probably because of the uncertainty about how the partner will respond, or perhaps because the fantasy involves someone other than the long-term partner. The most commonly reported fantasies for both men and women are (a) reliving an arousing sexual experience, (b) imagining having sex with the current partner, and (c) imagining having sex with another partner. Interestingly, and perhaps contrary to expectation, only a small percentage of fantasies involve celebrities. Gender preferences in fantasies match the real life preferences: heterosexuals generally imagine opposite-sex partners, while gay men and lesbian women imagine same-sex partners in their fantasies.

- Prevailing theory suggests that the detailed content of a person's fantasies depends more on their life history than on genetic and hormonal factors. What we have experienced, whether pleasurable or traumatic, what we have read, movies that we have seen, our relationships with parents, sibs, friends, or even unknown persons, all shape and condition our fantasy world. Our fantasies probably incorporate both conscious and unconscious elements. Freudian psychotherapists since Freud have argued that many sexual fantasies have their roots in psychological trauma. The fantasy may function as a way to alleviate the unconscious pain left by the trauma.

- In their fantasies both men and women may often explore different sexual practices or anatomical positions, which for a variety of reasons may not be available to them in real life. Consider one example:

"I start making love to a beautiful woman, only to find out that it's really a beautiful man done up as a lady. It's a transvestite! This fantasy really arouses me, but I wouldn't want to do it in real life. But in fantasy, I kind of get the best of both worlds." (13, p197)

- Contrary to Freud's and other psychoanalyst's views that sexual fantasies are a sign of sexual dissatisfaction, deficiency, immaturity, inhibition, or pathology, especially in women, the frequency of sexual fantasy increases with the rate of sexual activity in both men and women. In contrast to food deprivation that leads to increased frequency of daydreaming about food, the frequency of sexual fantasy declines with sexual deprivation. Moreover, sexual fantasies occur most often in those who exhibit the least sexual dissatisfaction or sexual problems. The frequency of sexual fantasy declines with age in both men and women, consistent with the general finding that decreased sexual activity is associated with decrease in sexual fantasy. This suggests that an important function for sexual fantasy is to stimulate or enhance sexual arousal.

- Adults report that their fantasies began around the time of puberty, and males appear to have more consistent fantasies earlier than female. Some studies suggest that some minimal level of testosterone is necessary for sexual fantasy. This would explain why sexual fantasies appear to begin around the onset of puberty. Although children often experiment with sexual play, fondling their genitals, for example, little is known about what would qualify as sexual fantasies in young children.

- Most people do not seem troubled by their fantasies, but about 25% experience considerable guilt, perhaps because they imagine that the fantasy is immoral, abnormal, or indicative of something wrong with them or their relationship to their partner. Guilt tends to lead to fewer fantasies and more sexual problems.

- There are significant gender differences in the content of sexual fantasies. Presumably these differences arise from the different ways in which men are socialized compared to women. Men wield power, They are the 'doers', while women are sought after, using their looks to incite desire in men. In men's fantasies, the female partners tend to be submissive, and easily aroused even if they might feign reluctance initially. The male is in charge and responsible for inciting desire and arousal in a partner and then bring both to orgasm. Men's fantasies have more visual and explicit imagery than women's. For men the fantasy reassures them that their partners desire them and that they can satisfy them sexually. Women have more romantic and emotional imagery, and more often focus on their own desirability and pleasure, sometimes enhancing their pleasure by imagining more than one partner. For example:

Another frequent sexual fantasy is having anal sex with a woman. I like the way it makes me feel, dominant and in control. Usually we're in a bed and both totally naked. Sometimes the woman is on "all fours" and sometimes I grab her breasts and squeeze them. Then I usually push her flat on her stomach and continue being rough until I climax deep inside of her. (14)

"I see a women in a bikini swimming close to me. I look appreciatively at her body and she half-blushes and halfbeckons me. I swim up to her and kiss her and fondle her. We then climb out of the water and then I notice that her wet suit is transparent. I begin fondling her and she requests me to stop. But her request only enhances my desire for fondling her more vigorously. This continues until we reach the car by which time I am so aroused that I strip her and myself and push her onto the backseat of the car and make passionate love to her." (14)

Two guys, paying all their attention to me, waiting on me hand and foot, doing whatever I wanted them to do to me. I would make them take off my clothes, smother me in lotion, then a full body massage. Making sure my whole body is tingling they would take their turns entering me. I wouldn't be satisfied until both of them have cum and then I would do the same. We would all sleep together in my bed, naked, listening to Miles Davis as the summer heat made us sweat. (14)

I often fantasize about being a submissive to a couple. In the fantasy I live with the couple or am hired out to the couple to do whatever they would like me to do. Often there is bondage and most often I am serving them orally. While I act as though I am humiliated and resistant, I am really enjoying it. (14)

Women can also fantasize about being sexually dominant. In these cases they are the ones who provide pleasure to their partner

I would love to drive to the factory where my husband is an engineer, walk to his office, pull his clothing off, push him onto the top of his desk and make love to him. I know he would be surprised

and pleased. A variation on this theme is that I would go to his office, hide under his desk and when he returns perform oral sex with him at his desk. Again he would be surprised and pleased. (14)

- Fantasies may sometimes be labeled 'forbidden', 'deviant', or 'perverse' by the fantasist. Some examples that might fall into these categories: imagining either submitting to or having anal sex; perhaps imagining sex with several partners; fantasies involving sadism (inflicting discomfort or pain in others) or masochism (self-inflicted pain); imagining having sex with children; a fantasy about having sex with an animal. Since none of these fantasies are that uncommon, these adjectives don't have an objective validity. While sadistic fantasies may be of special concern, the data available indicates that few people act out their fantasies. Brett Kahr comments: *"Fortunately, fantasy often exerts a strong containing function for the human mind; as a result, we manage to encapsulate some of the more aggressive and destructive aspects of our personalities into the fantasy content itself. I have talked to many doctors, priests, social workers, nurses, and other members of the 'caring professions' who have had very violent fantasies that they have never enacted and, most likely, never will enact."* (13, p435) According to Kahr, fantasies with a sadistic component may be a very effective way to 'discharge aggression' and relieve accumulated stress that might otherwise become dangerous. Sex offenders often report that their fantasies are related to their offenses. However, fantasies involving sexual offenses are not uncommon in people who never act on them. The boundary between fantasy and behavior remains quite fluid, and unless detailed information about a person's behavior is available, it is very difficult to predict for any given person when that boundary has been crossed, and the fantasy erupts into a dangerous pathology

- Fantasies in which submission and some level of force is involved or implied are fairly common. The use of force might be expected in men's fantasies given the tendency in men of linking arousal with dominance, that is, the male imposing his will on the female. Hence, dominance fantasies are much more common in men than women. Nevertheless, a small percentage of men admit to having fantasies in which they submit to force. Submission or rape fantasies are much more prevalent in women. In a study published in 2008, 31 – 57% of women had submission (or rape) fantasies, and for 9 – 17% of women this type of fantasy was their most frequent or favorite fantasy. This may be an underestimate because some women may find it embarrassing to report them, or because it may be socially unacceptable to do so. The high incidence of female rape fantasies can unfortunately be used to justify real rapes, the men arguing that the woman was 'asking for it'. Do many women want to be raped? There is no evidence that women actually want to be raped. Nevertheless, the high prevalence is paradoxical and poses a significant challenge in trying to understand them.

My favorite fantasy is kind of like a rape scene, but with no violence. I'm tied up, blindfolded and forced to have sex and perform all duties. I'm very frightened, but very turned on. I am completely dominated. There may be one or more people involved, or perhaps a whole gang of really horny, sexy young men. All very fit with not beer bellies The Brad Pitt type of man. Mmmmmmmmmm. I DO NOT WANT TO BE RAPED IN REAL LIFE THOUGH – IT'S A FANTASY. (13, p82)

Clearly this would have been a horrible and traumatic experience if it had happened in real life. Why would anyone want to imagine rape? It seems perverse to do so. The important question that the authors pose is "Why have a fantasy about an event that in real life would be horrible and traumatic?" Some investigators have suggested that there is a deep connection between rape fantasies and the popularity of erotic romance novels. Romance novels are erotic love stories written almost exclusively by women and read overwhelmingly by women. With more than 20 million loyal readers, they account for about 40% of the mass paperback sales in the U. S. The story lines, essentially the same can sometimes take place in exotic locales. The titles all evoke the novels' theme *Love's Wild Assault, Wicked Loving Lies, Love's Tender Fury,* typically the rape or forced sex of the heroine. The heroine is always beautiful and highly sensual, qualities that draw men to her. The hero is a strong, masculine, sexually bold, and somewhat dangerous man, irresistibly attracted to the heroine. The heroine in turn also finds the hero sexually attractive, and eventually in highly charged sexual scenes gives in to the hero. She uses her beauty to manipulate the hero to her advantage and eventually domesticates him.

Both rape fantasies and romance novels are really a form of pornography in which the female, rather than the male, is the important protagonist. Both are meant to be sexually arousing. In the rape fantasy the story line that leads to arousal and final climax is self-generated; in the romance novel, the reader identifies with the heroine and experiences the rape scenes vicariously. In both the fantasy and the romance the rape scenes are always safely violent and never resulting in physical injury. The inevitable rape scene becomes an exciting and sexually arousing event.

The transformation of the rape scene into something sexually stimulating is embodied in perhaps the first explanation proposed to account for submission fantasies in women. The psychologist, E. B. Hariton (1973) suggested that they are in reality power fantasies because the woman, although submitting, is really in control, affirming her desirability. The implied, but never realized danger of the rape scene, and the power of the male only serve to heighten the woman's arousal and pleasure.

Another hypothesis suggests that a woman can feel blameless when she submits, because she is not the instigator. Being forced to engage in otherwise improper or forbidden behavior may relieve guilt and lead to increased pleasure. If we look closely, however, both of these explanations reflect two different ways in which a woman enhances her power.

A third explanation is that in a culture of male sexual aggression and female sexual acquiescence, women are socialized to accept sexual submission and their fantasies reflect that. However, this hypothesis does not account for the submission fantasies in men. It has also been suggested that victims of sexual abuse during childhood may be conditioned to associate submission with sexual stimulation.

The available studies tend to support the first two proposals: that submission-dominance fantasies represent two sides of the same coin, that is, they both serve the same purpose – affirming sexual power and irresistibility. These fantasies satisfy some deep longing for sexual excitement that cannot be admitted openly without inviting societal disapproval or embarrassment. Women's rape fantasies may provide a way for women to experience enhanced sexual arousal in a manner they can control, while satisfying or fulfilling their sexual needs.

Their value or significance

Psychiatrists suggest that many, if not most, fantasies are 'wish-fulfillments', that is, they express or reflect a desire to escape what we may consider our mundane world. In the fantasy we are free to explore sexual acts or sexual situations that are beyond our reach in real life. We can have sex with people who are inaccessible to us in reality. In the fantasy we can give free rein to our erotic imagination, stimulating our sexual arousal when we are with a partner or partners.

Nevertheless, it is also clear that sexual fantasies have other important functions. Brett Kahr suggests that fantasies may function as 'over-the-counter' self-medicating agents. They are free and available anytime to provide physical and psychological release when we might feel overstressed or overwhelmed by anxiety, depression, or conflict. We may use them to bolster our self-confidence, and to help vent aggressive or sadistic impulses. For Freudian psychoanalysts, sexual fantasies enable us to maintain our equilibrium and a sense of self, especially in those cases when we have suffered psychological trauma. They can also alleviate the pain associated with the psychological trauma. The erotic is powerful, for as Kahr suggests, *"The eroticization of trauma can simply be a creative solution of a painful event."* (13, p374)

We don't know when, why, or how sexual fantasies first emerged in our species. However they came about, they are permanent elements of our psyche, and it would be difficult to imagine humans lacking the capacity for sexual fantasy. Sexuality is a powerful creative force not only in a biological sense, but also because its imagery – private and unconstrained by convention – may be the source of all types of artistic activity.

Do we have any influence or power to shape our own fantasies? Kahr suggests that we may not: *"Although we like to imagine ourselves as the architects of our own fate, choosing our own life paths and our own erotic preferences, my research has led me to the conclusion that large numbers of people do not command their own sexual minds. Rather, sexual preferences and sexual fantasies become forged by early impressions often as a result of shame, of humiliation and of sexual trauma."* (13, p, 311)

Why we have sex – *not a simple question*
What sex surveys tell us.

In contrast to food and water, we do not need sex to survive. For many of us, life without sex might be sad, tragic or boring, but many people have had happy and satisfying lives without sex. Despite what we may hear from self-appointed 'experts' on sex, there is no evidence that sexual abstinence has any adverse health effects or alternatively, or that some specified level of sexual activity is necessary for optimal health. In the 19th century medical experts recommended one intercourse per week as the upper limit, while in 1997 the recommendation was that one penile-vaginal intercourse per week should be the lower limit. Too much sex, on the other hand, can have adverse health effects, if many partners are involved. This is not because of the sexual activity itself, but because of the high risk of acquiring sexually transmitted infections.

Widespread public interest in, concern about, and even preoccupation with, our sexual practices, behavior, and problems is relatively recent, probably beginning during the latter half of the 20th century. This is not to say that there was no interest before, but it tended to be private or anecdotal. The 20th century ushered in a new era of sexual explicitness, liberation, and awareness in Western societies, and a curiosity to know more about the sexual practices of others led quite naturally to sex surveys. Katharine Bement Davis, a prison reformer who had served as New York City's first female commissioner of corrections, in her 1929 study of the sexual experiences of 2,220 women, carried out the first large-scale sexual survey in the United States. But the studies that gained the most notoriety were the Kinsey reports of 1948 and 1953. The most recent survey is the 2010 National Survey of Sexual Health and Behavior. It was conducted by the Center for Sexual Health Promotion, Indiana University. The largest nationally representative study of sexual practices and behaviors ever fielded, some 5,865 men and women between 14 and 94 years of age participated in the study. It has given us an interesting portrait of sexual practices among contemporary Americans. Among some of the findings:

- There is enormous variability in the sexual repertoires of U.S. adults, with 41 combinations of sexual activity describedvaginal intercourse, oral sex, anal sex, and other variations.

- For men between 25 and 39, and in women between ages of 20 to 29, penetrative sex was the most common, while oral sex (giving, receiving, or both) was also common in both men and women between 18 and 49.

- Although sexual activity declined progressively among the older age groups, some 20% to 30% of men and women continued having sex well into their 80s.

- Most men reported having an orgasm during their last sexual encounter, and 85% also believed that their female partners also had an orgasm, but interestingly, only 64% of women reported having had an orgasm. (A difference that is too large to be accounted for by some of the men having had male partners at their most recent event.)

- Men are more likely to orgasm when sex includes vaginal intercourse; women are more likely to orgasm when they engage in a variety of sex acts and when oral sex or vaginal intercourse is included.

- While about 7% of adult women and 8% of men identify as gay, lesbian or bisexual, the proportion of individuals in the U.S. who have had same-gender sexual interactions at some point in their lives is higher.

- At any given point in time, most U.S. adolescents are not engaging in partnered sexual behavior. While 40% of 17 year-old males reported vaginal intercourse in the past year, only 27% reported the same in the past 90 days.

Another revealing survey, titled *Why We Have Sex*, was published in 2007. In this case the premise of the study was that we are able to get an idea of why people have sex (or at least what they say when asked why they have sex) by asking them. The study queried 2000 students at the University of Texas regarding their motives for having sex and choosing their sexual partners. Characteristics of the participants: very few of the participants in the study were sexual novices, some 73% of the women and 68% of the men reported having had sexual intercourse in the past, 88% of both men and women reported having engaged in oral sex, and 95% had engaged in some form of sexual petting in the past.

Perhaps the most attention-grabbing aspect of the study was the reported number of reasons for having sex – an unexpected 237. Now keep in mind the limitations of studies based on questionnaires. In particular, self-reporting about sexual matters may be quite deceptive. Previous studies have suggested that self-reporting can be notoriously unreliable, and some scholars consider studies based on questionnaires of this type generally worthless. For example, presenting a favorable sexual image probably skews responses to those with more social desirability (expressing love, affection, or commitment), and away from low social undesirability (punish a partner, to make money, increasing the number of conquests). This tendency may be more important for females than males. Moreover, the population studied clearly does not represent a random sample of the general population. For example, the motivations of the university students could be quite different from those of 30 and 40 year old singles as well as those who are married.

Still despite these limitations, the remarkable aspect of the study was the large number of variables that influenced the sexual partner choice, leading the authors to remark, *"efforts to reduce sexual motivation to a small number of variables are doomed to fail"* (15).

The reasons given are both interesting and revealing. A list of 45 of the more common ones of the 237 reported gives you a sense of the range of responses.

I was bored I was married, and you're supposed to

It became a habit Sex was the only way my partner would spend time with me

I wanted to stop my partner's nagging I wanted to have more sex than my friends

Someone dared me I wanted to see what all the fuss was about

I wanted to defy my parents I was slumming.

I needed another notch on my belt It was an initiation rite

The person was famous The person was a good dancer

The person had beautiful eyes The person had a great sense of humor

The person bought me an expensive dinner I wanted a job

Someone offered me money I'm addicted to sex

My hormones were out of control I was tired of being a virgin

I wanted to feel closer to God I was trying to reaffirm my sexual orientation

It's considered taboo I wanted to get rid of aggression

I was physically forced I was verbally coerced

I was seduced I wanted to humiliate the person

I wanted to give someone an STD I was feeling lonely

I wanted the person to love me I thought it would help me trap a new partner

I was ovulating I wanted to get rid of a headache

I thought it would help me fall asleep I wanted to keep warm

I wanted to burn calories I wanted to relieve menstrual cramps

It's my genetic imperative I was curious about my sexual abilities

The person smelled nice I realized I was in love

I wanted to change the topic of conversation

Can we draw any conclusions from the responses? The authors make a brave attempt: they suggest that the responses can be grouped into four broad reason categories. The first category is the *Physical – stress reduction, pleasure, physical desirability, and experience seeking.* The second category is Goal *attainment – popularity, social status, revenge, and utilitarian.* The third category is *Insecurity – self-esteem boost, duty/ pressure, and mate guarding.* And finally the fourth category is *Emotional, - love and commitment, and expression of feelings.*

Men and women agreed on 20 of the top 25 reasons for having sex. There were some differences. For example, men gave much more importance on physical appearance as a measure of desirability. Men also rated higher "experience seeking' – wanted to increase the number of partners, and taking advantages of opportunities that presented themselves, the person was "available". Women, much more than men, endorsed emotional motivations, such as "I wanted to express my love for that person", "I was in love". In general, sex without emotional involvement, simply feeling "horny" was a stronger motivation for men than for women. Interestingly, men more than women, used sex as a way of gaining favors or treatment, contrary to the usual stereotype of women being "gold-diggers". They also used sex for increased self-esteem and status enhancement more frequently than women.

What is perhaps most interesting is that a large number of the reasons given reflected what we could call the *non-erotic incentives* for having sex. There was a curious absence of strong, consuming passion. Instead, the motivation for sex was for some type of explicit or implicit personal gain. We presume that some physical attraction was present in each case, but we learned very little about that, for example, what attracted them to one particular person or another. This is surprising, perhaps, because these were university students, and we might have expected them to be much more erotically, romantically driven.

A historical controversy

There is more to the question, *Why we have sex?*, than perhaps meets the eye. Half a century ago, Frank Beach, a well-known scholar of sexuality, identified the central dilemma with the question:

Since no animal mates in order to reproduce, but animals must mate in the service of species survival, we are faced with the problem of identifying the source of reward or positive reinforcement, which impels individuals to copulate. The problem has scarcely been recognized as far as sexual activity is concerned. (16)

We can rephrase the Beach's question as follows: since animals are not aware that they mate to reproduce, what is it that drives them to mate? To say that it is an instinct doesn't help us much, because we then turn around and define the sexual instinct as the drive to mate. We never get anywhere with this type of circular reasoning. The clue, according to Beach, is in identifying the 'reward' for having sex. The answer interestingly enough comes from us.

Humans are different from animals. We are certainly aware (and have been for several thousand years) that reproduction is one of the outcomes of mating. But we also know that sex is pleasurable, which is probably why we are obsessed with it. We are a pleasure-seeking species, and we will want to repeat any activity that gives us pleasure. Just think of all the hundreds of activities that we indulge in – sports, music, dancing, gambling, eating, drinking – and repeat over and over again. This is clearly the case for sex. Humans have been engaging in sex purely for the fun of it for thousands of years. Sex is pleasurable, whether or not pregnancy occurs. In fact, having babies is only an occasional outcome of having sex. In contemporary societies that practice birth control extensively the procreative aspect of sex has been almost completely eliminated.

The 'reward' or 'positive reinforcement' that Beach was looking for is 'pleasure'. Sex, in the language of psychologists, is intrinsically rewarding and has a positive affect. The motivation for sex is the pleasure we experience, and we want to repeat the pleasure. This type of reasoning probably applies to animals as well. Animals mate because copulation is rewarding, and not because they understand that they mate to reproduce. We don't know if what they experience qualifies as pleasure in the human sense or whether they experience orgasm, but it must be rewarding nonetheless.

But where does this leave sex for reproduction? It can't be ignored, for it is clearly important. In the grand scheme of things, how do we weigh or balance these two aspects of sex – procreation or recreation? This is not easy to do, for these two alternative, often complementary, views have been entangled in a complex web of commentary and controversy for most of our history.

Procreative sex – a perspective

The view that reproduction is the sole or primary justification for sex has been dominant during much of Western history in the last 1500 or so years. According to historians, its origins can be traced to the legacy of the early Christian thinkers during the 3rd – 6th centuries who were trying to fashion a new Christian social and moral order to replace the decaying classical Greek and Roman world. Perhaps the most influential of these was St. Augustine (354 – 430 CE). How he came to his views is related in graphic terms in his memoir, known now as the *Confessions of St. Augustine*. The *Confessions*, a complex work that mixes arcane theological arguments and personal history, is in some ways the typical archetypal Christian conversion story, but with a twist. Augustine's conversion, as related by the historian Garry Wills in his *Augustine's Confessions - a Biography*, was the second of the two most important in Christian history – the first was St. Paul's on the way to Damascus. St. Paul's conversion involved a change of religion; in Augustine's case, the conversion did not mean changing religion, but meant giving up sex. Augustine is very explicit in his decision

"Portray the woman as you will, endow her with every good thing, yet have I made up my mind that nothing is more to be shunned than union with a woman. . . I have therefore laid this demand on myself (rightly and usefully, I believe) – to protect the

freedom of my soul by giving up any concern or quest or contract with a wife" (17, St. Augustine, *Confessions* 5:66)

St. Augustine in his younger days led an active sexual life typical for a man of his social class in the cosmopolitan city of Alexandria in Egypt. He also lived with a woman he never married for 13 years and with whom he had one child. According to legend, his mother, St. Monica, prayed constantly that he would give us his profligate life-style, get rid of his mistress, and marry according to his social station. Before Augustine took his no-sex vows, his mother had persuaded his common-law wife to return to her homeland, and in turn selected a young woman of high standing to be Augustine's wife. However, at the time the young woman was still too young to be married. Augustine regretted the loss of his former mistress, and took another to assuage his sex drive.

His views on sex apparently began to change when he became embroiled in a question that was of central importance during that period: *Would Adam and Eve have had sex if they had not been expelled from Eden?* We may laugh about this now, but we tend to forget the energy we spend in controversies that will appear trivial to later generations. Augustine convinced himself and argued vehemently that sexual desire originated from Adam and Eve's disobedience in the Garden of Eden, and remained the permanent flaw in the human soul that kept humans away from God. Accordingly, sexual activity was to be shunned, and could be justified only if its purpose was procreation. Any sexual activity – masturbation, fellatio, cunnilingus, anal sex, sex with the same-sex individual - not leading to procreation was sinful.

Giving up sex was not easy for St. Augustine. His famous half-hearted appeal for strength to overcome his addiction has reverberated through the ages: *"and I, an unfortunate young man … would pray- 'Lord, give me chastity, and continence, but not now".* (18) Nevertheless, finally at the age of 31 Augustine committed himself to a life of sexual abstinence. Complete abstinence was not easy for St. Augustine, for as he writes, sexual desire was *"plucking at my garment, my flesh, these my past sweet joys softly murmured: 'Are you dismissing us? . . . from this moment, will you never be allowed to do this or to do that?' And, oh, my God, what was it they suggested in those words 'this' and 'that'?"* (18).

Augustine took on his no-sex vow with the tenacity and fanaticism of a new convert. Choosing a life of abstinence was not an unusual step in Augustine's day. During the early Christian centuries celibacy was considered a supreme virtue, a special way of coming to know God. Many men even took the extreme measure of castrating themselves to remove the temptations of the flesh and enable them to remain celibate. We don't have such practices anymore, but celibacy, as a special calling remains alive in the Roman Catholic Church.

Augustine resisted the temptations of the flesh and kept his vow of abstinence. In his old age he records an encounter with Julian of Elanum, a young, aristocratically educated, married bishop, who had problems with Augustine's theories of original sin. For Augustine, original sin represented the unrepressed sexual appetite. Julian, perhaps to get a rise out of old Augustine, tells him that he has sex with his wife whenever and wherever he feels like it. Augustine explodes in his response:

"Really, really: is that your experience? So you would not have married couples restrain that evil – I refer of course to your favorite good? So you would have them jump into bed whenever they like, whenever they feel tickled by desire. Far be it from them to postpose this itch will bedtime: let's have your 'legitimate union of bodies' whenever your 'natural good' is excited. If this is the sort of married life you lead, don't drag up your experience in debate!" (19)

Despite his vow of celibacy, Augustine understood that sex was necessary, but he argued that it could only be justified in the context of marriage. St. Augustine's views became the orthodoxy in the expanding Christian church, and remain the official doctrine of the Roman Catholic Church, and by and large his views on sexual morality even remained after the Protestant Reformation.

Repressive attitudes regarding sexual activity reached their peak in the 19th century, but these were largely due to some members of the medical profession who set themselves up as the moral guardians of sexual morality and feminine virtue. God had designed intercourse for the production of children and no other reason. Couples were often warned about seeking or prolonging pleasure since children conceived under such conditions would turn out to stupid or idiots. Females, in particular, should not enjoy sex because they were maternal, not sexual creatures. Many mechanical devices (medical appliances in the U.S. Patent Office records) to limit sexual pleasure were marketed and sold to men and women. The English physician, William Acton, author of the most widely quoted sexual-advice book in the 19th century English-speaking world proclaimed that *"the majority of women (happily for them) are not much troubled with sexual feeling of any kind. What men are habitually, women are only exceptionally"* (20). A story was told about a young woman who asked her English mother how she should behave one her wedding night, and her mother answered *"Lie still, and think about the Empire".* (20)

Theopilus Parvin, a prominent American physician, in his medical school lectures maintained: *"I do not believe one bride in a hundred, of delicate, educated, sensitive women, accepts matrimony from any desire for sexual gratifications; when she thinks of this at all, it is with shrinking, or even horror, rather than with desire."* (20). The historian Viola Klein summed up the 'official' attitudes regarding female sexuality: *"In the whole Western world during the 19th and beginning of the 20th century it would have been not only scandalous to admit the existence of a strong sex urge in women, but it would have been contrary to all observation."* (20). St. Augustine's anti-sex message cast a long shadow, and to some extent continues to have powerful reverberations in contemporary society.

More recently, in a strange twist, the Augustinian view has been given the patina of scientific validity by an unfortunate and erroneous tendency in some areas of evolutionary biology to explain physiological processes by reference to their function or purpose, rather than by analyzing cause and effect. Sexual behavior, in particular, is explained by linking sex and reproduction in a way that seems at first sight quite plausible. The evolutionary argument simply put is that sex evolved for reproduction, and that any sexual activity not leading to procreation is non-adaptive, that is, it would be eliminated by natural selection. In other words, sex without reproduction has no biological value.

Since we know that sex is necessary for species survival (although it is not necessary for our personal survival), the argument seems sensible. But evolutionary arguments of this type remain unverifiable. Moreover, it is difficult to explain the recreational aspects of sex. If the purpose of sex were only procreative, then the recreational aspects of sex would have been eliminated. If sex was only for procreation, we would then mate like animals do – just to reproduce. But we don't. Overwhelmingly we engage in sex for pleasure.

Even more pernicious are the corollary conclusions that are drawn from this mistaken evolutionary premise: sex between same-sex individuals, sexual activity of menopausal women are illegitimate and abnormal; sexual activity other than penile-vaginal sex – fellatio, cunnilingus, anal sex, masturbation – are all illegitimate activities and therefore deviant and abnormal. Projecting or imposing function and purpose in explaining natural phenomena is always dangerous. By doing so we tend to forget that our impositions are illusions, unscientific, and costly because they prevent us from understanding the world as it is.

Recreational sex – rewarding and heartbreaking

Marriage handbooks and sexual advice manuals, mostly written by physicians, were popular in the 19th century, and most of them carried anti-sex messages. They have contributed to the images that historians have given us of a sexrepressed society. Reality was different. A thriving prostitution industry coexisted along side the grave admonitions and warnings from many of the experts. While we know relatively little about the views, attitudes, and practices of ordinary folk, anecdotal information from diverse sources suggests that they, especially women, held views that countered those held by many in the medical establishment. It should be said that not all physicians in the 19th century held the view that women were sexless beings, incapable of or interested in enjoying sex. The historian Carl Degler in his informative study of female sexuality in the 19th century reviews the works of a few physicians who had what we would consider very modern views.

One can be found in the extraordinary study carried out during the latter part of the 19th century by a Stanford University professor, Clelia Duel Mosher (1863-1940). By any measure Dr. Mosher, a pioneer in the study of women's sexuality, was a remarkable person. She was an astute observer of women's predicament. Dr. Mosher in her writings noted that the anti-sex messages of the advice manuals did have an effect on many women. She attributed the difficulty women had in reaching orgasm to *"training has instilled the idea that any physical response is coarse, common and immodest which inhibits (women's) proper part in this relation."* (21)

Her study of female sexual attitudes and behavior was the first documented sexual survey in the history of the field. The study was never published but its details survive in her collected papers left to Stanford University.

Forty-six women participated in the study, a project that spanned some 20 years. All the women had attended college or a normal school; 17 were born before the Civil War, 33 before 1870, and all before 1890. Hence, their attitudes and practices were those of middle to upper class women who grew up and married within the 19th century. In addition to questions about family background and education, half of the questionnaire was devoted to their sexual behavior, including questions about frequency of intercourse, whether intercourse was 'agreeable', whether they had orgasm and the feelings they had with orgasm or its absence, purpose of intercourse, contraceptive use or not, ideal habit of sexual relations. Dr. Mosher was far ahead of her time, but so were the women who participated in the study.

Despite having a college education, the women reported having little knowledge of sexual physiology. What stands out is that all of the women accepted sexual relations with enthusiasm and frankness. Even more surprising and contrary to the views expounded by the medical profession about women's sexuality, the women were not at all sexless – 35 of the 45 admitted that they felt desire for sex independent of their husband's interest, and all had experienced orgasm, while 34 experienced orgasm always or usually. These numbers are quite amazing because of their contrast to findings of surveys of women in the late 20th and first decade of the 21st century as we will see in a later chapter.

Notably several women rejected reproduction as 'sufficient justification' for sex. One woman, born before 1850, commented after she had been married for ten years: *"I consider this appetite as ranking with other natural appetites and like them to be indulged legitimately and temperately; I consider it illegitimate to risk bringing children into the world under any but most favorable circumstances.* " (21) Another woman, also born a decade before the Civil War, denied that reproduction *"alone warrants it at all; I think it is only warranted as an expression of true and passionate love. This is the prime condition for a happy conception, I fancy."* (21) Another woman born before 1861, offered with considerable enthusiasm *"the desire of both husband and wife for this expression of their union seems to me the first and highest reason for intercourse. The desire for offspring is a secondary, incidental, although entirely worthy motive but could never to me make intercourse right unless the mutual desire were also present. . . My husband and I believe in intercourse for its own sake – we wish it for ourselves and spiritually miss it, rather then physically, when it does not occur, because it is the highest, most sacred expression of our oneness. On the other hand, even a slight risk of pregnancy, and then we deny ourselves the intercourse, feeling all the time that we are losing that which keeps us closest to each other."* (21)

Another woman, born in 1857, commented that sexual intercourse *"makes more normal people. . . Even if there are not children, men love their wives more if they continue this relation, and the highest devotion is based upon it, a very beautiful thing, and I am glad nature gave it us."* (21)

These women appear to have rejected the prescriptions of the marriage handbooks and other advice manuals that denied women sexual feelings and their legitimate expression. They are a gratifying reminder that ordinary people have always been able to defy the messages of fear and apprehension from the self-appointed guardians of the 'truth'.

Recreational sex has been incredibly fertile. A huge part of Western literature is devoted to extolling or describing the pleasures and agonies of sex and love. Consider the following poem by Sappho, ancient female Greek poet (ca. 600 BCE):

> *When I behold thee*
>
> *Even a moment;*
>
> *Utterance leaves me;*

My tongue is useless;

Runs through my body;

My eyes are sightless,

And my ears ringing;

I flush with fever,

And a strong trembling

Lays hold upon me;

Paler than grass am I,

Half dead for madness. (22)

What is the source of the sexual attraction that Sappho describes so marvelously, and which is the prelude of the sexual drama that is played out in almost infinite variations all over the world. The biologically oriented scholars of sexual behavior tell us that what activates us sexually is a stimulus that we interpret as a sexual incentive. For animals, the stimulus is the appearance and proximity of a potential mate. For us as well external visual stimuli are very important and common, but it remains for the mind to interpret and integrate the stimulus. Or as William Shakespeare put it:

Love looks not with the eyes, but with the mind,

And therefore is winged Cupid painted blind (23)

Let's say we are in the proverbial crowded room and a face catches our attention. Sometimes the impact of that stimulus can be overwhelming. Consider the first meeting of Dante Alighieri, the author of *The Divine Comedy*, and Beatrice Portinari, the woman who became his muse and inspiration, even though they only met two or three times during their lives. He was so taken by her (she was only eight years old at the time, and he was ten) that he wrote later in his autobiographical book *La Vita Nuova how he felt* **"Behold a god more powerful than I who comes to rule over me."** (24)

Or consider Romeo's reaction when he first meets Juliet

O, she doth teach the torches to burn bright!

It seems she hangs upon the cheek of night

Like a rich jewel in an Ethiope's ear;

Beauty too rich for use, for earth too dear (25)

Much closer to our time is Richard Burton's description of his first glimpse of the nineteen-year old Elizabeth Taylor:

"She was so extraordinarily beautiful that I nearly laughed out loud. She . . . was famine, fire, destruction and plague . . . the only true begetter. Her breasts were apocalyptic, they would topple empires before they withered . . . her body was a miracle of construction" (26)

Poor old Richard fell hard, and he probably never recovered his sanity.

The stimulus can be just as effective between same sex individuals. Marcel Proust in his novel *Remembrance of Things Past* has one his characters relate an encounter between Baron de Charlus, and a railway conductor at a train station:

"'Oh', the sculptor would whisper, seeing a young railway man with the sweeping eyelashes of a dancing girl, de Charlus could not help staring 'if the Baron begins making eyes at the conductor, we shall never get there, the train will start going backwards'" (27)

We don't always need the presence of an external sexual stimulus to be activated sexually. We can also be, and quite often are, stimulated by mental images, remembrances of past sexual encounters, or erotic fantasies of sexual intercourse either with a person we know or even with a person we don't know. Sometimes these images of sexual activity can be so powerful that they may induce orgasm. Some women can induce an orgasm by evoking images of sexual activity with some desired partner. These seem not to be faked since the mentally induced orgasms show the same hormonal and genital blood flow patterns as women who obtain orgasm by physical stimulation of the genitalia.

Our ability to respond to external stimuli or mental images depends on central nervous system processes about which we know little as yet. In animals certain brain regions that play an important role in processing sexual stimuli have been identified, but it is not yet clear whether the same brain regions – we might call them the *sex activation centers* - modulate our responses to sexual stimuli. It is even more difficult to identify the source of our selectivity – why we respond to some but not all stimuli.

We don't really know why we find one person more attractive than another, any more that we know why we have certain preferences – in cars, houses, paintings, music, etc. The strength of the sexual incentive evoked by different persons varies considerably, and our preferences can also change with time and place. Our preferences in sexual partners like our preferences in food and drink are also strongly culturally influenced, and our sexual behaviors are modulated by social learning – not only with respect to when, where, and how we have sex, but also with respect to the body expressions (gestures, facial signals) and words that we use to communicate our sexual readiness, and the way in which we respond to signals from others.

It is quite common nowadays to read that our sexual preferences in partners are determined by what is called the 'reproductive value' of our desired partner. Sociobiologists and evolutionary psychologists have been the main proponents of these views. For example, males are said to prefer female body shapes with a waist/hip ratio of 0.70 (somehow, males possess a calibrated eyeball that can calculate these ratios in every woman) because such a ratio is a marker of good health, good genes, and good fertility. Or that males like large breasts because a large breast is an assurance of abundant food for the infant. These stories always catch our attention, and often they are interesting to read. But we shouldn't take them seriously. Specifically, there is no evidence that women with a waist/hip ratio of 0.70 are more fertile than women with a different ratio. Much more likely is that this ratio reflects a Western (or American) cultural bias and preference rather than some biological imperative. In addition, there is no correlation between the size of the breast and ability to breast feed successfully. And, of course, these arguments don't apply for same sex preferences.

More generally, these evolutionary scenarios are the equivalent of "psycho babble" applied to physiological processes. We like to read about them because we have a weakness for trying to find meaning and purpose in the world around us. Laura Kipnis, author of a number of books on the complexities of human sexual behavior, likens these scenarios to Rudyard Kipling's *Just So Stories* written for children (examples: *How the camel got his hump, How the rhinoceros got his skin*). Despite their patina of science, they are fables, fanciful notions, and interestingly they all tend to ratify prevailing cultural views of men as the powerful, dominant ape and women as maternal, nurturing, and demure.

The strength of the incentives that motivate us for sex is not always stable. Initially we may be overcome by an intense desire - what we would term 'lust' or perhaps 'falling in love'. We all want that intense physical longing to last but perhaps more often than not, it doesn't. Falling in love is the first act of a drama that quite often ends in disaffection or tragedy. We can fall out of love almost as quickly as we fall in love. This seesaw is much more common during adolescence and early adulthood, but it can occur at any age.

The end of love is heartbreaking. The poem O do not love too long by W. B. Yeats expresses that poignancy

> **Sweetheart, do not love too long**
>
> **I loved long and long,**
>
> **And grew to be out of fashion**
>
> **Like an old song** (28)

The result of falling out of love can sometimes be overwhelming. Consider how one poet responds to his former lover's withdrawal:

> *Today . . . your mind moved back into your face, willing away Your last night's beauty. And the hard mask of resolution lies dull upon you like a bad make-up.*
>
> *There are no stars tonight to get my bearing by. What time is it? What season? What year? The sky sags . . . bellies. The city gargles*

dust in the streets. (29)

Love, what's left for us, and of us, is this Living remnant, loving revenant, brief kiss Like a bee flying completed dying hiveless (30)

The waning of the passion for one person, and the search for its replacement in another is quite likely an important reason for infidelity and divorce. William Simon, noted scholar of human sexual behavior, describes this waning in a way that may be very typical: *"I have a niece who is about forty: two of her female friends recently unnerved her by leaving what appeared to be very successful marriages. And when asked why did they leave, they replied almost identically – 'This may be the last time I will ever know being in love again.'"* (31).

But we also know that deep bonds of affection often develop even after sexual passions have diminished in intensity. One of the women of the Mosher study expresses this change:

"My ideas as to the reason (for intercourse) have changed materially from what they were before marriage. I then thought reproduction was the only object and that once brought about, intercourse should cease. But in my experience the habitual bodily expression of love has a deep psychological effect in making possible complete mental sympathy, and perfecting the spiritual union that must be the lasting 'marriage' after the passion of love has passed way with years." (21)

Shakespeare expresses this development in his insightful and exhilarating way:

Love's not Time's fool, though rosy lips and cheeks Within his bending sickle's compass come; Love alters not with his brief hours and weeks, But bears it out even to the edge of doom (32)

The British journalist, Claire Rayner, who wrote a column for a British newspaper in the 1970s dealing with emotional, medical, and sexual questions, ended an interesting article titled *The Meaning of Sex: A View from the Agony Column* as follows: *"These are the people who, I believe, stand happily at the end of the long, long line which runs through our history from Chaucer to Shakespeare to Fielding to Max*

Miller. For them, sex means simply fun. And I hope none of us ever forgets that meaning." (33)

Does sex have meaning?

Does sex have meaning in some ultimate, objective sense? Does it signify something beyond our own experience of it? The universe we inhabit provides no clue, and in this vacuum we have had to provide our own answers. Giving meaning and significance to our existence is perhaps the one common feature of all human societies. We find it almost impossible to consider that our existence has no meaning. The thought may be too frightening for most of us. And this may be true of sex as well. All human societies have invested greatly in creating the stories that give sex meaning and significance. Although these stories have been used as a way of controlling or containing sex's immense force, it is also the case that these stories – these myths – are an attempt to understand and interpret our sexuality, and they have great symbolic value.

Although the meaning and significance of sex, both individually and collectively, has varied throughout human history, two general ideas about the meaning of sex that have held sway In the Western world for several thousand years. One of the earliest contends that sex is a sacrament, an expression of religious faith. Interestingly, both the act itself and its denial (celibacy and chastity) have resonated powerfully in many cultures. A second general idea, equally ancient, is the view that sex has been a civilizing force in societies, especially because of its civilizing influence on males. More recently, with the increased secularization of contemporary society, we see emerging a more private, and less collective, meaning of sex as a search for intimacy, psychological comfort, and solace.

Sacramental sex

The sacramental or religious significance of sex may originate in the connection between sex and fertility, a connection that must have been noted very early in our history. This relationship may have become especially critical with the development of agriculture, with the cycle of planting, growth, and harvest so essential for the survival of the earliest farming communities. In ancient Mesopotamia (Sumer and Akkad) and Egypt yearly rituals enacted by the king and a priestess to ensure the fertility of the soil played an important part in the life of the society. The earliest written records that give us an insight into these ceremonies appear in a collection of poems from about 2500 BCE. They are called the Dumuzi-Inanna cycle, often referred to as the Sumerian 'love poetry' or 'sex poetry' or 'sexual lyrics' cycle. Inanna was the Sumerian goddess of love and war, and her consort, Dumuzi, was the priest-king and shepherd of the land. The poems themselves are very explicit evocations of passion and sexual abandon. At one point Inanna and Dumizi exchange these sentiments:

" this vulva ... of mine, clothed in beauty, my vulva the moist and well-watered ground – who will put an ox there? Lady, the King shall plough them for you. Her vulva is as sweet as her mouth, her mouth is as sweet as her vulva. Plough my vulva, man of my heart.
(34)

When my sweet precious, my heart, had lain

down too, each of them in turn kissing with the tongue, each in

turn, then did it fifty times to her, exhaustedly waiting for her,

as she trembled underneath him. " (35)

Although the full significance of these earthy and sensual poems is still debated among Sumerian scholars, the standard interpretation is that they allude to a ritual known as the "sacred marriage". This ceremony was part of the celebration of the New Year, in which the king, representing Dumuzi, would have sexual intercourse with a priestess representing the goddess Inanna. Their sexual union, apparently done in public, was essentially a religious sacrament, a prayer to the gods to assure a good harvest. Some verses refer clearly to this wish:

. . . with head high, the king goes now . . . to the holy embrace

of Inana. . . may he, like the farmer, make the fields productive . . . may he make the sheepfolds multiply. . . under him may there be flax, may there by barley, in the rivers may there be carp floods . . . in the marshes, fish . . . may the irrigated orchards produce syrup and wine." (36)

Lovemaking was transformed from a simple act between two people, especially during the time of the sacred marriage ceremony, into a transcendent religious experience, a communion with an appeal to the gods, in which everyone, in addition to the king and priestess, was expected to participate.

Two thousand years later the Greek historian, Herodotus, relates this story about a Babylonian practice (that probably both fascinated and appalled him) from about 1500 BCE

Every woman of the city has to go once in her life to the temple of Innana and give herself to a strange man . . . They all sit in rows, with gangways in between so the men can walk through and make their choice. Once a woman has taken her seat she is not allowed to go home until a man has thrown a silver coin into her lap and taken her outside to lie with her. It matters not what be the sum of money; the woman will never refuse, for that were a sin, the money being by this act made sacred. After their intercourse she has made herself holy in the sight of the Goddess and goes away to her home. Tall handsome women soon manage to get home again, but the ugly ones stay a long time before they can fulfill the law, some even as long as four years. (37, C. Miles and J. J. Norwich Love in the Ancient World)

In these rites and ceremonies sex was a collective act with many participants. Often they were wild exuberant celebrations in which all sexual prohibitions were lifted, and men and women had sex with many partners. The women often dressed as men and men dressed as women. The prophets of the Hebrew Bible railed mightily and continually against these practices. For some reason the exchanging clothes between men and women was considered a particularly abhorrent sin deserving of a special injunction as contained in Deuteronomy 22:5 *"The woman shall not wear that which pertaineth unto a man, neither shall a man put on a woman's garment; for all that do so are abomination unto the Lord thy god"*

Historians who have studied these pagan festivals and customs suggest that the exchange of clothes was a way for either sex to acquire the powers of the other sex. For men, in particular, it was to attain women's magic and powers, because women were considered to have special knowledge and to be much closer to the gods. The practice was so common even during the early Christian centuries that St. Augustine was driven to proclaim that men who wore women's clothes could not be saved. But in an ironic turn of events, the only men who were allowed to wear something like women's clothes were the priests of the church.

Many of these ancient practices were transplanted into the Greek and Roman worlds and evolved from approximately 800 BCE to about 600 CE into what historians call the Mystery traditions, of which the Bacchic, Dionysiac, Eleusinian, and Orphic are the best known. These practices were referred to as "orgies", derived the Greek word "orgia" meaning "secret worship", because they involved secret rituals in which only the initiated could partake. They were often celebrated at night with a frenzied religious and sexual fervor that may be difficult for us to imagine. Erotic dances with wild processions carrying an erect phallus were a common feature. There were many celebrations during the year, always bound up with the cycles of agriculture and fertility. The feast of the Saturnalia held at the winter equinox (December 21), celebrated the end of winter, and the hope of the coming of spring. The early Christians retained many of the dates of these orgiastic festivals but removed all the vestiges of their sexual nature. Christmas, for example, became the transformed Saturnalia festival. Valentine's day is a relic of the Lupricalia festivals, renown for wild, sensual dances in which the display of sausages had an important role. The Christian emperors of the 4th and 5th centuries finally had enough and took the unusual step of outlawing both dancing and sausages.

The Church's proscriptions against these festivals were never really completely successful, and some these festivals continued until the 15th and 16th centuries. One of these, the May festival, was celebrated after the spring planting to ensure the fertility of the soil. The festival would generally begin with dancing around the May pole, which according to historians represented a giant phallus inserted into Mother Earth.

Afterwards, the crowd would spread out into the plowed and planted fields and had sex with whoever was willing.

Although the origin of these festivals was religious, it is difficult to know whether the fervor of the participants was equally sexual and religious. We can easily imagine that the sexual motivation was predominant, and that the celebrations soon became 'debaucheries', as the early Christian critics called them, giving the pejorative connotation to the term 'orgy' that we have today. Remnants of these ancient practices remain today – just think of the annual spring break festivities in tropical resorts in which thousands of college age students participate, or the pre-Lenten festivals known as 'Carnaval' in Europe, or the Mardi Gras festivals in New Orleans or Rio de Janeiro. The religious aspect of these festivals has completely disappeared, and what remains is the public exuberance and celebration, a 'letting go' of sorts, with the sexual undercurrents still present, but greatly attenuated.

The polytheistic religions with their cult of the Earth Mother and their celebration of sex and nudity were eventually displaced in the Western tradition by the monotheistic religions, first Judaism, then Christianity. In these, sex was no longer celebrated openly and with such wild enjoyment, but was submerged, associated with sin, and no longer to be celebrated but to be carried out only for procreation. The sexual still retained its power, but in a strange twist, the denial of sex – celibacy and chastity - became the important virtues in the emerging Christian world. Sex existed for procreation and was therefore tolerated, but abstinence was a higher virtue. St. Paul in his Epistles praises widows and virgins for their chastity, devotion to the things of the Lord, and their church work. A consistent theme of the early Christian writers was their distaste for the married state. Soranus of Ephesus, a well-known physician of the second century, expressed it in medical terms:

Even among dumb animals we see that those females are stronger which are prevented from having intercourse. And among women we see that those who, on account of regulations and service to the gods, have renounced intercourse and those who have been kept in virginity as ordained by laws are less susceptible to disease. If, on the other hand, they have menstrual difficulties and become fat and illproportioned, this comes about because of idleness and inactivity of their bodies... Consequently permanent virginity is healthy, in male and female alike; nevertheless, intercourse seems consistent with the general principle of nature according to which both sexes have to ensure the succession of living beings. (38, Vern L. Bullough and Bonnie Bullough)

St. Jerome (died 420 CE) who repeatedly emphasized the inconvenience and tribulations of marriage, is famous for this passage:

I praise marriage and wedlock, but I do so because they produce virgins for me. I gather roses from thorns, gold from the earth, and pearl from the shell. (39, St Jerome *On marriage and virginity*)

Though the Church fathers could not bring themselves to declare that marriage was evil (it had after all been instituted by God), sexual abstinence, according to them, had much more value in the Lord's eyes. It was no surprise then that religious communities of both men and women who took vows of celibacy and chastity began to spring up during the early Christian centuries. They appeared first in the Middle East, and these became the antecedents of the monasteries and convents that became part of the religious landscape of Europe. For both the men and women who chose this path, sexual abstinence was not only a way of separating themselves from the rest of society, but was a special way to experience God and to achieve a spiritual closeness to Him. It was not a coincidence that from the earliest of times, nuns were known as the brides of Christ.

The cult of virginity was not a Christian invention for it had preexisted in the pre-Christian Greek and Roman worlds. Interestingly, it also coexisted with the sexual exuberance and sexual liberty of those times. The cult of virginity manifested itself at two levels – the familial and the societal. At the familial level virginity was an important virtue in order for a young woman to marry. Fathers watched over their daughters carefully, and punished them with great severity if they had sex before marriage.

In the Greek world, devotion to the two preeminent virgin goddesses, Athena and Artemis, expressed the societal importance of virginity. As was common with many of the gods and goddesses of Greek mythology, the stories of their births and roles varied from one region to another. Athena was both the goddess of war (a highly unusual role for a female deity) and also of wisdom. She was the one who inspired Odysseus with the idea of the Trojan Horse, that lead to the final defeat of Troy. She was also the goddess of weaving, needlework, and the domestic arts. In these roles she embodied both masculine and feminine traits. Artemis was the goddess of the hunt and wild nature, a symbol of freedom and independence. Artemis, in fact, chose to be a virgin, and asked Zeus to remain a virgin forever.

In the Roman world the societal cult of virginity rested on the Vestal Virgins. Although they had a number of functions, one of their main roles was the keepers of the sacred fire in the temple of Vesta, the symbol of the hearth and the Roman state. The six Vestal Virgins, chosen generally by lot from the best Roman families, when they were between six and ten years old, remained in their post for 30 years. Remaining a virgin was an absolutely essential requirement for the Vestals. Punishment for the fall from grace was swift and severe – being buried alive.

It may be difficult for us at this distance in time to understand the significance of the societal cult of virginity in the Greek and Roman worlds. Virginity was an immensely important aspect of Athena's and Artemis' character, as it was also for the Vestals. Virginity was valued not because of any practical importance. Its value was purely symbolic. Scholars suggest that in order to understand that symbolism we should keep in mind that the Greek myths and the cult of the Vestals were all created by men. Virginity represented something primeval, unsullied, uncontaminated, undefiled by men who are brutal and brutish. Perhaps the only vestige we have of ancient virginity devotions is the cult of the Virgin Mary celebrated in the Catholic countries of southern Europe and Latin America. The Virgin has thousands of devotees. Festivals in her honor, celebrated by men and women alike, are a moving testimony to the faith of her adherents. In Mexico, it is very common to see images of the Virgin of Guadalupe hanging in the rear view mirrors of taxis, trucks and buses. The Virgin represents unblemished purity, a refuge from the sordidness and corruption that surrounds them, the loving and ever forgiving mother to whom they can turn for solace, someone who preserves her identity, independence and is impervious to the influences of any other being. Perhaps this is why virginity has resonated so powerfully in the psyche of men.

Does sex civilize?

The earliest suggestion that sex has a civilizing influence comes from the first known work of literary fiction, *Gilgamesh,* an epic poem dating from about 2000 BCE. The story chronicles the life of a mythic king, Gilgamesh, of ancient Sumer. The first part of the story concerns the relationship between Gilgamesh, who has become distracted and disheartened by his rule, and a friend, Enkidu, who is half-wild man when he first appears in the story. Enkidu, runs with the wild animals and is creating havoc with the farmers and shepherds. The shepherds complain to Gilgamesh, and the king sends the woman Shamhat, a temple prostitute to deal with Enkidu. The meeting of Shamhat and Enkidu is perhaps one of the most interesting parts of the epic. Below is one recent translation of that encounter:

(Shamhat) stripped off her robe and lay there naked, with her legs apart, touching herself. Enkidu saw her and warily approached. He sniffed the air. He gazed at her body. He drew close, Shamhat touched him on the thigh, touched his penis, and put him inside her. She used her lovearts, she took his breath with her kisses, held nothing back, and showed him what a woman is. For seven days he stayed erect and made love with her, until he had had enough. At last he stood up and walked toward the waterhole to rejoin his animals. But the gazelles saw him and scattered, the antelope and deer bounded away. He tried to catch up, but his body was exhausted, his life-force was spent, his knees trembled, he could not longer run like an animal, as he had before. He turned to Shamhat, and as he walked he knew that his mind had somehow grown larger, he knew things now that an animal can't know. (40, Stephen Mitchell, *Gilgamesh*)

Sexual contact with Shamhat tames the beast in Enkidu, and transforms him into a human being. In this story sex has an ennobling, civilizing effect, a powerful force for good. This idea has resonated over much of Western history, and has survived the notions of sex as sinful or a necessary evil as exemplified in the story of Adam and Eve, or in the notions of the Church fathers. In the historical records, the civilizing of conquered territories or cities began with the arrival of women. What other message, if not the humanizing, calming, and refining effects of women, do we get from proliferation of love poetry, the chivalry romances of the Middle Ages, the focus on love in most novels. And keep in mind that this love literature has been written mostly by men.

The search for intimacy

Love is something far more than desire for sexual intercourse. It is the principal means of escape from the loneliness which afflicts most men and women through the greatest part of their lives. (41, Bertrand Russell)

It may be true that as Bertrand Russell indicates in this epigraph that we are continually searching for a way to assuage the loneliness that is an essential part of the human condition. Friends can help fill the abyss, but perhaps only sexual intimacy can satisfy us completely and fully. How else to explain the proliferation and popularity columnists of the Dear Abby type, of therapists of all persuasions that occupy the radio and television airwaves that offer advice and counsel. Entering *Sex* and *Intimacy* in Google search returns over 5 million entries. The British journalist, Claire Rayner, who wrote a column for a mass circulation newspaper in Britain, and dealt with a wide range of emotional and sexual problems, in 1977 described her conclusions from her many years of letters from her readers: *"For a great many people, the only real joy and sense of deep satisfaction they ever get is from sex."* (33, Claire Rayner, The meaning of sex: a view from the agony column).

Joan Miro, "Ohne title, 1924" (cSuccessio Miro/Artists Rights Society (ARS). New York/ADAGP, Paris 2013)

Chapter 3

Anatomy of Sex

The iconic tissues – *cultural obsessions*

A consideration of the genital members is very difficult, and everything should not be revealed particularly with youths, because sin makes the subject of generation diabolical and full of shame, and a discussion might excite impure acts (John Moir (1620) Anatomical Education in a Scottish University)

A 2000-year confusion

Generally, when we think about our sexual machinery, the external genitalia and the female breast immediately come to mind. These tissues not only define the most obvious anatomical differences between the sexes, but they also are the focus of much of our erotic imagination. Their images excite our imagination in ways that are generally unthinkable with images of other parts of the body. They are not simply a part of the body like the limbs, the head, the eyes, or the heart. They are the symbols – the *icons* – of our sexual universe.

The female and male genitalia look so different from each other that it is difficult to imagine that at one time they were considered inside-out versions of each other. The Greek physician Galen (2nd century CE), convinced that the two sexes were complementary, considered that the genitalia were two versions of an underlying substance, and one could be turned into the other. The anatomist Baldasar Heseler (1540) was quite definitive: ***"The organs of procreation are the same in the male and the female . . . For if you turn the scrotum, the testicles, and the***

penis inside out you will have all the genital organs of the female".
(2)

In the 18th century edition of a famous British sex advice manual, Aristotle's Masterpiece, the unknown author of the poem wrote:

Thus the Women's Secrets I have surveyed

And let them see how curiously they're made:

And that, tho they of different sexes be,

Yet in the Whole they are the same as we:

For those that have the strictest Searchers been,

Find Women are but Men turned Outside in:

And Men, if they but cast their Eyes about,

Many find they're women with their Inside out. (3)

You would think that this fanciful notion would have disappeared by now, but apparently it is still alive, because remarkably, it was resurrected in the 2003 movie *"Normal"* starring Jessica Lange and Tom Wilkinson. The film traces the complications of the decision of the husband (Wilkinson) after 25 years of marriage and two children to become a female. In one dramatic short scene their adolescent daughter, played by Haden Panettiere, entertains her girl friends by demonstrating with plastic bags and a banana how the male genitalia can easily be converted into the female genitalia. You have to see it to believe it.

The penis – *power and anxiety*

The word 'penis' is derived from an archaic Latin word for an animal's tail, perhaps because like an animal's tail, it can stiffen and rise, as well as hang down between the legs. Apparently, it was considered an obscene term, but somehow the word survived and became the accepted name. The penis stands out in its erotic potential, probably because of its size and its remarkable ability to transform itself from a small, flaccid tissue to a much larger stiff one. The erect penis has since time immemorial symbolized vitality, power, and fertility and has been celebrated in sculpture and painting in probably all cultures.

Perhaps the earliest, from 15,000 years ago, is found in the painting known as "The Man in the Well" in the cave of Lascaux in the Dordogne region of France. The scene depicts a dying bison, and next to it a very simple sketch of a man who appears to be lying down or falling backwards. To the left is the figure of a rhinoceros that appears to be running away. In contrast to the well-drawn figure of the wounded animal, the man is a stick figure, very childlike, but the most conspicuous aspect of the man, however, is his unmistakable erection. There have been numerous interpretations of the entire scene, but interestingly, this distinctive anatomical detail seems to have been ignored. Images of the erect penis, especially huge ones, are fairly common in primitive art, and they have been found in many parts of the world. Although we don't really know what these images meant or represented to the artist's audience, they suggest at the very least a preoccupation with the penis.

In ancient Egyptian and Sumerian societies the penis, especially the ejaculating penis, was venerated as life-creating. Impotence meant defeat and death. The cutting off of penises of the losers in battle was a common way to celebrate the victory. One inscription in the walls of Karnack from around 1200 BCE celebrated the victory of the Egyptians over the Libyans by enumerating the penises cut off and presented to the Pharoah - Libyan generals, 6; Libyan soldiers, 6,359; Sicilian soldiers, 222; Etruscan soldiers, 542; and Greek soldiers, 6,111.

In classical Greek and Roman times the erect penis also symbolized dominance and strength. Stone sculptures, with the head of the god Hermes and in the middle a huge erect penis known as Hermae were on display in every town and in many Greek homes. All Roman boys, as good luck amulets, wore a *bulla*, a necklace with a locket containing a replica of an erect penis known as a *fascinum*. A large fascinum hung in the chariot of the victorious general during the elaborate Roman victory parades. All Roman towns displayed sculptures of the god Priapus, a small, ugly figure but with an enormous erect penis. The name survives today as a medical term referring to an erection that lasts more than one hour (priapism). Fifteen hundred years after the fall of Rome, the Italian prime minister during World War I wore a fascinum on a bracelet to ensure victory by the Allies.

With the advent of Christianity the prominent display of such images went underground, and appear only in hard-core pornography. But there is no doubt that the linkage of the penis and power persists. One remarkable example occurred during an off-the-record encounter between President Lyndon Johnson and a number of reporters who were questioning him about the presence of the U.S. in Vietnam. Increasingly irritated by the refusal of his skeptical audience to understand his explanations, he finally unzipped his trousers, pulled out his penis, and shouted: "This is why!"

Even as men have flaunted the power of the penis, they have been beset by a deep, sometimes unsettling anxiety about impotence, a small penis, or its disappearance altogether. This latter gives rise to the condition known as *koro,* a pathological fear that the penis will somehow retract into the abdominal cavity. Epidemics of koro sweep across some Asian countries periodically. The men attach clamps or weighted strings to prevent penile retraction that they believe will lead to their death.

In contemporary societies many men worry about their penis size. Pathological worry about penis size is known as the 'small penis syndrome.' Which, of course, brings up the question: *what is the normal penis size?* One reliable study involving 80 physically normal men showed a mean size of the Flaccid penis 8.9 -+ 2.4 cm (2.5 cm equals 1 inch) and the Erect penis 12.9 -+ 2.9 cm. Smaller penises grow relatively longer than bigger ones during erection. From a statistical rule of thumb then, an erect length of less than 7 cm would be considered abnormally short, and an erect length of more than 19 cm would be considered abnormally long.

It is not clear that this information is a comfort to many men. Normal depends on the individual. It is also very subjective. Otherwise it is difficult to explain the explosion of penis augmentation surgery, especially in southern California, and apparently carried out on men with average size, rather than very small penises. The operation, which severs the ligament supporting the penis does not lengthen the penis, it merely appears that way because the penis hangs out farther from the body. The length of the erect penis does not change, however. Operations to increase the thickness of the penis, which often result in a lumpy and abnormal looking penis, are not particularly successful either. Vanity is not a stranger to males.

Given the symbolic significance of the penis throughout history, it is not surprising that it has suffered other culturally determined modifications. One of the most common and ancient is circumcision, the removal of the foreskin (prepuce) that covers the glans, the tip tissue of the penis, which is loaded with nerves that make it exquisitely sensitive to touch. We don't really know what the function of the foreskin serves. It must not be an essential function because it can be removed without any serious consequences.

Although we may associate this practice with a Jewish and Muslim religious tradition, circumcision has a much more ancient lineage, being described in Egyptian hieroglyphics dating back to the third millennium BCE. Currently, circumcision is often justified medically for hygienic or medical reasons – prevention of *smegma* build up (mucus-like substance that can build up underneath the foreskin), prevention of *phimosis* (in which the foreskin does not retract from the glans), or reduction in the risk of transmitting sexually transmitted infections. Perhaps the most compelling reason is to reduce the risk of urinary tract infections in infancy, some of which can be very serious. Of course, none of these explain the origin or continuance of the practice for non-medical reasons.

The real point about circumcision is that it is really a religious or cultural rite signifying membership in a group or marking entry into adult status. The significance of circumcision in different societies has elicited endless commentary, but of course, no resolution. Sometimes the decision to circumcise or not may present a dilemma, as given in a tongue-in-cheek way in a recent book *Foreskin's Lament* (2007), by Shalom Auslander, with respect to his son: *"I don't know what to do, I said. On the one hand, it's insane, it's mutilation. On the other hand, maybe he should have a connection to his past. On the other hand, I worry God will kill him if we don't do it. On the other hand, I feel guilty not circumcising him when so many Jews in history died for the chance to. I'm like fucking Vishnu here with all these hands."* (4).

A few groups, notably some Polynesian and Australian aborigine tribes carry out two other more extreme penile modifications. In one the foreskin is slit on the top side (*supercision*) permitting it to fall and hang below the tip of the penis. No tissue is removed. In the other, a slit is cut along the underside of the penis (*subcision*). The result is that the glans separates from the underside of the penis and flares out, giving the penis (to our eyes) an abnormally flat look.

The female genitalia – *"L'Origine du Monde"*

The female genitalia are not as distinctive anatomically as the penis or scrotum. Interestingly, an excellent description of the female genitalia comes from an entry of *The Diary of a Young Girl* by Anne Frank. This particular entry and many others were omitted in the original 1947 edition because of their openness about the sexual awakening of a young girl, but are included in the definitive edition of 1997. The passage, remarkable for its clarity and the knowledge it reveals in such a young girl in that society, reads in part as follows:

...I don't think boys are as complicated as girls. You can easily see what boys look like in photographs or pictures of male nudes, but with women it's different. In women, the genitals, or whatever they're called, are hidden between their legs. ...How on earth would I go about describing a girl's parts?

When you're standing up, all you see from the front is hair. Between your legs there are two soft, cushiony things, also covered with hair, which press together when you're standing, so you can't see what's inside. They separate when you sit down, and they're very red and quite fleshy on the inside. In the upper part, between the outer labia, there's a fold of skin that, on second thought, looks like a kind of blister. That's the clitoris. Then come the inner labia, which are also pressed together in a kind crease. When they open up, you can see a fleshy little mound, no bigger than the top of my thumb. The upper part has a couple of holes in it, which where the urine comes out. The lower part looks as if it were just skin, and yet that's where the vagina is. You can barely find it, because the folds of skin hid the opening. The hole's so small I can hardly imagine how a man could get in there, much less how a baby could come out. It's hard enough trying to get your index finger inside. That's all there is, and yet it plays such an important role! (5).

The *vagina* is the invisible part of the genitalia, and the term is derived from a Latin word referring to a 'sheath' or 'scabbard', thus describing its function as the scabbard for the penis. The term was first used in English in 1682. The older Greek term – *verenda* – meaning a part that inspires awe or respect somehow never caught on. The term, *vulva*, is generally used to describe the visible parts of the genitalia. *The mons veneris* (mound of Venus), is a small mass of fat that overlays the pubic bone which, after puberty, is covered with hair. Below the mons are the labia (the lips) divided into the outer labia, and the inner labia. The inner labia are not covered by hair and are extremely sensitive to the touch. The two sides of the labia come together at the top and form a hood of skin that covers the clitoris, a small, hard ball of tissue.

The clitoris is the counterpart of the penis, and is perhaps the preeminent erogenous tissue in a woman's body. The term 'clitoris', derived from a Greek word of possibly several meanings, one of which is 'little hill', first appeared in English in 1615. We don't know who discovered the clitoris in a scientific sense, but the Italian anatomist, Renaldo Colombo (1516-1559) who made that claim also provided an accurate description of its sensitivity. It was the *'seat of woman's delight'*, which *'if you touched it, you will find it rendered a little harder and oblong to such a degree that it shows itself as a sort of male member.'* (6). In a guide for midwives published in 1671, the clitoris *'makes women lustful and take delight in copulation'* and without it *'they would have no desire, nor delight'* (7). In addition, in its absence they would be unable to conceive.

According to another midwives guide published in 1675, *'It is reasonable both to reason and authority that the bigger the clitoris in women, the more lustful they are.'* (8) Recent studies indicate that in contrast to the penis, which stops growing after puberty, the clitoris continues to grow during the woman's lifetime. However, external clitoral size by itself does not affect its sensitivity. Masters and Johnson (1966) demonstrated that a small clitoris is as sensitive as a large one.

The female genitalia, like the penis, have their own complicated cultural history. Catherine Blackledge in her interesting book *The Story of V: Opening Pandora's Box,* reviews the complicated history of the way in which the female genitalia have been viewed in different societies. She points out that the display of the female genitalia has an old history. Carved female images with a prominent display of vulva have been recovered in many Paleolithic archeological sites and they have generally been interpreted as fertility symbols. Even more impressive have been tombs and places of worship modeled on female genitalia, such as the stone temples in Malta and Gozo (4500-2500 BCE) which appear to represent the genitalia of the goddess. We, of course, don't really know what these images represented, but perhaps these Paleolithic and Neolithic remnants are vestiges of our forgotten matriarchal vagina-worshipping past when the flagrant display of female genitalia was life affirming and celebrated rebirth.

In the transition from matriarchal to patriarchal cultures the display of the female genitalia began to take on a more negative connotation. Consider, for example, a passage from the Hebrew Bible, from Jerusalem 13: 26-27, in which Yahweh is railing against Jerusalem that unless she repents of her wicked ways *"I will also pull your skirts up as high as your face and let your shame be seen. Oh! Your adulteries, your shrieks of pleasure, your vile prostitution."*

In an old Gaelic legend, the Irish leader, Cuchulain, decides to battle his Ulster countrymen. Many of his supporters try to dissuade him, but without success. Finally, in desperation, 150 women led by the female warrior chieftain, Sannlach, *". . . and they all exposed their nakedness and the boldness to him. Cuchulain lowered his gaze away from them and laid his face against the chariot, so that he might not see the nakedness nor the boldness of the women."* (9).

In Greek legend, Bellerophon, the invincible warrior – the tamer of the winged horse, Pegasus, killer of the Chimera, the ferocious she-monster, and conqueror of the race of women warriors, the Amazons - was finally defeated by a raised skirt. According to legend, in his attack on the city of Xanathas, Bellerophon calls on Poseidon to flood the city, but the women of Xanthas charge en masse at him, lifting their skirts to their waist, exposing their vulvas. Magically, the waves recede, and

Bellerophon and Pegasus retreat.

Since the advent of Christianity women have been coerced into being ashamed of the display of their genitalia. Painted images of female nudes always appeared with their genitalia covered, and no depiction of pubic hair was permitted. Perhaps this is why the painting *L'Origine du Monde* (1866) by the French Realism painter Gustave Courbet generated such a storm of protest that it took almost a century before it could placed on permanent public display. The painting offers a close-up view of a naked woman in bed with her legs apart and showing a full shock of pubic hair and a clear display of the labia. The title of the painting itself harks back to the ancient days of the venerated Earth mother, and the association of the female genitalia and rebirth.

Controversy has followed the painting even in recent times. In 1994 the novel *Adorations Perpetuelles* by Jacques Henric showing the painting on its cover was removed from the windows of French bookstores because it was considered to be too stimulating to passers by. We can understand why. The powerful and flaunting erotic nature of the work is evident even today when we are surrounded by images of naked women. Perhaps the reason is that the images of female genitalia today have been so sanitized and neutralized for public consumption that they have lost most of their erotic potential, almost the equivalent of the traditional painted nudes with their covered genitalia. It may be that the erotic significance of the painting lies precisely in the beauty and mystery of the unadulterated genitalia.

Most feminists have no doubt that men have been the most responsible for limiting the display of the female genitalia. Erica Jong in her book, *Fear of Flying (1973)*, puts it this way: ***"That was the basic inequity that could never be righted: not that the male has a wonderful added attraction called a penis, but that the female had a wonderful all-weather cunt. Neither storm nor sleet nor dark of night could faze it. It was always there, always ready. Quite terrifying when you think about it. No wonder men hated women. No wonder they invented the myth of female inadequacy."*** (10).

The female genitalia, like the penis, have not escaped culturally dictated surgical interventions. Surgical modification of the genitalia, known as *female circumcision, female genital mutilation,* or the currently preferred term, *female genital cutting* (FGC), is widely practiced in many countries in Africa, the Middle East, and Indonesia, and is especially associated with Islamic societies. Three main types of procedures are carried out. In the least invasive, generally known as *sunnah,* the clitoral hood is removed, although in most instances part of the clitoris is excised as well.

More invasive is the complete removal of the clitoris and the hood, a *clitorectomy,* in which it is common to remove portions of the minor labia close to the clitoris. Finally, in the most invasive procedure, known as *infibulation,* includes a clitorectomy, the removal of the entire minor labia, and parts of the major labia as well. In addition, the remaining parts of the major labia are sutured together leaving only a small opening for the flow of urine and menstrual blood. In effect, the vaginal opening is greatly reduced, which means that it has to be enlarged in preparation for the female's first intercourse.

To Western eyes, these procedures are barbaric, which is why they are generally referred to as genital mutilation. No medically reasonable justification can be provided for these practices. We may forget, however, that most deeply engrained cultural traditions don't need justification. Women in these societies generally do not view these practices as abhorrent, but view them as a rite of passage into womanhood. Without it the woman is not marriageable.

We, on the other hand, interpret these practices as an extreme and gruesome form of the culturally determined subjugation of women. Their ultimate purpose is to limit or abolish their sexual life and pleasure. However, several studies that have examined the consequences of the operation have found that the women's desire for sex (in fact the incidence of premarital sexual intercourse was not affected by the circumcision), is not reduced, and ability to experience orgasm is retained in some women. It is interesting to note that while the American Academy of Pediatrics has taken a strong stand against FGC, it has taken a neutral position with respect to male circumcision. Through pressures by the U. S. and other Western countries, many African countries have banned the practices, but it is difficult to know how effective the bans are.

FGC, however, is not unknown in the West – it goes by another name, *female cosmetic genital surgery* (FCGS), and has become a new growth industry in the field of cosmetic surgery. The most common procedures are *labioplasty* – reduction or correction of irregularities of the labia; *vaginoplasty* (tightening the vagina) - narrowing the vagina introitus; *clitoral unhooding* – removing the tissue surrounding the clitoris; hymenoplasty – reconstruction of the hymen; *G-spot amplification* – injecting the anterior vaginal wall with collagen. All these procedures have been marketed as increasing sexual sensitivity and satisfaction. These procedures are carried out every year, and their number has been increasing significantly every over the last decade. And of course, genital cosmetic surgery is one more version of other types of cosmetic surgery common in women – face lifts, nose alterations, liposuction, and breast augmentation. From an anatomical perspective FCGS and FGC are essentially the same. The critical difference according to the supporters of FCGS is that the adult female 'freely' chooses to undergo their surgery, whereas FGC is imposed on young girls without their consent.

The breast – eros and nurturance

For why do you exhibit your 'milky way,' your uncovered bosoms? What else is it but to say plainly, Ask me, ask me, I will surrender; and what is that but love's call? (11)

The breast has been a cultural obsession in probably every human society. In ancient times the breast was a symbol of life, the source of the life-giving milk that made human life possible. The most ancient depictions of the breast are the Venus statuettes and breast-shaped pendants found in many Paleolithic sites from different parts of the world dating to about 20,000 years ago. The statuettes are typically faceless, armless, and legless, but with enormous breasts – potent symbols of their power to sustain life. The enduring symbol in many primitive societies was the earth mother, the giver and sustainer of life, and depicted with large breasts. The Egyptian goddess, Isis, whose breast milk nurtured not only the living but also in the afterlife, was worshipped for almost

4,000 years. In many cultures our galaxy, the Milky Way, was imagined to have originated from the spilled drops of milk the mother goddess' breasts.

Echoes of this ancient veneration of the breast and breast milk existed even into the medieval period in Christian Europe where the Virgin Mary's milk was said to contain miraculous curative powers. Saint Bernard, given up for dead, was restored to life when the Virgin appeared in a dream, put her breast to his lips, and gave him three drops of milk. Many holy shrines, scattered over Europe, were said to have obtained vials of the Virgin's milk by some miraculous intervention. So much of it was available that John Calvin, the French Protestant theologian of the 1500s and the founder of Calvinism, exasperated at the practice commented *"There is so much that if the holy Virgin had been a cow, or a wet nurse all her life she would have been hard put to it to yield such a great quantity."* (12).

The veneration of the earth mother eventually gave way to malecentered religions in which male gods were predominant, and with this change the breast began to be seen more and more as a symbol of sex and pleasure, but still somehow mysterious and elusive.

Revealing the complexity of our cultural obsession with the breast is Woody Allen's film *Everything You Always Wanted to Know About Sex but Were Afraid to Ask* (1970) in which a giant breast cup begins rampaging the countryside and becomes a threat to civilization, and in Phillip Roth's enigmatic novel *The Breast* in which a man is transformed into a breast. Much more explicit are the incessant images of large breasted women and advertisements promoting breast uplifts and breast augmentation surgery. Breasts have become a commodity, rather than an object of veneration. Marilyn Yalom, in her exhaustive *A History of the Breast* traces the complicated vicissitudes of the depictions, images, and symbolic significance of the breast in human societies, puts it this way – *". . . babies see food, men see sex, doctors see disease, businessmen see dollar signs . . ." The much more difficult question, however, is what do women see?* (12) For this question there is no single, straightforward answer.

The sexual sensory apparatus
Where is fancy bred?

Tell me where is fancy bred,

Or in the heart or in the head?

How begot, how nourished?

Reply, reply (13)

How would you answer Shylock's poignant questions? Although we often speak about "affairs of the heart", as if the heart were independent of our head, we all understand that the heart cannot be the source of our fancy. Any adult recognizes that our brain is the command center controlling our sexual interactions. Lest we flatter ourselves with this bit of understanding, we should remember that recognizing the importance of the brain is not recent. As Hippocrates, that crusty old Greek physician from the fourth century BCE, put it *"From the brain, and from the brain only, arise our pleasures, joys, laughter and jests, as well as our sorrow, pains, griefs and tears"*. **(14)** He would also quite likely agree that the brain is both the source of our sexual imagination and the command center through which all aspects of our sexual lives are realized. Emily Dickinson had her own way of expressing the mystery of the brain:

The Brain is wider than the Sky –

For – put them side by side –

The one the other will contain

With ease – and You – beside (15)

The brain, however, does not exist in a void. It is continually receiving from a sensory nervous system, the network through which our five senses inform our brain about the world outside. Sexual arousal and excitation can be elicited from visual, tactile, olfactory and possibly other cues. These signals are channeled through different sets of sensory neurons to the sexual centers in the brain.

Physical stimulation of the genitalia probably elicits the most intense sexual arousal and activates sensory nerves in the penis, scrotum, and rectum. The genital sensory nerves – the pudendal, the pelvic, hypogastric, and genitofermoral nerves – which transmit their impulses through the spinal cord, and vagus nerve which bypasses the spinal cord, receive information from a number of genital sites. These include the clitoris and clitoral sheath, the anterior vaginal wall, the labia, the cervix, the penis, scrotum, perineum and thigh, the anus and rectum, the nipples, and the prostate. Tactile stimulation of the genitalia activates a special class of skin receptors known as *Ruffini* endings, which are especially sensitive to pressure. The clitoris and the penis glans (the tip of the penis) have the highest concentration of the Ruffini receptors.

Stimulation of the tip of the penis will activate the pudendal nerve, while touching the shaft of the penis, the scrotum, or the rectum will activate the pelvic nerve. Interestingly, even stimulation of the prostate can be sexually arousing. In this case the hypogastric nerve carries the arousal signals. The genitofemoral nerve carries information from the thigh and perineum. In broad outline the female sexual wiring diagram is very similar to male wiring diagram, although the partitioning of sensory input by these three nerves appears to be more intricate and complex than in the male. The pudendal nerve, for example, innervates the clitoris primarily, the pelvic nerve, the vagina wall, cervix, and rectum, while the hypogastric nerve innervates the uterus and cervix. The vagus nerve, which bypasses the spinal cord, innervates the upper vagina and cervix. This suggests that physical stimulation of the female genitalia may generate both distinct and complementary signals that are then transmitted to multiple sex centers of the brain. In addition, stimulation of the nipple will activate sensory nerve fibers that transmit signals to the same brain sex centers that receive information from the genitalia. This diversity of sensory signals has suggested to some investigators that sexual response of females may be more nuanced than that of males.

Hormones – the chemical messengers

In both sexes, the brain's ability (or more correctly, specific structures within the brain) to respond to stimuli with sexual responses depends on a number of chemical messengers, a broad class of compounds that for our purposes here we divide into hormones and neurotransmitters. In the first group are the sex hormone, testosterone, and the pituitary hormones, oxytocin and vasopressin; in the second group the neurotransmitters, dopamine and serotonin. The neurotransmitters, dopamine, serotonin, and the pituitary hormones, oxytocin, vasopressin, have been discussed widely in the popular media, often with extravagant claims about their functions. Oxytocin, for example, has been called the "cuddle hormone', vasopressin, the 'bonding' hormone, and dopamine and serotonin the "feel good chemicals". Most of what we know about these compounds comes from animal studies. Their role in humans is still unclear. On the other hand, the universal role of testosterone in sexual activity is the best understood.

Importance of testosterone – *in the male*

Probably all human societies have known that a great reduction in sexual activity in the male is a major consequence of the removal of the testes (castration). Many recent well-controlled studies of men castrated for medical reasons (prostate or testicular cancer) have shown quite clearly that the intensity of sexual behaviors, erotic dreams and fantasies is greatly reduced. The testosterone dependency also shows a threshold effect, that is, a certain minimum level of testosterone is needed to elicit sexual behavior, but increasing the levels of testosterone does not increases the intensity of the sexual behavior.

This means that administering testosterone to men with normal testosterone levels does not increase the intensity of their responses to sexual stimuli. An interesting demonstration of this threshold effect came out of a study in which genital response in castrated men to sexual stimuli was monitored directly by using strain gauges that measured penile circumference while the men viewed pornographic movies. From many other studies it is known that penile circumference increases reliably in most men by watching pornographic movies. An interesting observation in this study was that penile circumference increased in 25% of the castrated men. The testosterone levels in these responders were two-fold greater than the levels measured in the non-responders.

Since the only source of testosterone in the castrated men is the adrenal gland, this result indicated that in some men adrenal testosterone may be sufficiently high to maintain some level of sexual functioning. This experiment also provides a way of understanding anecdotal reports of castrated men preserving some sexual function.

We can summarize a large amount of data by saying that in the human male the ability to respond to diverse sexual stimuli is dependent on testosterone action. What we don't yet know is where and how testosterone enables different structures in the brain to respond to diverse sexual stimuli.

Importance of testosterone - *in the female*

The role of sex hormones in female sexual behavior has been the subject of dozens of studies. Many of these have examined variations in sexual behavior during the ovulatory cycle or have compared pre-menopausal with post-menopausal women. Unfortunately, the vast majority of these studies have relied on subjective measures of response (questionnaires and self-reports). The conclusions from such studies can be unreliable, and this may account in part for the conflicting data they have generated. A few recent studies have used objective measures of female response, such as an increase in vaginal vasocongestion (increase in genital blood flow which can be measured accurately – see below) to sexual stimuli (for example movies depicting sexual intercourse).

The results from these studies, in contrast, are quite consistent. First, they show that the variation in responses to sexual stimuli during the ovulatory cycle is negligible. Moreover, no significant differences were seen in the genital blood flow response of premenopausal compared to post-menopausal women, despite studies in which post-menopausal women report diminished sexual satisfaction. The most straightforward explanation is that the subjective experience of diminished sexual responsiveness is not physiological, but depends on the context of the situation. Many other factors may influence the way in which postmenopausal experience sex. In any case, since estrogen levels vary during the cycle, and since post-menopausal estrogen levels are very low, these observations indicate that estrogen, an absolutely critical hormone in many other respects, does not have an important role in female sexual behavior.

What about testosterone? The sources of testosterone in the premenopausal female are the ovaries (25%), the adrenal glands (25%), and peripheral tissues (50%). The adrenal glands have more importance than their 25% contribution might suggest. This is because they also produce the progenitor compounds that are used by the peripheral tissues to produce testosterone. Testosterone levels decrease with age so that 40-50 year old women have about half the testosterone levels as 20 year olds. Thereafter, the decline is slower or may cease. Quite interestingly, menopause does not seem to have a significant effect on testosterone levels, possibly because the postmenopausal ovaries produce important levels of testosterone. In fact, blood testosterone levels generally increase from age 50 – 90 when the values are adjusted for body mass index. These data show that the female maintains important testosterone levels through her reproductive and later non-reproductive life. This means that the dissatisfaction that some post-menopausal women report with their sex life is generally not due to testosterone deficiency.

The most definitive evidence that testosterone plays an important role in female sexual behavior has come from analysis of women who have had both their ovaries and adrenal glands removed (generally as therapy for aggressive forms of breast cancer), or have been treated with agents that destroy adrenal gland function. The women have extremely low testosterone levels and suffer from greatly reduced sexual responsiveness, and which can be restored by testosterone supplementation. These studies have shown quite convincingly that female sexual behavior is dependent on testosterone. And, as in the case of males, we don't yet know the precise function of testosterone in regulating sexual responsiveness in females.

Oxytocin and vasopressin – *the social bonding hormones?*

Oxytocin and vasopressin, two pituitary hormones, have made the popular news in the last few years because of their connection to social bonding and parental care in prairie voles, a hamstersized rodent species. In contrast to other vole species or to most other mammals, female and male prairie voles establish lifelong pair bonds, maintain a nest and rear the young together. This highly unusual feature has been shown in a remarkable series of studies to depend on olfactory signals between the members of the pair, and high concentrations of receptors for oxytocin and vasopressin in the nucleus accumbens and ventral pallidum areas of the brain, respectively.

It is this social bonding feature that has led some writers to refer to oxytocin as the 'cuddle hormone'. Oxytocin is an interesting hormone in other respects. It is a good example of a multi-tasking hormone. In humans oxytocin triggers the uterine contractions that lead to childbirth, and it also is needed for the release of milk from the mammary gland when the infant suckles at the breast. Popular reports of the prairie vole research have tended to extrapolate the prairie vole data to humans, particularly because long term partnerships and combined parental care are fairly common in humans. Social conservatives who have been pushing for sexual abstinence have argued that the prairie vole should be the model for humans, and some have suggested that the absence of oxytocin and vasopressin signals may be the cause of divorce and absentee fathers. Might we be able to stabilize human relationships, and reduce divorce and single parenting, for example, by somehow tweaking our oxytocin and vasopressin levels? Intriguing idea! A few very preliminary studies have been considered to suggest that a connection may exist. For example, oxytocin levels have been reported to increase during sexual intercourse and during breast feeding in humans, and it has been suggested that the relaxed feeling after intercourse may be due to the release of oxytocin. In addition, the intranasal infusion of oxytocin has been reported to decrease stress and increase trust among humans. However, the full significance of these preliminary studies remains unknown.

Unfortunately, the prairie vole, it turns out, may not be the apt model to which humans should aspire. The prairie vole's fall from grace came when it was discovered that both male and female prairie voles commonly have extra-marital relationships. The prairie voles have established an interesting modus vivendi. Both members of the pair routinely mate with other members of the extended group. Social monogamy does not imply sexual monogamy, and sexual infidelity does not affect the reproductive success of the cheating partner, nor does it interfere with social stability. The authors of this key study concluded, perhaps in a tongue-in-cheek way: *"Ironically, the dissociation of social and sexual infidelity leads us to suggest that prairie voles are even better models of human attachment than has been appreciated."* (16)

Dopamine – *does it stimulate desire?*

Much has been written about dopamine. Its release has been considered something like an all-purpose trigger for sexual motivation, sexual arousal and reward. This view has led to the development of compounds that enhance dopamine or stabilize dopamine levels in the brain to try to stimulate sexual desire. One such drug, known as apomorphine (trade name Uprima), originally developed for the treatment of Parkinson's disease, was initially approved as therapy for erectile dysfunction. However, after reports of serious side effects, the manufacturer of Uprima withdrew its application for FDA approval. Dopamine it seems is not a specific activator of sexual behavior.

Serotonin – the inhibitor

On the other hand, serotonin, generated in the hypothalamus, does appear to inhibit sexual behavior and function. Drugs that belong to a wide class of compounds used to treat depression, the selective serotonin reuptake inhibitors (SSRIs), such as Prozac or Paxil, work by stabilizing serotonin levels in the brain. A common side effect of taking SSRIs in men is erectile dysfunction or delayed or absent ejaculation, and in women, decreased sexual desire and difficulty in reaching orgasm.

Melanotan II – *the ultimate aphrodisiac?*

One of the more interesting of newly identified factors that appear to have a role in sexual function is -melanocyte stimulating hormone (-MSH), which has long been known to stimulate melanin (the red, brown, and black pigments) production in the melanocytes of the skin, and thereby control skin pigmentation. Studies in the late 1980s in which -MSH injected directly into the brains of animals elicited sexual behaviors indicated that -MSH might also be involved in sexual function. More recently, a small fragment of -MSH, known as *melanotan II* (MTII) has been shown to have more powerful effects than -MSH itself. That MTII acts as a potent erection promoter was reported by the biochemist, Mac Hadley, in the time-honored way of scientists using themselves as guinea pigs. What follows is a short excerpt of his description of what happened when he injected himself with MTII:

. . .MTII caused a rather immediate, unexpected response: nausea and, to my great surprise, an erection. While I lay in bed with an emesis (vomiting) pan close by, I had an unrelenting erection (about 8 hours duration), which could not be subdued even with a cold pack. When my wife came upon the scene, she proclaimed that I "must be crazy." In response, I raised my arm feebly into the air and answered, "I think we may become rich". (17)

Melanotan II works differently than compounds like Viagra that are used to treat erectile dysfunction. The site of action of compounds like Viagra is the penis, and hence, these drugs sustain an erection by preventing the outflow of blood from the penis. They work only if sexual motivation and arousal are present, that is, if genital blood flow takes place. Melanotan II, on the other hand, appears to induce an erection even in the absence of sexual motivation. Melanotan II, in a sense, preempts sexual motivation, probably by activating the brain regions that normally stimulate penile erection in response to sexual stimuli.

However, extensive clinical trials, did not pan out as Mac Hadley would have wanted. Clinical development ceased in 2008.

In general the medicalization of sexual desire has not been particularly successful. The various compounds that have been tested do not generate sexual desire, whose source is external stimuli and erotic fantasy.

Genital blood flow – *objective measure of sexual arousal*

Penile erection

Does the penis sometimes have a mind of its own? Leonardo da Vinci must have thought so when he wrote:

The penis disputes with the human intellect, and sometimes has an intellect of its own. . . Thus be he sleeping or waking it does what it desires. Often a man is asleep and it is awake, and many times a man is awake and it is asleep. Many times a man wants to use it, and it does not want to; many times it wants to and a man forbids it. (18)

All men since time immemorial would concur with Leonardo da Vinci's observation of the complex and often irascible behavior of the penis. Irascible it may appear, but there is certain logic to its madness. Erections, and even ejaculation, during sleep (clinically referred to originally as 'nocturnal penile tumescence' and more recently as 'sleep-related erections' (SREs)) occur commonly in all sexually mature males. These erections are involuntary and unconscious. For a long time SREs were considered to be the consequence of 'impure', erotic, or otherwise unhealthy thoughts or dreams during sleep. Sigmund Freud in his theory of dreaming favored this explanation. In many religious orders special devices, known as 'spermatorhea rings', designed to prevent the nocturnal erections were used routinely. These ranged from teeth-embedded metal rings to expansion-triggered, electrical sensors that triggered buzzers or minor shocks. The pain inflicted by these devices must have traumatized their subjects for life.

Various studies show that SREs occur cyclically about every 80 minutes and each episode lasts about 20 minutes. SREs occur during the rapid-eye movement (REM) stages of sleep. They are not triggered by the need to urinate, and are not associated with sexual dreams. The regularity and ubiquity of sleep-related erections in healthy men of all ages, as well as their non-volitional nature, means that failure to obtain SREs is taken as good evidence of organic erectile pathology. SREs then are important not only because they indicate a healthy erectile response, but because of what they tell us about the control of penile erection. Let's look into that more closely.

Penile activity depends on a dynamic balance of opposing signals of the sympathetic and parasympathetic nervous systems. In the penis these two systems regulate blood flow in and out of the small chambers between the smooth muscle cells of the penis. Regnier de Graaf, a Dutch anatomist, discovered in the late 1600s that injecting water into the penis of a human corpse generated an erection. Da Vinci, who dissected penises from executed criminal, was perhaps the first to recognize that during an erection the penis fills with blood. When a man is sexually aroused, the parasympathetic system stimulates the release of two transmitters, vasoactive intestinal polypeptide (VIP) and nitric oxide (NO) and leads to relaxation of the smooth muscle cells permitting blood flow into the chambers resulting in an erection.

Nitric oxide, in particular, controls the penile muscles that control the flow of blood into and out of the penis. The spectacularly financially successful drugs prescribed for erectile dysfunction - *Viagra, Levitra, and Cialis* - work as nitric oxide boosting compounds that keep the penile muscle relaxed and the penis full of blood and erect. The erection is lost when the sympathetic system predominates. Its effect is to stimulate smooth muscle cell contraction, thereby pushing blood out of the chambers and preventing blood to flow back into the chambers. Penile erection, it turns out, is fundamentally a plumbing problem – an amazingly low-tech solution to a process so crucial to our reproduction.

Sexual arousal can take place in many different and interconnected ways. In addition to tactile stimulation of the penis, the list of cues that can turn men on seems almost endless - by the sight, thought or anticipation of a potential partner, or by the memory of a past erotic encounter. *Victoria's Secret* and countless other magazines know that in men lingerie is sexually arousing; so are high-heeled shoes, a well-turned ankle, different hair-styles, certain types of dresses, and a whole assortment of fetish objects.

Some erections, referred to as 'reflexive erections', do not appear to involve any command centers in the brain, but are triggered entirely by a region of the spinal cord known as the 'spinal erection-generating center', the source of parasympathetic neurons and located just above the tail end of the spine cord including sacral, lumbar, and thoracic vertebrae. In humans the existence of this center has been suggested by close examination of paraplegic men who retain the ability to have erections, a few of whom can also have vaginal intercourse and ejaculate. In such men the spinal cord injury that prevents the flow of nerve signals from the brain to the peripheral regions of the body is located above the region of the spinal cord that contains the putative erection-generating center. However, a special nerve circuit involving the pudendal nerve from the penis and spinal parasympathetic nerves is preserved. Hence, as long as this nerve circuit is intact, physical stimulation of the penis will result in an erection even in the absence of any contribution from the brain.

Although the erect penis gets all the attention, the penis spends most of its life in a non-erect, flaccid state. Leonard Bloom, in James Joyce's *Portrait of the Artist as a Young Man*, contemplating his penis floating in the bath water, referred to it as *"the limp father of thousands, a languid floating flower."* To maintain the penis in a non-erect state requires the continual activity of a system designed to keep the penis under control. It makes sense that the penis be kept under control. Walking around with an erect penis would certainly be uncomfortable and would interfere with normal work activities.

A long lasting erection would also be dangerous to the health of the penis. Erections that last longer than four to eight hours, medically referred to as priapism, require medical treatment because the blood trapped in the chambers of the penis is depleted of oxygen. If not replenished within a reasonable time severe tissue damage will occur. Priapism can occur as a consequence of certain diseases, and can also be drug-induced. Many cases of priapism have been reported after drugs for treating erectile dysfunction, such as Viagra and Cialis, were first made available.

It may be that the strength of this inhibitory control over the penis will vary from one individual to another. In some men, it may be particularly strong leading to problems in achieving or maintaining erections sufficient for successful intercourse. In others, a weaker control may possibly lead to risky or excessive sexual adventures. The nature of this erection-suppressing network remains unclear. Animal experiments points to a region of the brain stem known as the paragigantocellular nucleus (PGN). Signals generated by the neurons in this center suppress the activity of the erection-generating center in the sacral spinal cord. The flaccid penis contrary to what we might have imagined represents a very active, rather than passive, state.

Vaginal vasocongestion – *the counterpart of penile erection*

The control of penile erection, particularly through the spinal control centers is understood reasonably well. It is not hard to guess why. The penis is hard to miss, and its response to sexual stimulation is obvious and easy to measure. It has therefore received most of the scientific attention. The female genitalia are another matter. The vagina is not visible, the clitoris is very small, and the labia, although visible, do not appear as responsive as the penis, all of which have made the study of the female genital response more difficult. The counterpart of penile erection is the engorgement (vasocongestion) of the labia, vagina, and clitoris with blood. Vasocongestion of the vagina is not visible, but it can be measured with a small photocell with the very complicated name – photoplethysmograph. This instrument tracks the change in the color of the vaginal walls from pink to purple as it fills with blood.

An additional physiological response to sexual arousal is vaginal lubrication, the release of fluid throughout the vaginal wall. The indefatigable Regnier de Graaf was one of the first to describe the lubrication triggered in the human vagina during sexual arousal. An

American obstetrician and gynecologist in landmark but little known studies carried out in the late 1800s, but only published in 1930, described vaginal lubrication in detail. His two innovations were to use a penis-shaped glass tube inserted into the vagina during sexual arousal stimulated by a vibrator. Nothing is new under the sun.

Vaginal vasocongestion and lubrication are controlled by the relaxation of sympathetic, and activation of parasympathetic signals.

Like penile erection, both vasocongestion and vaginal lubrication can be induced by genital stimulation, but also nontactilely – erotic images or thoughts. Interestingly, nocturnal arousal also occurs on a regular basis in women, like in men four or five times a night during REM sleep. The similarity of these physiological responses to sexual stimuli suggests that the female sexual circuitry, at least at the genital periphery, is similar to that of the male.

A surprising discovery, made during the last decade is that another nerve, the vagus nerve, which regulates breathing, swallowing and vomiting - functions not associated with sex arousal - can also function as a genital sensory nerve. This discovery came about by investigating reports of orgasm in women who had suffered a spinal cord injury above the ninth thoracic vertebra. This is above the entry of these three nerves into the spinal cord, and hence, the injury would be expected to prevent sensory information from these nerves from being to experience an orgasm by genital stimulation suggested that another genital sensory pathway not affected by the injury was operative.

Experiments in both animals and humans have shown that this additional pathway is the vagus nerve, which innervates the genitalia but bypasses the spinal cord as it travels up to the base of the brain. The experience of one patient who recovered the ability to have orgasms is described:

A single 30-year old woman paralyzed from the waist down in a car accident assumed she'd never enjoy sex again either. Ten years later she fell in love and the couple tried to have sex. "I was fulfilled. I had orgasms, it was like I was reborn," she said. (19)

Even more interesting perhaps is that the discovery of the sex arousal capabilities of the vagus nerve provides a way of explaining scattered reports of non-genital orgasms in women with spinal cord injuries. Orgasms can be induced in such women by stimulating small hypersensitive areas above the level of the injury – in the shoulder, chest, or even in the chin. It is not yet clear what nerves are involved in inducing the orgasm, but it does suggest the mind-blowing possibility that other parts of the body may be capable of generating the signals that activate the brain regions responsible for producing an orgasm.

The brain – does sex matter?

". . . popular portrayals of sex differences in the brain are riddled with claims that are highly extrapolated, misinterpreted, or just made up but are nonetheless used to justify the differential treatment of boys and girls in school or men and women in the workplace." (20)

Men and women differ not only in their sexual anatomy, but also behaviorally in a multitude of ways. We may remember when we were children and adolescents how different girls were from boys in their interests, their play preferences, and behavior, and we know that these differences persist into adulthood. It is part of our common lore to say that males are *aggressive* while females are *caring; females are cooperative,* while males are *competitive;* boys prefer *outdoor* play and like *roughhousing,* while females prefer *indoor* and *less active* play. Girls who prefer roughhousing and outdoor play are referred to as 'tomboys'.

Although on tests of general intelligence males and females on average are the same, other tests that examine different aspects of cognitive function are said to reveal differences between the two sexes. For example, males on average do better than females on spatial navigation and map reading, targeting, mental rotation tests. They are more likely to play with mechanical toys as children, and they tend to score higher on engineering and physics problems as adults. Girls on average start to talk earlier than boys and are more likely to play with dolls, and they score higher on tests of emotion recognition, social sensitivity, and verbal fluency. Males typically tend to be more analytical, be more adept at systemizing, think narrowly, more obsessive, and are more forgetful of others, while females are better at communicating, think broadly, and are more empathetic.

Are these differences real, and if so, how do we account for such cognitive and behavioral differences? This has been the subject of a long and sometimes acrimonious debate among scientists who study human behavior. Sociologists and anthropologists have tended to favor the idea that many gender traits are socially conditioned. We know that society and culture mold and affect behavior. We learn or are taught, implicitly and explicitly, to behave in a manner that is appropriate for our sex. Boys even from a very young age are rewarded when they exhibit boyish behavior, and strongly discouraged from expressing what we consider girlish or sissy behavior. What we call feminine and masculine traits may simply be arbitrary products of a sustained educational (some would say brainwashing) program that begins soon after birth, and that in fact continues throughout our lives.

The other point of view – the *biological reductionist* view – is that the sex differences in cognition and behavior may be innate, a consequence of subtle sex differences in brain anatomy, neural wiring, hormones, all of which ultimately depend on differences in gene function. According to this view, female and male brains, although very similar in many respects, are also different in others. The molding of the female and male brain is not a single event but a process that begins very early during our embryonic life, and is probably completed during puberty. The brain sex differences may have enormous consequences for us because they may affect many aspects of our behavior (both sexual and non-sexual) and many different aspects of cognitive function.

A large array of new techniques developed in the past 5 to 10 years are beginning to document in increasing detail sex differences in memory, emotion, vision, hearing, recognizing faces, pain perception, navigation, and sexual behavior. Advances in human brain-imaging techniques such as positron emission tomography (PET scans) and functional MRI (fMRI), for example, which make it possible to look into the brain in live subjects, have revealed hitherto unsuspected differences between males and females in the anatomy, chemistry, and function in brain regions involving language, memory, emotion, vision, hearing, and navigation. Sex differences in brain anatomy and neural circuitry, in particular, have been notoriously difficult to validate, and only a few have are currently accepted. What effect they have on behavior or cognition remains unknown.

Nevertheless, many neuroscientists consider that sex brain differences will eventually help us in understanding striking sex differences in the incidence and/or nature of many central nervous system (CNS) disorders. For example, dyslexia and stuttering are three to four times more frequent in boys than girls, and attention deficit hyperactivity disorder is diagnosed 10 times more often in boys. Autism and autism spectrum disorder are up to four times more prevalent in males, as is early-onset schizophrenia. In contrast, major depressive disorder, anxiety, panic disorders are diagnosed two times more frequently in females than males. Anorexia bulimia is about three times more prevalent in females, and anorexia nervosa (a disorder characterized by the failure to eat sufficiently for normal health) is 13 times more prevalent in females. In general, developmental onset mental disorders are more frequent in males, while adult onset disorders are more frequent in females.

Discussion of inherent differences between men and women is often discouraged because we may fear that whatever differences are found may be used to justify continued gender discrimination and the preponderance of males in high-level positions of power in industry, government, and science. Many neuroscientists worry that the focus on the biological origin of brain sex differences are being distorted and exploited by nonscientists and even some scientists who are making wild, unsubstantiated claims, and making a lot of money to boot. A few examples: The 1992 book *Men Are From Mars, Women Are From Venus* that attributes disparities in gender roles in education, marriage and parenting, the business world to brain sex differences. *Why Gender Matters* (2005) argues for gender segregation in schools because of presumptive brain and sensory differences between boys and girls; *Leadership and the Sexes* (2008) which makes the astounding claim that males have sixtimes more gray matter related to cognition and intelligence than females; *The Female Brain* (2006) that makes the claim that

> *"The female brain has tremendous unique aptitudes – outstanding verbal agility, the ability to connect deeply in friendship, a nearly psychic capacity to read faces and tone of voice for emotions and states of mine, and the ability to defuse conflict. All of this is hard-wired into the brains of women.*

These books are replete with bold, outlandish claims, for which there is no evidence to support them. Neuroscientists would label such outlandish claims as 'pseudoscience' or 'nonsense neuroscience'. Yet, these views have permeated our culture, and in many ways they have become the standard popular way in which we think about male-female differences. We as a society seem to be very receptive to this mish-mash of unfounded claims that perpetuate stereotypical notions of male – female differences.

Ignoring the continual and complex interaction between genes and experience will always diminish our understanding of ourselves. Rather than being dismayed by differences between the sexes, we should celebrate the diversity and take advantage of it. We should not fear exploring fully the disparities between the two sexes not only because it will help us understand the mysteries of brain function and lead to therapeutic benefits. Just as importantly we may come to understand that only a society that incorporates the differing talents and aptitudes of its male and female citizens will prosper. We need to keep in mind a view expressed in a 2001 report from the medical branch of the National Academy of Sciences: *"Sex does matter. It matters in ways that we did not expect. Undoubtedly, it matters in ways that we have not yet begun to imagine."* (22)

Gonzalo Maecha Valenzuela, "Adriana" Marble relief, painted in oil, 60 x 20 x 1.8 cb. With permission of the artist.

Chapter 4

Our Sexual Theater

Sexual intercourse began
In nineteen sixty-three
(which was rather late for me) -
Between the end of the Chatterley ban
And the Beatles' first LP.

Up to then there'd only been
A sort of bargaining,
A wrangle for the ring,
A shame that started at sixteen
And spread to everything.

Then all at once the quarrel sank:
Everyone felt the same,
And every life became
A brilliant breaking of the bank,
A quite unlosable game.

So life was never better than

In nineteen sixty-three

(Though just too late for me) -

Between the end of the Chatterley ban

And the Beatles' first LP. (1, Philip Larkin, *Annus Mirabilis*)

Nothing is new

Philip Larkin's famous poem about sexual intercourse beginning in 1963 expresses in a tongue-in-cheek fashion the conceit of every generation that what they experience and discover is unique and new. This is true in some areas of human activity – science, for example – but certainly not new when it comes to sexual matters. For most of us the term 'sexual revolution' refers to the widespread changes in sexual behavior and experimentation that took place in the 1960s – the rise in feminism, gay liberation, and living together without marriage. We may not be aware, however, that sexual revolutions have been taking place periodically during our history. Two recently published books, one by Deborah Lutz, *Pleasure Bound. Victorian Sex Rebels and the New Eroticism,* and another by Evelyn Lord, *The Hell-Fire Clubs: Sex, Satanism and Secret Societies,* remind us that sexual experimentation among the respectable upper classes in 19th and 18th century England was as audacious and uninhibited as we might find today. Sexual rebels have always existed. The search for new and different erotic possibilities outside what is considered the norm, although sanctioned or marginalized, appears to be a constant in human societies. Sex is continually renewing and reinventing itself – it is always new and always old.

Our individual sexual encounters are often full of tension and anxiety, and even disappointment. We may anticipate a big bang, but often we have to settle for a whimper. This, at first sight, seems strange.

Sexual intercourse is, after all, not rocket science. Most everyone learns how to do it with relatively little instruction – you just learn by doing, and maybe watching pornographic movies - and like riding a bicycle, you get better at it the more you practice. Still, we must be very insecure: how else to explain the vast inventory of how-to magazine articles, internet sites, books, and sex therapists that describe new anatomical positions, new foreplay methods, new sex toys that promise to increase our pleasure. Here are a few titles from the DoubleDay book club: *Advanced Techniques for Driving a Man Wild in Bed, Daily Sex, Superhotsex, The 10 Secrets to Great Sex, The 10 Golden Rules for Great Sex, The Best of Best American Erotica 2008.*

It is difficult to know how useful or helpful these books are, but they feed our persistent interest in and curiosity about things sexual. Perhaps one important role they play is that they bring our sexual behavior into the open, and we understand that we are not the only ones who are sex-obsessed. Everyone else is as interested in sex as we are. These publications foment an almost obsessive concern for our sexual wellbeing. Sexual gratification looms almost as important as our concern for our health. In this post-modern world of sexual information-overload is there anything new to learn? Perhaps a good response is that we know a lot, but understand very little.

The coital drama – *in four (three) acts*

The publication in 1966 of *Human Sexual Response* by Masters and Johnson marked the beginning of the modern scientific examination of human sexual intercourse. Their decisive, and at the same time, scandalous, innovation was to measure a number of physiological responses of couples in the throes of intercourse – blood pressure, heart rate, increased blood flow to the genitalia, the muscular contractions associated with orgasm in both males and females, and the relaxation that follows intercourse – in a way that had never been done before. Perhaps as important as the physiological data collected was that a taboo subject could now be read by everyone and was no longer relegated to obscure medical journals.

Their signature proposal was that intercourse (by which they meant male-female, penile-vaginal), which they referred to as *the human sexual response* – could be separated into four phases – excitement, plateau, orgasm, and resolution. For a decade or more afterward these phases were discussed widely in the media, and they became part of the lexicon by which sexual intercourse was understood.

However, the idea of sexual intercourse taking place in stages was not new. The American physician, J. Chapman in 1883 summarized a woman's sexual response beginning with a preparatory stage, which he wrote *may be reached by any means, bodily or mentally, which, in the opposite sex, causes an erection. Following upon this, then, is a stage of pleasurably excitement, gradually increasing and culminating in an acme of excitement, which may be called the stage of consummation, and the analogue of which in the male is emission. This is followed in both sexes by a degree of nervous prostration, less marked, however, in the female, and . . . by a relief to the general congestion of all the genital organs which has existed, and perhaps increased, from the beginning of the preparatory stage. (2)*

In 1926, the Dutch gynecologist, Theodore Henrik van de Velde, in his very successful marriage manual, *Ideal Marriage Its Physiology and Technique* divided the act into a sequence of four stages. Since van de Velde does not report any studies that led to his conclusions, we probably can assume that they are based on personal experience. In van de Velde's portrayal, human sexual intercourse is an elaborate, drawn-out performance. Maybe thinking about it as a drama may not be so far off the mark.

Van de Velde labeled the acts of the drama as the *prelude,* passing into *love-play,* followed by *coitus,* and ending with the epilogue or postlude. He describes the prelude in part as follows: *"As soon as the first stirrings of the impulse of approach are perceptible, the prelude to sexual union begins",* and a couple of pages later *"In the prelude the impulse of approach works through the three senses of sight, hearing and smell. Taste and touch come into play at closer range, and it may be said that touch, once in action, soon becomes paramount".* (3)

Love-play begins with the erotic kiss (a peculiarity of Western cultures, according to van de Velde), and proceeds with touching of the entire body, eventually focusing on the genitalia. Love-play, if successful, will lead to erection in the man and vaginal lubrication in the female. Van de Velde suggests ways of inducing sufficient lubrication in the female if she is not responding appropriately: *"And this may best, most appropriately, and most expeditiously be done without the intermediary offices of the fingers, but through what I prefer to term the kiss of genital stimulation or genital kiss, by gentle and soothing caresses with lips and tongue"*. (3) Similarly, if the man's arousal is lacking, the woman may provide oral stimulation to the penis. Van de Velde was lucky that he published his book in the Netherlands for what he was advocating – cunnilingus and fellatio – were felony acts in the U.S.

The third stage, coitus, begins with the insertion of the penis into the vagina, followed by accelerating thrusting, increasing 'sexual tension', and ending with ejaculation and orgasm. Finally, if the encounter was ideal, the fourth stage, the *postlude "should echo, and vibrate, and reawaken in the preliminaries of a new act of sexual communion'.* (3) Since he was also a practical man, he accepts that without love or affection between the partners a satisfying postlude will be absent.

Masters and Johnson reworked and renamed van de Velde's stages, dropping the *prelude* stage, love-play became *excitement, coitus* became plateau; *orgasm* was given its own stage, and *postlude* became *resolution*. It soon became clear, however, that a significant limitation of their model was that it focused almost exclusively on the mechanics and genital responses during intercourse, and ignored the motivation that normally brings two individuals to initiate a sexual interaction. The motivation in van de Velde's terminology was expressed in the prelude - "the first stirrings of approach". Masters and Johnson ignored the motivation, perhaps taking it as a given, or possibly because it referred to a subjective and emotional experience that could not be measured physiologically.

Omitting sexual motivation, however, left out one of the most important aspects of human sexual encounters. To correct for the omission, the psychologist and sex therapist Helen Singer Kaplan in 1974 modified the Masters and Johnson model, resurrected van de Velde's prelude stage, renaming it *desire*. *Excitation* became *arousal*, and *plateau* was eliminated, simplifying the coital drama into three acts – *desire, arousal,* and *orgasm.* Her modification had intuitive appeal because it agreed with the prevailing notions of how sexual encounters begin. Kaplan's phases also seemed to have some clinical relevance as well. For example, her phases could be matched to problems frequently reported to psychiatrists and psychotherapists by their patients, such as the lack of sexual desire, inability to get aroused (get an erection, for example), or orgasm difficulties. Kaplan's model seemed so eminently plausible and was so widely accepted that it was incorporated into the American Psychiatric Association's (APA) *Diagnostic and Statistical Manual of Mental Disorders (DSM)* as defining the 'normal' sexual response pattern.

What may not have been appreciated at the time was that the relationship between desire and arousal, although it seemed straightforward, was anything but. Let's turn to that now.

Desire / Arousal – a Pandora's jar

What is it men in women do require?

The lineaments of Gratified Desire.

What is it women do in men require?

The lineaments of Gratified Desire. (4, William Blake, 1793)

Arousal and the experience of desire – gender differences

We don't really know the precise meaning of William Blake's intriguing poem about 'Gratified Desire', but maybe that's the source of its charm. It evokes multiple meanings and sensations about what is probably a universal human quality - sexual desire. Many of us might claim that we have an intuitive understanding of what sexual desire is. It's like the old saw - we know it when we feel it. Often we make use of terms – love, covet, crave, need, yearn, lust, want, hanker, excitement, long for, drive, horny, libido, fantasy, attraction, turned-on – to help convey what it means to us. Often, as these terms do, we mix two different concepts – *desire* as a subjective, internal state, and what brought us to that state – excitement or *arousal*. Although making that distinction seems reasonable, we might be hard pressed to define them more precisely.

We shouldn't feel too bad about this. Ambiguity and inconsistency about what these two concepts refer to and how they can be measured validly has characterized the scientific literature of the last three decades or so. Sexual desire has been notoriously difficult to define. Consider just a few that have been offered: desire is *"the sum of the forces that lean us toward and push us away from sexual behavior"* (5); or *"a psychological state subjectively experienced by the individual as an awareness that he or she wants or wished to attain (presumably pleasurable) sexual goal that is currently unattainable"* (6); or *"consists of fantasies about sexual activity and the desire to have sexual activity"* (7); or Kaplan's proposal that desire is *"experienced as specific sensations which move the individual to seek out, or become receptive to, sexual experience. These sensations are produced by the physical activation of a specific neural system in the brain. When this system is active, a person is 'horny', he may feel genital sensations, or he may feel vaguely sexy, interested in sex, open to sex, or even just restless."* (8)

These definitions are not particularly satisfying: first, they are circular, and therefore, uninformative; and secondly, they attempt to describe sensations or feelings, but they don't tell us how those sensations or feeling come about. *How in fact does desire come about? What is the relationship between desire and arousal? Does desire (however defined) always precede arousal (however defined)?* Rosemary Basson, a psychologist from the University of British Columbia, on the basis of her studies, proposed that women follow a sequence different from men's: *"A woman reports that when her sexual experience began, her main incentive was to please her partner and increase their ongoing emotional closeness. Kissing, hair stroking, and gentle breast caressing, followed by oral genital stimulation, led to her subjective sexual excitement and orgasm. She experienced desire for the sexual stimulation per se, close to her orgasm."* (9)

On the basis of studies, Basson concluded that women may not often feel 'spontaneous' sexual desire in the way Kaplan defines it, but initiate sex out of a wish for intimacy or to please a partner. The desire itself may be triggered later after the sexual encounter has begun and she is being aroused. Basson called this type of desire, *responsive sexual desire,* and suggested that it was more typical of women, *while spontaneous sexual desire* (as described by Kaplan) was more typical of men. Some population surveys based on questionnaires appeared to support this difference. For example, in studies reported in 1980 and 1994, about 30% of sexually experienced, orgasmic women reported that they had never experienced the spontaneous sexual desire as defined by Kaplan. In a 1991 study, 97% of American college student females 25 years and older, who had engaged in sexual behavior reported that they did it without spontaneous sexual desire. These questionnaire studies also indicated that for some women, sexual desire does not appear to be imbued with the intense sexual thoughts, or fantasies, that are considered far more typical of men. Sexual desire in women may not as sharply focused, but more amorphous and diffuse, and associated with emotional feelings, wanting be feel close to a partner or wanting to be intimate with a partner through sex. Sexual desire may be less a feeling of being 'turned on', than a whole-body readiness to participate in sex.

The bifurcation of desire into these two forms – spontaneous and responsive – seemed plausible at first sight, possibly because it agreed with a cultural bias that male sexuality was intrinsically different from female sexuality. One serious problem in interpreting clearly the difference between these two types of desire, however, was that desire was not properly distinguished from arousal - the two terms remained imprecise and ill-defined - and as indicated in the excerpt noted above were often used interchangeably. What was needed was a way of distinguishing desire from arousal in an empirical, objective way.

Fortunately, the development of a new instrument, the *plethysmograph,* provided a means to make a meaningful distinction between arousal and desire. The *plethysmograph* measures vasocongestion (enhanced genital blood flow) in the pelvis. In the male, the increased genital blood flow leads to a swelling of the penis, and swelling of the penis is a measure of the extent to which the male has been sexually (genitally) aroused. The penile plethysmography wraps around the penis and measures penile circumference, volume and rigidity.

In females, a similar instrument, the vaginal photoplethysmograph carries a plastic probe that is inserted into the vagina, and measures vaginal lubrication. Increased vaginal lubrication and swelling of the external genitalia is a sign of sexual (genital) arousal in the female. Plethysmography has provided a well-validated instrument to measure genital responses in both men and women.

The set up of the experiments with this instrument was straightforward. Sexual (genital) arousal in both men and women in response to watching erotic films was measured with plethysmography. At the same time, the researchers assessed the enhanced sexual feelings elicited by the erotic films – referred to as subjective arousal – using questionnaires, with questions such as "how sexually aroused do you feel when you watch the different images?" The advantage of this approach was that a physiological and psychological response could be evaluated simultaneously.

A brief summary of the findings:

- Both men and women become equally (quantitatively) genitally aroused in response to erotic films. The intensity or strength of the genital response varied with the explicitness of the film, increasing with the close depiction of the sexual organs.

- The increased genital blood flow occurred within seconds after the film is started, suggesting an autonomic response not requiring conscious cognitive evaluation.

- Men, in general, responded genitally in 'category specific' ways, that is, men who identified themselves as straight had a significantly greater genital response to heterosexual or lesbian sex and while watching masturbating and exercising women, than when viewing male-male sex. Gay males respond in the opposite way.

- The female response was different. Irrespective of their reported sexual preference, women responded genitally more or less equally when watching male-male, male-female, or femalefemale sex.

- Subjective arousal differed significantly between men and women. In men, subjective arousal was highly correlated with genital arousal. In women, the genital responses were not highly correlated with their subjective sexual feelings. Even when the erotic film was disliked and induced no subjective feeling of arousal, the genital responses still occurred in females.

- This important aspect of the female sexual response has been tested in the following way: 30 men and 30 women were shown a 'woman-friendly' and a 'man-friendly' erotic film. In the 'man-friendly' film the focus is on the genitals and the male actors while pleasure, romantic aspects between the male and female actors are absent. In contrast, in the 'woman-friendly' film, while the focus is on the genitals and on the female actor's pleasure, it is also on the relationship between the actors. The finding: the genital response was the same in both sexes; subjective arousal of the men did not differ between films, but in the women the sexual arousal elicited was higher in the 'womanfriendly' film than in the 'man-friendly' film.

Provisional conclusion:

The genital response of women to sexually relevant stimuli is not quantitatively different from that of men. Sexual (genital) arousal and subjective arousal arise from a stimulus that our brain interprets as being sexually meaningful. Sexual arousal is an autonomic (non-cognitive) physiological response. How that comes about remains unknown. Subjective arousal represents the emotional and psychic expression of the enhanced genital blood flow. In the absence of a sexual stimulus there is no desire. This means that all desire is responsive, and that there is no such thing as spontaneous sexual desire. It may be reasonable to equate what we call *sexual desire* with subjective arousal. In contrast to Kaplan's formulation, these psychophysiological studies indicate that *arousal* precedes, rather than follows *desire*, but they may not be fundamentally different – they are parts of one another.

Men's subjective arousal is generally correlated with the *intensity* of the genital arousal, and the sexual feelings elicited are typically positive. Women's subjective arousal appears to be more determined by the *meanings* associated with the stimulus or the context that is generated by the stimuli, and not always by the strength of her genital response. For women, quite often, subjective arousal can be strongly negative despite registering a genital response.

The disparity between objective (genital) and subjective arousal in women has been noted in many other circumstances. Rape victims have noticed increased vaginal lubrication despite the aversive and violent nature of the act, and there are even reports of women experiencing orgasm under such violent circumstances. Surges of vaginal blood flow have been reported in women who listen to descriptions of rape scenes. These are troublesome observations, for they can be used by the ignorant or malicious to argue that women invite or consent to rape because they are genitally aroused by the aversive act. How do we counter that allegation? *How do we explain genital arousal in unwanted sex?* We don't have a definitive answer as yet, but the concept of 'reflexive sexual readiness' may provide an explanation. Genital lubrication is essential in reducing discomfort and possibly injury to the vaginal tissues during penile penetration. Reflexive sexual readiness refers to the predisposition of women to lubricate as a protective measure any time they sense sexual stimuli whether wanted or not. *". . .Ancestral women who did not show an automatic vaginal response to sexual cues may have been more likely to experience injuries during unwanted vaginal penetration that resulted in illness, infertility, or even death. . ."* (10). The important lesson which needs to be emphasized continually: *sexual (genital) arousal is not always consent.*

Complications:

Although this model provides a more coherent way of relating sexual arousal (increased genital blood flow) to subjective arousal (enhanced sexual feelings, and equated with sexual desire), it is important to think of it as a first approximation of a more complex reality. For the physiologically driven investigators, subjective arousal is too imprecise and illdefined to be scientifically useful. Referring to the subjective experience sometimes associated with genital arousal, one harsh critic states: *"It could, without prejudice, be left to psychologists attached to the employment of questionnaires. . . The additional meaning given to sexual arousal inherent in the expression subjective sexual arousal seems to refer to some esoteric state of mind, accessible only through introspection. It has probably no explanatory value whatsoever and should be allowed to enter the oblivion of history." (11)*

Of course, for most of us it is the subjective feelings – esoteric they may be - that are of primary importance. But there are other concerns. Consider the following. In males, sexual (genital) arousal and sexual desire (subjective arousal) are closely correlated when watching erotic films under laboratory conditions. However, in other circumstances, that correlation may be absent. Erections – the normal sign of genital arousal - can occur without subjective arousal, for example, such as during Rapid-Eye-Movement (REM) sleep, or in other circumstances, such as accidents. Psychophysiological studies have shown that men can get erections watching rape films while reporting no subjective arousal. The opposite occurs as well – in strip clubs despite being subjectively aroused, many men do not get erections. Other studies have found that genital responses to diverse sexual stimuli can vary significantly among men. In one study, about one-quarter of the participants were classified as 'non-responders', yet the reported subjective arousal reported did not differ between the 'non-responders' and the 'responders'. Taken together these diverse findings tell us that in both men and women the relationship between genital arousal and subjective arousal is much more complex and multi-faceted than we might have imagined. No generalization is likely to do justice to this complexity.

Cupid's arrows – triggers of desire

What enslaving cocktail have I sucked

From your full mouth . . . to leave me so totally yours?

I need love more than ever now . . . I need your love,

I need love more than hope or money, wisdom or a drink (12, Walter Benton (1943) This Is My Beloved)

In Roman mythology, *Cupid* was the god of desire; his Greek counterpart was *Eros*. A constant feature of his portrayal in painting and sculpture is a quiver with two sets or arrows, one set is gold-headed, and other is lead-headed, with opposite effects. The gold-headed arrows were responsible for desire and love, while the lead-headed arrows triggered disillusionment or hatred. It's also interesting that in some literature Cupid was portrayed as capricious, fickle, and wicked. Cupid and his arrows are good metaphor for the illusive, esoteric nature of sexual desire and the triggers of desire – stimuli that are interpreted as being sexually relevant.

Sexual stimuli come in many different forms, and sensitivity and response to these triggers may span a wide spectrum. It does appear that there are gender differences in the range of responses to sexual stimuli. For women, perhaps more so than for men, a complex range of contextual factors – biological, personal, situational, cultural – give meaning to the sexually relevant stimuli that she receives or perceives, and modulate the strength and final effect of the stimulus.

It seems likely that humans have known about the power of tactile stimulation since the beginning of their existence. All of the self-help books and articles on improving our sexual enjoyment provide detailed instructions for caressing or otherwise stimulating the clitoris or penis to elicit maximal arousal. This is not really new. In the 1920s when 'marriage manuals' were finding a receptive audience (such as van de Velde's described above) clitoral stimulation either with the tongue or fingers was recommended as a way to stimulate a sexually inexperienced wife and prepare her properly for intercourse. Although clitoral or penile stimulation are probably the most effective stimuli, other types of tactile stimulation may also be useful, at least in a preliminary way – kissing on the lips (or so-called French kissing), or suckling the nipples, or massaging.

Even non-sexual touching can be extremely sexually arousing. One of the best examples is described in Jane Austen's novel *Persuasion* when Captain Wentwork, without touching the heroine, Anne, but by picking up a bratty nephew off her back, produces in her **"such a confusion of varying, but very painful agitation, as she could recover from"** (13). Her arousal is so strong that to pull herself together, Anne has to leave the room.

Some stimuli may function unconsciously, triggering a reflex action, a rapid, unconscious response, akin to that generated when we touch a hot object. From experience we know that visual stimuli – a face, a gesture – are crucially important in stimulating desire.

Consider Robert Burton's ruminations on the causes of love in his *The Anatomy of Melancholy*:

But the most familiar and usual cause of love is that which comes by sight, which conveys those admirable rays of beauty and pleasing graces to the heart. (14)

Isabel Arundell describes her first sight of Richard Burton, the 19th century British explorer, intrepid adventurer (who had himself circumcised so that he could pass as a Moslem to visit Mecca during the annual Hajj), and linguist (translated the Kama Sutra and *Arabian Nights*):

The most remarkable part of his appearance was two large, black flashing eyes with long lashes, that pierced me through and through . . .I was completely magnetized; and when we had got a little distance away, I turned to my sister, and whispered to her – 'That man will marry me'. (13)

Or consider how Charles Homar, the narrator in William Giraldi's novel, *Busy Monsters,* describes Gillian Lee, the woman he rescues from a stalled Ferris wheel:

Her odd beauty was the injurious kind, radioactive – it had physical effects on me, my anatomy in quake . . . She was as if the word gustatory had grown legs and got a dress. (15)

Other elements of this system may function consciously, for example, a voice, an erotic image, the memory of a past erotic encounter, or even a wished-for erotic encounter. Reading about unusual types of sexual practices can be extremely arousing. Consider the following response by a woman reading about bondage and submission:

What is happening to me? Suddenly, I found myself reading blog upon blog about D/S, BDSM, Taken in Hand, and other alternative sexual pursuits. I am fascinated by the woman's perspective and experiences in these kind of consensual, loving marriages. I find myself drawn to these women and their stories. I find myself walking around with this warm, excited feeling between my legs. (16)

Some stimuli may have a delayed impact, with desire experienced hours or even days after exposure to stimuli. The stimulus may also include other cues that we receive from the other person (does the other person respond to our own signals? Is the other person receptive?). Mental images of sexual activity can also be generated in the absence of direct visual stimuli. We may conjure up images of sexual encounters as we do in sexual fantasies, or from movies, or previous sexual encounters, and these can under the right circumstances stimulate arousal. In some cases, some women report that the arousal can be so intense that orgasm can take place.

Both sexes respond to certain types of auditory stimuli also, for example, listening to erotic or pornographic audiotapes - hence, the popularity of telephone sex. We don't know if the stimulus is the auditory stimulus itself, or the mental images of sexual activity that the audiotapes were inducing in the recipients. Interestingly and perhaps contrary to expectation, response to olfactory signals – perfumes and the like – is very weak or non-existent. Perfumes may be pleasant, but evidence that they are effective in stimulating sexual arousal is lacking.

Being desired can be a powerful sexual stimulus for women. This has been a perennial theme in Western literature since its origins: the wayward or unfaithful wife, the sexual rebels who forsake husband and family for erotic pleasure. The most famous females in our literature have been sexual rebels. Such tales have become a staple in our movies and TV dramas and they have a particular hold on our imagination. The story line is always the same – a woman is overwhelmed by a man's desire for her – but we seem never to tire of it. Shakespeare in his inimitable way expresses that feeling:

Careless lust stirs up a desperate courage, Planting oblivion, beating reason back (17)

For Marta Meana, professor of psychology at the University of Nevada, Las Vegas, "being desired is the orgasm." (10) Female desire may not always be driven by relational factors, the search for comfort and emotional intimacy, but by a narcissistic need, a drive that may in certain circumstances overcome the normal constraints that modulate her sexual arousal. A woman may choose intimacy and closeness for marriage, but relationships may not always be the primary source of her desire. A need for excitement and sheer lust may take over in many circumstances. Isabel Arundell who renounced the values of her devout Catholic family, fell passionately in love with and married Richard Burton, atheist and sexual libertine, wrote in her diary: *"They say it is better to marry one who loves and is subject to you than one whose slave you are through love. But I cannot agree to this – where in such a case is the pleasure, the excitement, the interest."* (13)

The narcissistic face of female Eros, its unpredictable and impulsive nature, has probably been disturbing and troubling, especially to men. They could easily accept that quality in themselves, but not in women. That anxiety and fear that this produced is perhaps one of the primary sources of the demeaning and severe constraints that sought to control, stifle and misrepresent female sexuality. It is not difficult to understand why discussions of female desire are fraught with cultural, political, and religious imperatives.

Orgasm – summa voluptas (the greatest delight)

According to the Oxford English Dictionary the word **orgasm** comes from the Greek *orgasmos* "to swell with moisture, be excited or eager". Somehow this simple definition doesn't capture the complexity of either the physiological reactions or the pleasure and emotional release that orgasm brings. The term first came to be applied in 1899 to the unique pleasure humans experience at the end of sexual intercourse, while 'climax' as a synonym for orgasm was coined in 1918. 'That sensation' was used earlier by the quack doctor John Marten who started a crusade in the 1700s against masturbation *"the unnatural practice by which persons of either sex . . . endeavor to imitate and procure for themselves that Sensation, which God has ordered to attend the Carnal Commerce of the two sexes"* (18)

Many descriptions of orgasm have been written over the centuries. One, tinged with cosmic significance, was penned by Galen (129-199/217 CE), the Greek-Roman physician, surgeon, and philosopher:

In a single impact of both parties, the whole human frame is shaken and foams with semen, in which the damp humor of the body is joined to the hot substance of the soul . . . I cannot help asking, whether we do not, in that very heat of extreme gratification when the generative fluid is ejected, feel that somewhat of our soul has gone out from us? And do we not experience a faintness and prostration along with a dimness of sight? This then, must be the soul producing seed, which arises from the out drip of the soul, just as that fluid is the body producing seed which proceeds from the drainage of the flesh. (19)

An ancient and perennial question: *Is the sensation of orgasm the same in women and men?* The Greeks had an answer, as they did for most questions. In Greek mythology, Tiresias, a prophet of Thebes, according to one story, was changed into a woman for angering one of the gods. He lived for seven years as a woman, apparently even having a family. Eventually he was forgiven, and turned back into a man. Zeus and Hera, the king and queen of the gods, were having an argument as to who had the most pleasure in sex, a man or a woman. Hera, interestingly, said it was the man, while Zeus, said it was the woman.

They turned to Tiresias who because he had had sex both as a man and as a woman, would know. Without hesitation, Tiresias, replied that women did by far: ***"Of ten parts a man enjoys one only, but a woman enjoys the full ten parts in her heart"*** (20) Hera, who would not tolerate anyone contradicting her, blinded poor old Tiresias for his impertinence. Although the legend doesn't specify, the pleasure referred to was most likely orgasm, and perhaps this legend contributed to the prominent view in the classical world that women had a stronger sex drive.

It's an intriguing story, but was Tiresias right in his assertion? A number of studies raise some doubt. In one study, psychologists, obstetricians, gynecologists, and medical students were unable to guess the sex of the author of 48 anonymous, written descriptions of orgasm. In other words, the 48 women and men produced indistinguishable descriptions of orgasm. In another study, 1000 students were asked to describe their orgasm experience in two different contexts, masturbation and sex with a partner, by using 60 adjectives. The results were that the sexes did not differ qualitatively in their descriptions or orgasm. There were some minor differences in the intensity of the experiences reported. Women reported stronger emotional responses than men, while men described 'shooting sensations' as more intense than women. In general then, it appears that the subjective experience of orgasm is the same in both sexes.

Orgasm as therapy

The social historian, Rachel P. Maines, reminds us in her engaging book, *Hysteria, the Vibrator, and Women's Sexual Satisfaction,* that orgasm as a healing therapy has a long history in Western medicine. The origin of this idea arises from the historical preoccupation of men with women's sexuality, in particular the affliction known as 'hysteria'. In the ancient world, hysteria, thought to arise from the upward movement of the uterus, was characterized by weeping, irritability, depression, morbid fears, headaches, mental confusion, constant worry, and so on. Maines describes one particularly interesting practice - the genital massaging of women to orgasm (or *paroxysm,* as it was called before the term orgasm was adopted), a practice that can be traced as far back as Hippocrates (4th century BCE).

Consider the following excerpt from a book published in 1653 by the Dutch physician, Peter van Foreest, describing the therapy for hysteria:

When these symptoms indicate, we think it necessary to ask a midwife to assist, so that she can massage the genitalia with one finger inside, using oil of lilies, muskroot, crocus, or something similar. And in this way the afflicted woman can be aroused to the paroxysm. This kind of stimulation with the finger is recommended by Galen and Avecenna, among others, most especially for widows, those who live chaste lives, and female religious; it is less often recommend for very young women, public women, or married women, for whom it is a better remedy to engage in intercourse with their spouses. (21)

Many physicians in the 19th and early 20th centuries felt that hysteria was often due to the neglect by husbands of their wife's sexual needs. This neglect generated the need for the "titillation of the clitoris" to relieve the symptoms of hysteria. Despite what we might think now, for many doctors this therapy was time-consuming and considered onerous, and was delegated to nurses or assistants. Females, however, were warned about self-therapy, since this would impair their health and ruin their marriages.

But for many other physicians the therapy was also quite lucrative, and many had practices that specialized in the genital relief of hysteria. A godsend for physicians who specialized in this therapy was the invention of the electrical vibrator (1880) – hailed as a great labor saving device, reducing fatigue on the part of the physician. Many women liked it because it induced multiple orgasms. Vibrators for home use quickly became available. In the 1915 General Electric mail order catalog, fullpage ads described the properties of the vibrators that made them especially useful "for women's needs". Vibrators fell out of favor when the porno film industry began using them in the late 1920s. Their sale was illegal in many states, but they reappeared in the 1970s with the feminist revolution.

Orgasm therapy itself also disappeared (interestingly the American Psychiatric Association did not drop hysteria as a disorder until 1952), and is now considered an extreme example of unprofessional conduct. Remnants of this therapy survive, however - witness the news reports of psychiatrists who have sex with their patients as part of the psychotherapy.

The connection between sexuality and disease received its imprimatur from Freud and the school of psychoanalysis that he founded. The origin of psychic disorders or afflictions according to Freud is sexual dissatisfaction. *"The symptoms of the disease are nothing else than the patient's sexual activity. . .. I never find it otherwise—that sexuality is the key to the problem of the psychoneuroses and of the neuroses in general"* (22). Hysteria was no longer seen as a symptom of a dislocated uterus, but rather a symptom of compromised sexuality, just as neurosis and anxiety were. Freud early in his career would apply strong pressure to the patients' 'body armor' hoping to overcome their rigidity.

Wilhelm Reich, a student of Freud, relates the following story of the Viennese physician Chrobak who referred a patient to Freud. The patient had been married for 18 years to an impotent man, was still a virgin, and she was suffering from severe anxiety attacks. Chrobak comments to Freud: *"We know only too well what the only prescription for such a case is, but we cannot prescribe it. It is 'Rx: Penis normalis, dosim. Repetatur'"* (23) In other words, the proper therapy for this poor woman was to get laid repeatedly.

Reich, according to Christopher Turner, author of *Adventures in the Orgasmatron*, coined the term 'sexual revolution' in the 1930s to express his conviction that "a true political revolution would only be possible once sexual repression was overthrown". Sexual repression would be eliminated only when everyone was sexually healthy, that is, was able to have an orgasm. *"The elimination of sexual stasis through orgastic discharge eliminates every neurotic manifestation"* (23) Reich became the apostle of the orgasm. *"The actual goal of therapy was making the patient capable of orgasm"*. He became so extreme in his views that the International Psychoanalytical Association expelled him in part because of his insistence that his patients undergo therapy in their underwear. Freud too, eventually repudiated him.

Nevertheless, Reich's tireless proselytizing of his view that political liberation required sexual liberation, and that a healthy democracy depended on a vibrant sexuality found a receptive audience during the 1930s. James Baldwin, in his essay *The New Lost Generation,* comments on that period when *"people turned away from the idea of the world being made better through politics to the idea of the world being made better through psychic and sexual health like sinners coming down the aisle at a revival meeting."* (24)

After fleeing Nazi occupied Europe, Reich eventually landed in the U. S. Industrious and driven as ever, he founded the Orgone Institute Diagnostic Clinic and the American College of Orgonomy, and dedicated himself to exploring his new obsession – orgone energy, which he conceived as primordial cosmic energy. Reich designed a machine to trap the energizing and healing force of orgone energy. The machine, a telephone boothlike box lined with metal sheeting and steel wool, became known as the Orgasmatron or orgone box. *"Reich considered his orgone energy accumulator an almost magical device that could improve its users 'orgastic potency' and by extension their general, and above all, mental health,"* Turner writes (25).

The whole concept of the Orgasmotron is laughable in retrospect, but the orgone box instantly acquired famous devotees: J.D. Salinger, Allen Ginsburg, Jack Kerouac, William Burroughs, Saul Bellow, and Norman Mailer, among others. There were cynics, critics, and unbelievers, of course – Einstein tried it for two weeks, and found it useless. James Baldwin tried to put the orgone box frenzy in perspective when he wrote *"the discovery of the orgasm – or rather, the orgone box – in retrospect seems the least mad of the formulas that came to hand"* at the time (25). Finally, in 1954, everyone came to their senses: the Food and Drug Administration ruled that Reich could no longer rent or sell his orgone box. Reich refused to comply, and was sentenced to two years in a federal penitentiary. He died in prison in 1957 at the age of 60.

Orgasm in the male – a long PERT

The terms orgasm and ejaculation are often used synonymously, but it is important to make a distinction between the two. Orgasm in the male is the subjective experience of pleasure associated with ejaculation.

The brain interprets ejaculation as a pleasurable event, perhaps in the same way that we have a sense of pleasure when we drink water if we are very thirsty, or when we eat food when we are very hungry. The pleasure associated with ejaculation is its most interesting aspect, but also the one we know least about. It remains a profound mystery.

In men the principal trigger of orgasm is penile stimulation, whether by masturbation, fellatio, or penetrative (vaginal or anal) sex. Continued penile stimulation induces a sensation of mounting tension attributed to increasing pressure in the wall of the prostatic urethra. As the tension increases sperm and seminal fluid are forced into the prostatic urethra causing it to expand and contracting the bladder neck to prevent semen going into the bladder. These events are referred to as the *emission* phase of ejaculation, at the end of which, a point of no return ('reaching the edge as it sometimes referred to) is reached. At this point, voluntary control over ejaculation has ended.

The *expulsion* phase begins with the sudden release of tension and the rhythmic contractions of the prostatic urethra and the pelvic muscles (a 'pumping' feeling) that eject the semen from the prostatic urethra through the penile urethra and to the outside. Emission and expulsion are not isolated events, but 'whole body' changes, since they are accompanied by an increased heart rate, rise in blood pressure, hyperventilation, sweating, and involuntary groaning or grunting at each contraction. The peak sensation of pleasure – orgasm – may occur slightly before or at the same time as ejaculation. The ecstatic pleasure of the climax is very brief, three to four seconds, although some men claim that their climaxes last more than thirty seconds. Finally, as the tensions built up before are dissipated, a feeling of calm and relief follows, sometimes referred to in marriage manuals as the "after glow". This sensation is capture beautifully in the following poem:

When love empties itself out,

it fills our bodies full.

For an hour we lie braiding

pulse and skin together,

like infants who sigh

and doze, dreamy with milk (26, Donald Hall, After Love)

Why can't the point of no return (staying at the edge) be prolonged indefinitely? Doing so might possibly intensify the pleasure of orgasm. We don't know the answer, but some investigators have speculated that prolonging the tension for too long a period could "overload" the nervous system and could lead to permanent damage, maybe akin to an epileptic seizure. So that aborting the point of no return may be thought of as a mechanism to protect us from excessive stimulation.

The time for ejaculation to occur can vary significantly, generally being short in adolescents and young men, but increasing with age. In older men difficulties in ejaculating is a common complaint. In younger men, on the other hand, premature ejaculation can be a problem because the male partner climaxes significantly before the female partner is satisfied. The force with which the ejaculate also diminishes with age – in young men, the ejaculate can cover a distance of a foot or more if no obstructions are placed in it way. In older men, the ejaculate just "drips out". Presumably, this diminished force may be due to the aging of the pelvic musculature, or possibly to the expulsion of the ejaculate into the bladder due to incomplete blockage of the bladder neck during the emission phase. It is not clear whether the quality of orgasm is correlated with the diminished force of ejaculation.

Two nerve networks – the cerebral and spinal – control ejaculation, but the cerebral centers override spinal control under normal conditions. In men with certain types of spinal cord injuries that render them unable to ejaculate nevertheless can progress through the emission phase. If these men are administered SSRI (selective serotonin reuptake inhibitors) antidepressants (whose site of action is cerebral, and not spinal), no effect on the emission phase is seen. However, SSRIs given to normal men, depending on the dose can delay or inhibit ejaculation. This indicates that the initial response to stimulation of the penis is assumed by the spinal control centers, Orgasm is followed by a post ejaculation refractory time (PERT) during which further stimulation leading to orgasm is not possible. Apparently, eight successive ejaculations in a fairly rapid succession have been recorded in one male.

This would be impossible for the huge majority of men. The PERT can vary considerably from one individual to another (from tens of minutes to hours), and is generally short in younger males, and increases with age. A long PERT, or the inability to experience multiple orgasms is a crucial difference between men and women.

Why the long PERT in men? Can it be reduced or even eliminated? In the 1970s and 1980s there was considerable interest in Taoist techniques of self-control that proposed that men could be trained to have multiple orgasms without ejaculation. In other words, they could be taught to will themselves to have a series of orgasms without the physical stimulation that leads to ejaculation. Female non-genital orgasms have been documented quite often in the clinical literature, but male non-genital orgasms are extremely rare. We hear relatively little about these techniques currently, most likely because the hype didn't live up to the reality.

Still the question of the long PERT in men is an interesting one. One possibility is that the PERT depends on the rate at which semen is restored after ejaculation to regain some critical volume that may be necessary to resume sexual activity. Although the normal ejaculate volume is considered to be 2.5 to 5 milliliters (ml), it can vary from individual to individual, presumably because the amount stored and/ or the rate of replenishment varies from one person to another. The ejaculate volume also decreases with age. Hence, it is conceivable that men who have a greater store or greater replenishment rate of seminal fluid can maintain the critical volume for more ejaculations than men who have a smaller store. This would be consistent with the observation that the PERT is longer in older men and their ejaculate volume is also diminished.

Orgasm in the female – a multicolored tapestry

Female orgasm inspires interest, debate, polemics, ideology, technical manuals, scientific and popular, solely because it is so often absent unlike the male orgasm which exists with monotonous regularity and for the most part interesting only to people directly involved in it. (27, Donald Symons, *Evolution of Human Sexuality*)

Orgasm in the female has always attracted more attention than orgasm in the male. Perhaps this has been because until very recently most of that attention has come from men, many of whom feared women's sexuality, considered it scandalous and dirty, and who have tried in different ways to keep it under control. How else to explain the sexual taboos, the sexual codes of conduct, distinctions between 'good' and 'bad' women, and even the existence of the pornography industry. Repression of women's sexuality has been the historical norm and is still evident in some religions and cultures today.

Much of the earlier literature is full of wishful thinking and pronouncements that have no biological foundation – sex is bad for women, enjoying sex will destroy the maternal instincts of women, or that women exist for men's pleasure. Even old Benjamin Franklin fell into that trap with his **"Women were designed to gratify our Passions"**. (28) British medical journals during the 18th and 19th centuries considered that "women's bodies were receptacles for male-centered sexual practices."

It is only since the Kinsey and Masters and Johnson studies that some of the fog that kept us from truly understanding female sexuality and female orgasm has begun to lift. We have also come to appreciate the inherent complexity and variability with which women experience orgasm, seemingly much greater than that of the male. In certain respects females vary more among themselves than males vary among themselves because of the spectrum of silenced genes on the X chromosome. The recognition of this variability has led one researcher to comment *"men are woven from a single piece of cloth, while women are woven from a multicolored tapestry."* (29)

Different roads lead to Rome

Definitions of a female orgasm abound – some focus on the physiological aspects, and others on the psychological (emotional) aspects. One definition, a mouthful, that tries to combine the two is:

"A variable, transient peak sensation of intense pleasure, creating an altered state of consciousness, usually with an initiation

accompanied by involuntary, rhythmic contractions of the pelvic striated circumvaginal musculature, often with concomitant uterine and anal contractions and myotonia that resolves the sexually induced vasocongestion, generally with an induction of well-being and contentment. " (30) Let's try to pick out the main points.

Several physiological changes take place in preparation for and during orgasm. The first is "vasocongestion," the rushing of blood in the breasts and genitals as a response to a sexually relevant stimulus. This results in the breasts and genitals becoming larger, the body feeling warm or hot to the touch, a change in color of the breasts and genitals, and enhanced vaginal lubrication. The second is "myotonia" or "neuromuscular tension," the build up of energy in the nerve endings and muscles of the entire body. Accompanying these is an increase in heart rate, increase in blood pressure, and hyperventilation. The myotonia increases until the point of no return, at which time the tension is released, and, according to Masters and Johnson, immediately followed by three to fifteen involuntary rhythmic contractions of the pelvic musculature with concomitant uterine and anal contractions. The explosive release of tension and the intense pleasure that is induced lasts from 3 – 26 seconds, or in some cases up to 2 minutes, and is accompanied by involuntary shouts and cries. Orgasm is also typically associated with a momentary clouding, or altered state of consciousness.

This complex mind-body experience can be elicited in three different ways. Stimulation of the clitoris (the equivalent of penile stimulation in the male) appears to be the principal means of triggering an orgasm. This can occur directly by manual (or through the use of a vibrator) stimulation of the clitoris, or indirectly as occurs during penile-vaginal intercourse (in this case the penile thrusting indirectly stimulates the clitoris).

Vaginal orgasms, independent of clitoral stimulation, may also occur, presumably through stimulation of the so-called Grafenburg or G-spot (a region of the upper vaginal wall). Despite dozens of papers that have been published on the subject, the existence of the G-spot as a distinctive region or site in the vagina remains highly controversial. It does seem possible, however, that certain sites within the vagina may be more sensitive in some women, but not in other women. Recall that four different nerve pathways carry sensory signals from the vagina, cervix, clitoris and uterus, and they all can contribute to orgasms. Hence, some variation in sensitivity of these different tissues may not be unexpected.

Much ink and paper has been wasted in rather useless arguments, again by men, about which type of orgasm is 'inferior' or more 'mature'. Freud, in particular, was perhaps the first to maintain that clitoral orgasms were a characteristic of an immature woman, while vaginal orgasms were the signature of a mature one, and hence, superior. The Masters and Johnson studies demonstrated clearly that the vaginal and clitoral orgasm dichotomy is completely false.

Stimulation of non-genital sites – the nipples, the mouth, the ears, the anus, even the hand – can trigger orgasm in some women. Even more interesting is that orgasm can be triggered by mental images, sexual fantasies, or during sleep without any physical stimulation. Reports of these types of orgasms have appeared in the clinical literature for many years, but their anecdotal nature make it difficult to confirm them as true orgasms.

Women in contrast to men are naturally multi-orgasmic. They have a very short or non-existent PERT, which means that continued stimulation of the clitoris can elicit multiple orgasms in rapid succession. Consider one especially graphic description of multiple climaxes:

I can't recall how long it had been since I had a romp with JM but it finally happened last night. (Thank You!). It was kind of odd as I wasn't really expecting it but did have a brief moment of thought through out my day how it would be so nice to just get laid without all the formalities. Without even trying for it or hinting about it. He did in fact, take the initiative and I got my wish. He touched me more than usual. He kissed more than usual. He even worked on me a little longer than usual, bringing me very close to the point of no return and back down again. As he [sic] making the attempt to bring me up one more time, I reached around him and grabbed him by his backside, wanting him inside me . . .NOW-NOW-NOW. He obliged, of course and within minutes I had the first of three wavepounding, earth shattering, thunder crashing orgasms. After that, I took control and climbed on top. Here comes another one from waaaaay deep within me. So much so, I shook and writhed uncontrollably. He braced me from my own collapse and while doing that, he had his mouth feverishly all over my breasts. His heavy breathing was like fire on my breasts, my shoulders, my face . . .. he was clearly out of control as well. It was such a magnificent turn on to see him actually enjoying himself while he completely devoured my upper body! He finally flipped me back onto my back and took his position as the pilot in his cock pit. Slowly he worked himself within me, pinning my wrists down, arching his back upward so he could watch his show. The occasional nibbling at my breasts, his heavy breath in my ear and the sporadic speeds of thrusts and stops brought me to my finale. He timed it with great skill as he came with me, releasing those ever so sexy grunts and gasps that come from his throat. God, I love that! (31)

Interestingly, descriptions of orgasmic-like experiences in the absence of genital stimulation have appeared in literary form. For example, consider St. Teresa of Avila's: *"In his (the angel's) hands I saw a long golden spear and at the end of the iron tip I seemed to see a point of fire. With this he seemed to pierce my heart several times so that it penetrated to my entrails. The pain was so sharp that it made me utter several sharp moans; and so excessive was the sweetness caused me by this intense pain that one can never wish to lose it."* (32) Her incisive description certainly sounds like an orgasm.

Closer to our time is Emily Dickinson's enigmatic poem, *I started Early – Took my Dog*, a poem that at the literal level tells of a woman who walks to the sea with her dog, and enjoys herself until the tide catches and overwhelms her, but which at a symbolic level tells a more intriguing story.

I started Early – Took my Dog –

And visited the Sea –

The Mermaids in the Basement

Came out to look at me –

And Frigates – in the Upper Floor

Extended Hempen Hands –

Presuming Me to be a Mouse –

Aground – upon the Sands

But no Man moved Me – till the Tide

Went past my simple Shoe –

And past my Apron – and my Belt

And past my Bodice – too –

And made as He would eat me up –

As wholly as a Dew

Upon a Dandelion's Sleeve –

And then – I started – too –

And He – He followed – close behind –

I felt his Silver Heel

Upon my Ankle – Then my Shoes

Would overflow with Pearl

Until We met the Solid Town –

No One He seemed to know

And bowing- with a Mighty look –

At me – The Sea withdrew (33)

Two veteran sex researchers, Beverly Whipple and Barry Komisaruk, from Rutgers University, have spent the better part of the last two decades documenting orgasms elicited from nongenital sites and through mental imagery. Using brain-imaging techniques, they have shown that orgasms triggered by genital and non-genital stimulation, and mental images activate the same brain regions, and in that sense are equivalent.

The frequency, type, and intensity of orgasm vary significantly among women and even in the same woman. In a 1990 population study 5 to 10% of women in the U. S. reported that they had never experienced an orgasm by any means. At the other extreme are women who in some circumstances can have one orgasm after another (serial multiple orgasms) and/or a series of orgasms 2 to 10 minutes apart (sequential multiple orgasms), and in other circumstances only one orgasm.

Many factors influence the sensitivity and threshold necessary to elicit an orgasm. A woman may fail to achieve orgasm with one partner, but may be multi-orgasmic with another. The emotional contexts of each encounter appear to play a critical role - quality of relationship with partner, education, sexual experience, self-esteem, body image, culture, age, level of stress or fatigue. It's also the case that many women fake orgasms. Estimates suggest that two-thirds of women admit to faking orgasms at some point in their lives, not only during vaginal intercourse, but during oral sex as well. What are their reasons for faking orgasm? Several reasons are given: stroking the male ego, embarrassment over failure to achieve orgasm, insecurity, fear of intimacy, simply wanting intercourse to end.

Although the ease with which an orgasm can be elicited is not fixed in any real sense, it does also seem that women are distributed along a continuum: at one extreme are women who have a difficult time achieving orgasm by any means, and at the other extreme are women who can reach orgasm with little or no genital stimulation or via fantasy, or women who are characterized by a persistent genital arousal disorder. Brain imaging studies conducted by Drs. Komisaruk and Whipple suggests that in the latter women the brain regions normally activated by genital stimulation are continually being activated endogenously, or originating within an organ. Presumably, in women who are unable to reach orgasm – anorgasmic women – the normal pathways that carry information from genital stimulations to the proper brain regions are blocked.

New research suggests that we may be in store for more surprises. Consider, for example, the case of the phantom foot orgasms described by the neuroscientist V.S. Ramachandran from the University of California, San Diego. In this case a man who had his foot amputated began experiencing orgasms in his phantom foot. Dr. Ramachandran suggests that nerve cells from other regions of the brain began to replace the ones that had been lost after the amputation. By chance, nerve cells that process information from the penis may have repopulated the lost ones, leading to the orgasms from the phantom foot.

In addition to demonstrating that an orgasm originates in the brain, these studies also show that the brain has an amazing plasticity, that is, that nerve cells can be rerouted and acquire new functions. The mind-boggling possibility is that in the near future we may learn how to train the brain to generate an excitation that culminates in intense pleasure in the absence of external physical stimulation. Maybe in a few years we might take a course in, say *Ten easy steps to reach orgasm*. Satisfaction guaranteed. Would you sign up for one?

Le petit mort and other questions

Most of us probably take orgasm for granted, but for evolutionary biologists it has always been a mystery, maybe a pleasurable mystery, but a mystery nonetheless. A number of "how" and "why" questions have been posed over time, and debated vociferously in the scientific literature. Let's consider a couple of these just so that you can get an idea of the problem.

Recall the definition of orgasm given above, one part of which reads:

a *variable, transient peak sensation of intense pleasure, creating an altered state of consciousness.* The pleasure of orgasm can be remembered, but it cannot be re-experienced. The sense of pleasure fades incredibly quickly. We may struggle to recapture it, but it vanishes. Maybe the ultimate motivation for sex may lie in reliving that sense of intense pleasure. But pain has the same property: we may remember past pains – breaking a leg, a blow to the head, and injuries in an accident – but we don't relive them. It would be terrible if we did, for we would be constantly reliving all the pains of our past. A life like that would be unbearable.

Pleasure and pain are very similar in that respect, and they may have a similar underlying neurological basis. Recent brain-imaging studies by Beverly Whipple and Barry Komisaruk suggest at least one connection between the two. They have found that two brain regions -- the insula and cingulate cortex - are activated during orgasms in women are also activated during response to pain. Moreover, there is a strong inhibition of the response to pain during orgasm. These findings indicate there is a very important interaction between the orgasmic experience and the pain experience, one of which may be that both activate some other site or sites in the brain that renders both experiences unrelieveable.

But let's go back to pleasure. Suppose we were able to elicit the pleasure of orgasm at will – could we live with constant pleasure? A troubling connection appears, however. The nucleus accumbens, a brain region activated during orgasm in women, is also activated by pleasure-producing drugs. Would we become like drug addicts constantly in search of the next fix, the next orgasm? Would we ever do anything else? Maybe it's better that we parcel out our orgasmic pleasure in small doses.

Second, what about the 'altered state of consciousness', what the French refer to poetically as 'le petit mort' or 'the little death' to describe the very brief state of diminished consciousness coincident with orgasm. This transient loss of the faculties has been known since ancient times and commented upon by many writers. St Augustine understood it well when he stated

Sexual lust not only takes possession of the whole body and outward members, but also makes itself felt within. . . . So possessing . . . is this

pleasure, that at the moment of time in which it is consummated, all mental activity is suspended (34)

An old Yiddish joke expresses the same idea in a more humorous fashion

When the penis steht, the brain goes out the window or "when the penis is hard, the brains are soft" (35)

What's the explanation for *le petit mort?* Gert Holstege and his group in the Netherlands have found that several areas of the brain are deactivated in women during an orgasm - the prefrontal cortex, just behind the left eye-ball, the part of the brain that governs conscious action, the amygdala, which governs fear and anxiety, and the amygdala which governs emotional control. What made their study particularly convincing was that they compared the brain scans of women who were faking an orgasm, and observed that no general deactivation takes place. This indicates that an integral part of an orgasm is a "letting go", a deep relaxation, free of anxiety. Turning off the conscious part of the brain, if only for a few seconds, may be the key to understanding how an orgasm can be elicited without physical stimulation.

This shutting down of key areas of the brain may also explain why autoerotic asphyxiation enhances the intensity of orgasm. Depriving a brain of blood during sex (by restriction of breathing) shuts down key brain regions and results in particularly intense and additive orgasms.

Finally, does orgasm serve any purpose? What is it for? This is a question that evolutionary biologists like to think about, but it is also a treacherous one because only speculative answers are possible. For males, ejaculation is necessary for reproduction, but not necessarily true for orgasm. Orgasm is a brain-driven event, independent of ejaculation. Why, then does it exist? Do animals experience orgasm? We suspect that our primate cousins experience something like it, but we don't really know. Maybe, as some biologists have suggested, orgasm helps to strengthen the male-female bond, important for child rearing. But as we saw with the prairie mole voles, social fidelity does not imply sexual fidelity. Maybe what drives males to copulate or masturbate is the intense pleasure of orgasm. A side benefit in the case of copulation is reproduction.

For females, the question is even more difficult to answer. Orgasm in females is not necessary to conceive. Probably the vast majority of women throughout human history have conceived without orgasm. In evolutionary lingo, this indicates that orgasm is not an adaptive trait, that is, it was not a trait that was selected for because it improved the reproductive success of the female. Elisabeth Lloyd, a philosopher of science, in her meticulously researched book, *The Case of the Female Orgasm,* examines 21 different explanations for the origin and evolution of female orgasm. She eliminates all but one, and concludes that because the clitoris and penis derive from the same embryonic tissue, female orgasm is a by-product of development of the orgasm potential of the penis. But, of course, this doesn't account for the non-genitally driven orgasms, whether from non-genital sites or from mental imagery.

The unsatisfactory answer is that we don't know if orgasm has a "purpose", and we will probably never know. Maybe all of these evolutionary arguments are examples of "just so" stories, fables that keep us entertained, but that we shouldn't take too seriously.

The one character play – a cultural taboo

The word, *masturbation*, has such a harsh and abrasive sound that that by itself may contribute to our reluctance to talk about it. The practice, perhaps because it is secretive and solitary, is a highly taboo subject, at least in our society. From a biological point of view, masturbation is of no particular interest, but it has acquired in certain periods and societies enormous moral significance. Why that is so is an enormously complex and interesting story, one that reveals much about our society. Let's begin by first considering the practice in children.

In children and adolescents

Childhood masturbation (CM) (self-stimulation of the genitalia in a pre-pubescent child) has probably always existed, but it was first recognized and acknowledged clinically by Felix Gattel, a pupil of Freud in 1898 as being common in young girls. The finding was ignored for almost a century, but came into prominence in the 1980s and 1990s when it was linked to sexual abuse. CM is now considered a common and developmentally normal sex behavior in children. Infants, especially boys, as young as 5 months of age who are learning how to grasp will often manipulate their genitalia. At around two children began to explore their bodies more explicitly and touching or fondling their genitalia is quite common. Touching the genitalia at home, in public, using the hand, or a toy or other object, and rubbing the body against objects or their parents is fairly typical. A 1998 study of 1114 two to twelve-year old children reported the following: in the 2-5 year olds, 60.2% of boys and 43.8% of girls, in the 6-9 group, 39.8% of boys and 20% of girls, and in the 10-12 year old group, 8.7% of boys and 11.6% of girls, masturbated at home (as rated by their mothers). CM diminishes with age in pre-pubertal children as they learn and assimilate culturally appropriate rules for sexual behavior. Children masturbate in most cases because it is pleasurable, but it can also be a mechanism to cope with anger, anxiety, boredom, family stress, and lack of affection.

Even when parents may accept CM as normal behavior, an important concern for many is: when does normal pass into abnormal or excessive? Unfortunately, there is no completely satisfactory answer to this question. What is normal in a statistical sense for a population may be considered unacceptable behavior by particular familial, cultural or religious groups. Moreover, the absence of solid epidemiological information on normal childhood sex behavior precludes clear-cut clinical definitions of 'abnormal' or 'excessive'. The *DSM-IV* does not include 'abnormal CM' as a psychiatric disorder because such a diagnosis has been difficult to validate. Nevertheless, most clinicians rely on fairly common sense markers. For example, masturbating in public would typically be considered normal in a toddler, but not in a twelve-year old. Anal, vaginal, or oral penetrations or other aggressive or adult-like sexual behaviors before puberty, extremely uncommon in normal childhood populations, would certainly be considered abnormal by most clinicians. In most cases these types of behaviors are indicative of serious emotional disturbances, often arising from sexual abuse. Psychological evaluation is clearly important in such cases.

As children enter adolescence masturbation generally becomes more frequent and may lead to orgasm in the female and ejaculation in the male. Studies from the 1970s report that the prevalence of masturbation was 60% to 90% among male and about 40% among female adolescents. Although masturbation is among the most secretive of human behaviors, adolescents need to be reassured that masturbation is a normal part of development. According to clinicians, masturbation in the adolescent has several beneficial functions: it is an effective way of releasing sexual tension and anxiety; it permits the exploration of sexual feelings and thoughts; and it is an efficient way of controlling and channeling sexual urges safely.

Solitary sex – *unmentionable (almost)*

Solitary sex, an apt description of masturbation in adults, remains in the U.S. an even more unmentionable subject than homosexuality, transsexuality, or Internet sex. How it acquired its importance gives us an insight into how a harmless practice of no biological importance came to be viewed with such singular opprobrium. The historian, Thomas W. Laqueur, in his informative and exhaustive work, *Solitary Sex: The Cultural History of Masturbation,* provides a fascinating historical perspective on an ancient, universal, and often reviled practice. Laqueur points out that the biblical passage in the Hebrew bible (Genesis 38, 8-10) that many have used as the religious basis for the injunction against masturbation is somewhat obscure, and religious scholars are divided over whether Onan, who "spilled his seed upon the ground", was being punished for masturbation or for withdrawing from the female before ejaculating.

The ancient classical world seemed not to pay any attention to masturbation. Some Roman physicians advised their women patients to rub their genitals (clitoris) to relieve tension. The early Christian church, other than considering it a carnal sin, did not pay much attention to the practice either. In the latter part of the 12th century it was included along with sodomy and bestiality as 'contrary to nature'. Interestingly, a major Catholic medical-theological guide of the 19th century mentions that women "found great relief from pains through pressing and manipulating of (the clitoris)" and was accompanied by "voluptuous sensations." (36)

Laqueur traces the modern obsession with masturbation with the publication in 1712 of a book entitled, *Onania; or, The Heinous Sin of Self Pollution and all its Frightful Consequences, in both SEXES*

Considered, with Spiritual and Physical Advice to those who have already injured themselves by this abominable practice. And seasonable Admonition to the Youth of the nation of Both SEXES. The book sold hundreds of copies becoming the equivalent of a best seller.

The author of this treatise remains unclear, but Laqueur suggests that it was John Marten, an archetypal snake oil salesman and all round con man who, although having been jailed for obscenity, managed to pass himself off as a surgeon. *Onania's* titillating description of 'onanism' and 'willful self abuse' had all the features of a modern day confessional, and according to Laqueur *"was basically soft-core medical porn – 'how I learned to do it,' and then, 'it was really bad."* (36). *Onania* was followed by another blockbuster for the time - *L'Onanisme,* written by a respected French physician, Samuel Tissot (1728-87). While *Onania* focused on the sinful aspects of masturbation, Tissot's treatise set the stage for the transformation of an old, harmless, and ignored practice into a disease syndrome - solitary sex not only is sinful, but causes disease.

A huge literature on masturbations dangers followed. According to Tissot, the waste of semen would lead to **"cloudiness of ideas, and sometimes even in madness; acute pain, decay of bodily power; pimples of face, suppurating blisters on the nose, breast, thighs, disordering of the intestines"** (36). In the U. S. much later, John Harvey Kellogg, the breakfast foods impresario, assured everyone that masturbation would lead to **"acne, shifty eyes, bed-wetting, finger nail biting, nervous shock"** (36). For him even procreative sex had it dangers – too much would lead to insanity. Even Freud put his word in, referring to masturbation as 'the primary addiction', a stage from which most graduated unless they suffered from 'arrested erotic evolution'.

The dangerous effects of solitary sex reverberated everywhere and among all social classes. The famous German philosopher, Immanuel Kant, maintained that masturbation was worse than suicide. In the list of charges against Marie Antoinette that justified her execution were that she had taught her son how to masturbate. In St. Elizabeth Hospital (a federal insane asylum in the U.S.) 108 men between 1855-1878 were admitted because they were suffering from masturbation-induced madness. The Greek poet, George Cavafy, wrote in 1897 in his diary about his own practice:

And yet I see clearly the harm and confusion that my actions produce upon my organism. I must, inflexibly, impose a limit on myself till 1 April, otherwise I shan't be able to travel. I shall fall ill and how am I to cross the sea, and if I'm ill, how am I to enjoy my journey? Last January I managed to control myself. My health got right at once, I had no more throbbing. (37)

The young Wittgenstein (who later would become one of the important philosophers of the 20th century) while a soldier in the eastern front during World War I agonized not about the death and destruction that he witnessed, but because he masturbated.

Even in our times the proscriptions against masturbation could have lasting influences in a sensitive soul:

"I was just hitting puberty, or puberty was just hitting me, when they told me I was committing genocide, on average, 3 or 4 times a day. They told me that when I died and went to Heaven, I would be boiled alive in giant vats filled with all the semen I wasted during my life." (38).

The anti-solitary sex frenzy led to a lucrative trade during the late 19th and early 20th centuries in devices such as erection alarms, sleeping mitts, and even hobbles to keep girls from spreading their legs. This last device was evidence that the epidemic had spread to women as well. For physicians in the 19th and early 20th century female masturbation was a sign of a disturbance in her sexual instincts. Contrary to what we might imagine, the role of the clitoris in sexual excitement and orgasm (known as *paroxysm*) was well known to physicians of that time, but they felt that the organ was to be aroused only by the woman's husband. Excessive masturbation indicated an unhealthy clitoris, and interestingly, a failure to respond to the sexual ardor of her husband, was also seen as clitoral problem. Excessive masturbation in girls and women was considered to lead to a variety of severe disturbances – insomnia, epilepsy, blindness, insanity, convulsions, melancholia, paralysis, and possibly even death. This combination of problems was given the name of 'masturbatory melancholia' or 'masturbatory paralysis'.

The French physician, Colombat d'Isere, argued that *'onanism, that execrable and fatal evil, soon destroys her beauty, impairs her health, and conducts her almost always to an early grave'* (39). Since the clitoris was the source of the problem, it had to be removed or destroyed. A variety of treatments were carried out – applying leeches to the vulva and anus, cauterizing the clitoris, and even using X-rays to irradiate the clitoris. The most popular procedure for excessive masturbation, however, in both Europe and the U. S. was the clitoridectomy – the surgical removal of the clitoris. On the other hand, for women who failed to orgasm with her husband, a *circumcision* (removal of the hood that covers the clitoris) was performed – the logic was that the clitoris would now be more exposed to stimulation by the penis during sexual intercourse.

Things began to change when the Kinsey reports and Masters and Johnson's *Human Sexual Response* demonstrated that everyone, or almost everyone, does it. The feminist movement and the sexual revolution, the gay-lesbian movement brought to an end the opprobrium and turned the tables: 'selfmanipulation was the gold standard of pleasure', 'the first, easiest, and most convenient way to experiment with your body', 'our primary sexual life'. Masturbation even made the major media: in movies such as *American Pie, American Beauty, Something about Mary,* and *Bad Lieutenant*, the male protagonists are shown masturbating. In the TV comedy Seinfeld, the protagonists in the episode entitled "The Contest" make a bet to see who can keep from masturbating the longest.

But masturbation in prime time has had a limited appeal – the taboo remains remarkably strong. The former U.S. surgeon general, Joycelyn Elders, was forced to resign because she had suggested that masturbation was after all not that harmful. She was accused of fomenting a 'selfish, depraved society'. Laqueur's *Solitary Sex* itself had to be printed in Canada because the American printer refused the job. In an era when hard-core sex is easily available on the Internet, public discussion of solitary sex has been completely suppressed. Laqueur ends his book with the following observation: ". . . *solitary sexual pleasure touches the inner lives of modern humanity in ways that we still do not understand. It remains posed between selfdiscovery and self-absorption, desire and excess, privacy and loneliness, innocence and guilt as does no other sexuality in our era"* (36).

Times do change, however. Clinicians are now touting the benefits of masturbation for women at least, not simply because it is pleasurable, but even better, because it is beneficial, especially for older women. According to Dr. Cathy K. Naughton, director of the Metropolitan Urological Specialists' Center for Sexual Health in St. Louis, *"Masturbation, which may include stimulation of the clitoris, urethra, and vagina, activates various neural pathways responsible for clitoral swelling, vaginal congestion, lengthening of the vagina, and lubrication"* (40) They even suggest that for women without a partner masturbation can be a satisfying substitute for sexual intercourse.

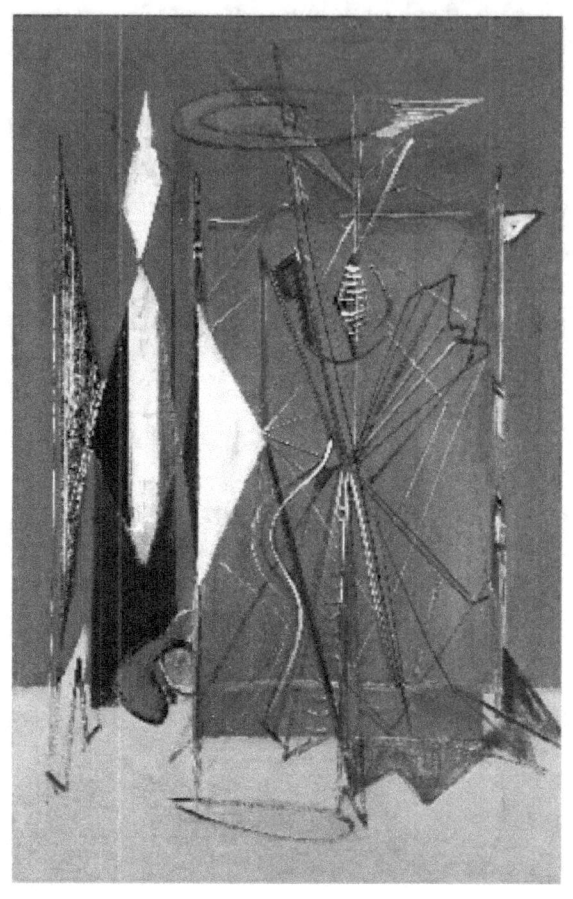

Mark Rothko, "Phalanx of the Mind, c. 1945" (c1998 Kate Rothko Prizel & Christopher Rothko/ artist Rights Society (ARS), New York)

Chapter 5

Erotic Preference and Gender Diversity

The mind is its own place, and in itself Can make a Heav'n of Hell, a Hell of Heav'n (1, John Milton, Paradise Lost)

Human sexuality – what is normal

A great multitude of people are continually talking of the Law of Nature; and then they go on giving you their sentiments about what is right and what is wrong; and these sentiments, you are to understand, are so many chapters and sections of the Law of Nature . . . [such and such an act, they say] is unnatural, that is repugnant to nature: for I do not like to practise it: and, consequently, do not practise it. It is therefore repugnant to what ought to be the nature of everybody else. (2, Jeremy Bentham, *Introduction to the Principles of Morals and Legislation)*

The enormous repertoire in our sexual practices and behaviors must have been perplexing and troubling to our ancestors, as it is to us now. John Milton's "the mind is its own place" is a particularly apt metaphor for locating the source of that repertoire. In this and the following chapter we tackle the immensely difficult subject of human sexual behaviors and practices that are considered taboo and deviant, or seen as difficult to understand, and those that are dangerous and criminal. A constant theme in our efforts to understand our sexuality has been the continuing tension between 'normal' or 'natural' and therefore, acceptable, behaviors, and, on the other hand, 'abnormal' or 'unnatural', and hence, unacceptable and forbidden, sexual behaviors.

Since time immemorial al societies have invested greatly in regulating our sexual behavior.

In Western Christendom, according to the historian Vern Bullough, the regulation of sexual conduct was very important to the early Church fathers. They were reacting not only to what they considered the sexual licentiousness of the pagan world, but they were also establishing norms of sexual behavior consistent with their interpretation of scripture, norms which developed as the Christian world expanded. He estimates that 20 to 30% of church canon law was devoted to defining appropriate sexual practices and relations between spouses. In the Judaic world, the sources of authority on sexual matters were the rabbinical writings collected in the Talmud, large sections of which analyzed sexual questions and incidents. Important parts of the religious writings in the other world religions were concerned with the questions of human sexuality. In the pre-literate societies appropriate sexual behavior was codified by oral tradition and custom. As a consequence, our views about when, where and with whom we have sex, the anatomical positions and the type of sex we indulge in, the roles and behavior of men and women, are all invariably shaped and more often then not, determined by the cultural and/or religious traditions in which we were raised. We learn both explicitly and implicitly what our society considers 'normal' and 'abnormal'. These views may be so deeply embedded in our psyche that we think of them as self-evident and quite often fail to realize that they are cultural conventions without a biological rationale. But if history tells us anything it is that we need to be very careful about labeling a practice as 'normal' or 'abnormal'. Let's consider one example. An extreme case perhaps, but instructive.

This view of sex and its practices was held and conducted among the Sambia tribe in New Guinea. A peculiarity in this society is that all boys between the ages of 7 to 10 are separated from their parents. They live in all male clubhouses separate from women until they marry. During their time in the male house the boys are required to fellate older boys and adult men. The justification is that ingesting sperm will allow them to mature sexually and they will be able to impregnate their wife when they marry. Not all the boys take to this practice voluntarily, and those that don't are coerced. In our society, we would be appalled by this practice and would judge it completely unacceptable; the males who were fellated would be considered pedophiles and would be punished severely. The Sambian justification for the practice would be dismissed as unscientific and unacceptable.

Aside from feeding our prurient interests, learning about unusual sexual practices may have an important benefit. It may lead us to reconsider our own definitions of what is acceptable and not acceptable, and to examine critically our justifications for the views we hold. We may come to understand that our sexual universe is immensely complex, and coming to grips with it is a work in progress. We are far from the finish line (if in fact there is one), but we have made some progress, especially in loosening the bonds that tie us to the mythologies of the past, mythologies that codified our sexuality and defined what was appropriate and what was not.

Erotic preference and gender – perceptions of ourselves

We are all now socially pressured to privately believe in and publicly proclaim our 'sexual identities' as the defining truth of whom we are. (3, J.N. Katz, The invention of heterosexuality)

In a study published in 1994, 99.7% of American men and 99.9% of American women reported an identity that was heterosexual, bisexual, or homosexual, indicating that the idea of one's identity being defined at least partly by one's sexual orientation was a meaningful and important concept to almost all contemporary Americans. In general, questions about sex and gender have assumed great currency in the last five or six decades. Many of our contemporary concerns about our sexuality tend to focus on four new ways of seeing ourselves, perceptions that have emerged quite recently in our history – *sexual orientation, sexual identity, gender role,* and *gender identity.* These concepts have captured the imagination of many contemporary societies. They represent another way of imagining ourselves, in much the same way that we might use race and ethnicity to define ourselves, that is, they are an essential part of our identity. Why that is so is itself an interesting and complicated story, but as it is with new ideas or concepts that periodically sweep across societies, we don't really have a definitive answer.

Homosexuality and transsexuality, both of which loom large in the public imagination in some societies around the world are seen to be particularly troubling. Although neither homosexuality nor transsexuality poses any real threat to the society at large, the commentary that we often hear, especially from many religious leaders in the U. S. make it seem as if these are responsible for the coming demise of Western civilization. Witness the statement of a prominent Protestant minister who blamed the 9/11 attacks on the Twin Towers in New York City on U.S. tolerance of homosexuality. In the U.S. both homosexuality and transsexuality are at the center of the so-called 'culture wars' that have polarized not only the public at large, but the scientific community as well. Many people find them troubling because they call into question our concepts of what are considered the acceptable relationships between sex and gender. They contribute to a pervasive sense of collective anxiety because they force us to examine more deeply our notions of what is normal. Sexual/gender nonconformity does raise complicated questions for all societies, but in our ignorance and out of frustration we very often deal with the non-conformers by ostracizing, marginalizing, and often punishing them.

Let's begin by defining what these terms mean in contemporary discussions. *Sexual orientation* is generally understood to refer to the nature of an individual's erotic preference. Three categories are typically considered – opposite-sex attraction (heterosexuality), same-sex attraction (homosexuality), attraction to both sexes (bisexuality). Generally they tend to be seen as separate, distinct categories. Erotic preference means that, for example, a heterosexual presumably responds to sexual stimuli from individuals of the opposite sex, while a homosexual responds to sexual stimuli from persons of the same sex, and a bisexual responds to sexual stimuli from both sexes. Response to sexual stimuli can be assessed by fairly reliable physiological procedures, such as penile plethysmography (measures penile engorgement) or vaginal photoplethysmography (measures vaginal lubrication), in response to sexually stimulating images. These methods measure genital responses to sexual stimuli. In other words, they are reasonably objective criteria for assessing response to sexual stimuli.

Distinct from erotic preference (sexual orientation) is *sexual identity.* An individual may have a same-sex erotic preference, but yet consider herself or himself a heterosexual. Males who identify themselves as heterosexual often have sexual relations with other men. This is often the case with male prostitutes. There have been many reports of males who married, had children, and outwardly were heterosexual, nevertheless come to realize that their sexual identity is homosexual.

Sexual identity and sexual orientation, then, do not always match. Sexual identity is a tricky, nebulous concept, difficult to define in any objective way. The term, sexual orientation, has its own problems. For example, we generally assume that it refers to a stable characteristic. In fact, sexual orientation is more fluid and flexible than previously considered, and may vary in time and context, and probably exists along a continuum. Terms such as *erotic preference* or *sexual preference* may be better alternatives. Erotic or sexual preference does not necessarily imply stability. Consider, for example, a heterosexual male who at one time might prefer slim, athletic females, and at another time, full-bodied, buxom females. Such an individual can respond to sexual stimuli from different types of females. Similarly, a male who identifies as heterosexual may on occasion, or possibly even frequently, may also engage in homosexual acts, but yet not consider himself homosexual. We could say then that it one case he had a heterosexual preference, and in the other, a homosexual preference, without implying any permanence to his preference. These examples illustrate the difficulty in trying to fit sexual behavior into rigid categories that do not correspond to the complexity and diversity that we observe.

Gender role and *gender identity* are two other aspects of our sexuality that have received much attention in the last few decades. Gender identity, a term introduced into the psychological literature in the 1960s, refers to a person's intrinsic sense of being either a female or male. Noncongruence between anatomical and psychosexual sex (a type of mind-body dissonance) is known clinically as *gender dysphoria or gender identity disorder* (GID). More commonly, persons with this discordance are said to be transsexuals. Many may want to undergo *sex reassignment surgery* to normalize their gender identity with their anatomical sex.

Gender role, on the other hand, refers to behaviors and traits that in a given society are typically assigned to one sex or the other. We often tend to think of these gender roles, for example, in play, in work, in the respective duties in marriage, as fixed, as if they were an innate characteristic of each sex. We don't have to look very far to realize that such gender roles are artificial, the product of particular circumstances and habits in any given society. A few examples: the mass mobilization of women during World War II to work in factories in jobs traditionally thought to be a 'man's job', the entry of females into high level positions in industry, government, academia, finance, and the expanding role of males in sharing the raising of children.

The fluidity of gender roles goes even much farther, as Claude Levi-Strauss reminds us in his informative lecture "Parenthood Revisited". Among the Nuer people of Sudan, for example, an infertile woman can purchase a 'wife' who will give her children using the services of a man, often a stranger. The infertile woman, considered the equivalent of a man, is the legal father. In other groups couples composed of two women employ males to have children, and one of the women will be the legal father, and the other the biological mother. A review of the anthropological literature describing the complex forms of parenthood and gender roles in many societies around the world may help us understand that aspirations and practices in our own society that may trouble us – assisted reproduction for single women, bachelors, widows or homosexual couples – ***have their equivalents in other societies, which are none the worse for it."*** (4)

Is there a biological reality behind these terms? That is, do we have a biological/chemical test that measures any of them? The simple answer is no. This is not so surprising - essentially all descriptions of human behavior fall in the same category, yet many researchers feel that there is an underlying biological reality to all behavior. The difficulty has been in defining what that reality is. What follows are those topics that I think will give you an insight into the questions and issues that are being raised and discussed currently.

Sexual orientation / identity – a *cultural obsession* The vicissitudes of history

A study of the history of opinion is a necessary preliminary to the emancipation of the mind (5, John Maynard Keynes)

Questions about the nature of homosexuality, its causes, and the extent to which it is innate or chosen have assumed great importance, becoming almost an obsession in the U.S. The importance attached to these questions seems out of proportion to the incidence of homosexuality, which is relatively low. Some recent estimates suggest that in the United States 3 to 4 percent of males and 1 to 2 percent of females identify themselves as exclusively homosexual. Even more alarming from a societal point of view is the extreme hostility with which homosexuality is seen by many sectors of contemporary American society. For many in the Christian right, homosexuality is an evil that must be eliminated. This extreme hostility was particularly evident in the 1980s. For example, Anita Bryant, leader of the "Save Our Children" campaign, declared *"God puts homosexuals in the same category as murderers."* The Reverend Jerry Falwell, head of the Moral Majority, in a mass mailing called on readers to *"Stop the Gays dead in their perverted tracks."* Dean Wycoff, head of the Santa Clara branch of the Moral Majority, declared on television that he believed *"that homosexuality should be included with murder and other capital crimes so that the government that sits upon this land would be doing the executing."* (6)

It was not a coincidence that more than a hundred vicious assaults were reported in a three month-period in San Francisco in 1981. The antigay attacks reached their peak in the late 1980s, declined for a number of years, but have reemerged in the last few years. In 2010, Fred Phelps, founder of the Westboro Baptist Church in Topeka, Kansas, and members of his church picket military funerals to spread their belief that U. S. deaths in Afghanistan and Iraq are punishment for the nation's tolerance of homosexuality. Their inflammatory rhetoric - "Thank God for dead soldiers" – make them perhaps the most extreme of the anti-gay groups. Other religious groups, the Orthodox rabbinate, the Roman Catholic hierarchy, and other conservative Protestant denominations, while less strident and inflammatory, still continue to oppose the expansion of gay rights.

Why the obsession with homosexuality? What is the source of this unremitting, often virulent hostility and intolerance toward homosexuality that we see in some sectors of American society? Why is a sexual act that injures no one so terrible? Why is sexual behavior that involves a rather small fraction of the population responsible for such moral indignation, public debate, and vast amounts of writing? Has it always been like this? How have other societies at different times in history viewed homosexuality? Why some societies make prejudicial distinctions based on religion, race, sexual preference, or other personal characteristics and others do not is not always an easy question to answer. Many Christians typically divide the world into Christians and non-Christians, a distinction that for non-Christians is pointless and makes no sense. And many Jews divide the world into Jews and Gentiles. For societies marked by racial prejudice distinctions based on the color and shade of the skin –'black', 'colored', and 'mulatto' – assume great importance. With regard to same-sex preference the historical record paints a very complex history – widespread acceptance in many societies, and hostility and intolerance in others. The diversity of acceptance versus intolerance across time and space in societies is not always easy to understand, but in fundamental ways must arise from the way that sexual behaviors and beliefs are organized in different societies.

Same-sex sexual preference has been found consistently in all societies. Historians point to writings from the ancient classical civilizations, and we have many descriptions of what is sometimes called 'gender atypical' sexual behavior (defined in contemporary Western terms) in indigenous societies in many parts of the world. Although most of this evidence is anecdotal, the general inference is that same-sex sexual behavior (typically involving males) has probably existed for thousands of years in different times and cultures. In some cultures, this type of behavior was accepted and practiced by many in the society some of the time. Examples that come to mind are the Sambian practice mentioned above, homosexual relationships between soldiers in the Spartan army in ancient Greece, or the practice in ancient Greece of older men having young male lovers. Although in most of these cases the males also had sex with females (wives, prostitutes, concubines), in many of these societies, a few individuals seemed to experience a compelling sexual attraction toward their own sex. In other instances, sex taboos against behaviors that included same sex erotic inclinations existed, but none portrayed same sex preferences with the singular horror that is seen in contemporary society. Homosexuality then, is not 'unnatural' in some intrinsic, biological, and universal sense.

The modern codification of the trait that we call sexual orientation into categories such as homosexual and heterosexual is a relatively recent phenomenon. The term homosexual was coined in 1869. These concepts were not part of the consciousness of Greek and Roman societies. What we now call homosexual interests and practices were seen as part of the normal range of human eroticism. In the Judaic world, opposition to homosexuality is linked to the specific injunctions in Leviticus (18:22 and 20:13) of the Hebrew Bible – *"Thou shall not lie with mankind, as with womankind; it is abomination"* – a sin punishable by death of both parties. But the force of this injunction varied in the different Jewish communities in the ancient and classical world.

Despite the Leviticus threats, allusions to same-sex love appear in the Hebrew Bible. Probably the most well known is that between David and Jonathan, the eldest son of Saul. Jonathan is struck with love for David on their first meeting:

And it came to pass, when he had made an end of speaking unto Saul, that the soul of Jonathan was knit with the soul of David, and Jonathan loved him as his own soul. And Saul took him that day, and would let him go no more home to his father's house. Then Jonathan and David made a covenant, because he loved him as his own soul. And Jonathan stripped himself of the robe that was upon him, and gave it to David, and his garments, even to his sword, and to his bow, and to his girdle.

Sometime later, Jonathan is killed by the Philistines, and David laments his death:

O Jonathan, thou wast slain in thine high places. I am distressed for thee, my brother Jonathan: very pleasant hast thou been unto me:

thy love to me was wonderful, passing the love of women.

In the early and emerging Christian world, the picture was more complex. The New Testament itself does not take any position with respect to same sex sexual preferences. None of the objections to homosexual acts can be traced to specific teachings of Jesus or the Apostles, and few early Christian writers based their oppositions to homosexual acts on the Leviticus injunctions. In contrast, many modern day Christians justify their anti-gay rhetoric citing the Leviticus passage from the Hebrew Bible, but they typically ignore essentially all of the other Leviticus precepts, such as circumcision, dietary laws, clothing of more than one type of fabric, and cutting of the beard or hair. The signaling out of homosexuality suggests that the Bible is used to justify an anti-gay hostility that stems from some other source.

In some early Christian circles there was no general prejudice against homosexuals. Some prominent and respected early Christians, some of them canonized, were involved in relationships that today would easily be considered homosexual. No early Christian writer considered same-sex sexual attraction 'unnatural'. St. Aquinas, for example, was very even-handed: *"Because of the diverse conditions of humans, it happens that some acts are virtuous to some people, as appropriate and suitable to them, while the same acts are immoral for others, as inappropriate for them"* (7). St. Augustine confessed his love for a friend of his youth whose death desolated him: *"For I felt that my soul and his were one soul in two bodies, and therefore life was a horror to me, since I did not want to live as a half; and yet I was also afraid to die lest he, whom I had loved so much, would completely die."* (8) But later, St. Augustine regretted the sexual aspect of his passion for his friend: *"Thus, I contaminated the spring of friendship with the dirt of lust and darkened its brightness with the blackness of desire."* (9)

Other influential writers censured homosexuality, but they also railed against lending at interest, sexual intercourse during menstruation, wearing of jewelry or dyed fabrics, shaving, regular bathing, wearing wigs, serving in the civil government or the army, manual labor on feast days, eating kosher food, and circumcision. For some early Christian writers homosexual acts were considered a sin because they were nonprocreative. For others the opposition stemmed from the act itself.

St. Augustine, despite his early sexual passion for his friend, came later to object to the act because it allowed a man's body to be used "as that of a woman" since *the body of a man is superior to that of a woman as the soul is to the body."* (6)

John Chrysostom, another of the early Christian writers and anti-homosexual propagandist, wrote in a similar fashion: *"For I maintain that not only are you made into a woman, but also cease to be a man; yet neither are you changed into that nature, nor do you retain the one you had"* (6) For both Augustine and Chrysostom their opposition stemmed from violations of gender expectations rather than from a Biblical injunction.

In general, an uneasy tension between tolerance/acceptance and opposition/intolerance existed in different parts of the early Christian world, and much of the hostility to homosexuality stemmed from sources other than the Bible. Some scholars trace the opposition in part to the influence of different ascetic schools of sexual morality, which tended to oppose all forms of sexuality. The anti-sex pressures of these movements increased significantly during the transition from the early Christian centuries to the early Middle Ages. Hostility to homosexuals increased during the dissolution of the Roman Empire (third to sixth centuries) for reasons that have not been elucidated. A few scholars suggest that the disappearance of prosperous urban centers throughout this period contributed to rise in intolerance.

An efflorescence of a gay subculture in Europe took place during the 11th and 12th centuries. This was marked by artistic conventions and literature in which monks celebrated same sex love in the monasteries, and Muslim, Jewish, and Christian poets wrote openly about homosexual love. Although an exuberant gay subculture prospered in many cities throughout Europe, hostility remained important in the rural areas. Some of the temper of the times can be seen in the poem *Purgatory* (Canto 26) by Dante (1265- 1321), who placed homosexuals in the highest rung of purgatory, along with persons guilty of "too much" heterosexual passion, far, far above the majority of other sinners. The tolerance didn't last, however. Shortly after Dante died, legislation passed in most of the Italian states punished homosexual acts.

What changed? For reasons that remain only partially understood, a virulent hostility began to manifest itself in the 13th and 14th centuries in popular literature first and then in legal and theological writing. The historian, John Boswell, suggests that the anti-homosexual fervor was related to the spread of a widespread intolerance to groups that were considered deviant and ideas that went counter to the prevailing majority norms. This increasing intolerance was manifested by the expulsion of Jews from many parts of Europe, the establishment of the Inquisition, the long-term noxious effects of the Crusades, and the campaigns against sorcery and witchcraft. The anti-gay sentiments were increasingly codified into civil and church law throughout most parts of the Christian world.

Before the end of the nineteenth century, both civil and church law in Europe proscribed homosexual acts, but the person who committed the forbidden act was not generally considered to belong to a special category of persons. A significant change in the perception of homosexual acts came with the development of psychiatry, which began to consider that a person who committed such acts was an "invert," a deviant. Only sexual activity that could be productive (that is, penile-vaginal intercourse) was seen as normal or natural, while sexual activity that precluded procreation was seen as unnatural.

Homosexuality began to be seen as a pathological condition. This concept of sexuality was reinforced in the 1920s with the discovery and gradual appreciation of the role of the gonadal hormones, estrogens and androgens. Maleness and femaleness began to be considered as two dichotomous hormonal states. The newly developing science of endocrinology helped to define the standard way of looking at human sexuality, the conviction that there are only two natural types or categories: *". . . one with female reproductive capacity, feminine behavior and a sexuality oriented towards men, the other with male reproductive capacity, masculine behavior, and sexuality oriented towards women."* (10)

These notions were buttressed by psychoanalytic theories that emphasized the roles of the mother or father, or family dynamics in the genesis of homosexuality. However, things began to change in the 1960s when the psychoanalytical underpinnings of the prevailing views of homosexuality began to be questioned in the medical and scientific communities. Many studies of sexual behavior and psychosexual orientation have shown that neither a hostile or distant father, nor an overly protective mother could be considered the cause of homosexuality.

The attitudes that shaped society's view of homosexuals have changed since the 1970s. Until the early 1970s, homosexuality was considered by the American Psychiatric Association (APA) to be a mental disorder. It was listed in the APA's 1968 edition of the *Diagnostic and Statistical Manual of Mental Disorders (DSM)* in the section on sexual deviations as an example of aberrant of sexual interests that "are directed primarily toward objects other than people other than the opposite sex." As such, physicians (mainly psychiatrists) had an obligation to "cure" it. Treatments that today would be considered completely unacceptable -- electric shocks linked to photographs of nude males, hormone injections, castration of homosexual men and transplantation of testicular tissue from heterosexual men, removal of the hypothalamus -- have been carried out at different times to cure homosexuality.

All of this is a sad commentary on the psychiatry profession. The psychologist, Margaret Nichols, recounts this history in quite forceful terms:

> *"Psychiatry has a long, shameful history of participating in the stigmatization and abuse of disenfranchised people. Beginning with the 19th century diagnosis of "drapetomania" (the desire of a slave to run away from his/her master), for well over a century psychiatric diagnosis has tended to reinforce the prejudices of society against women and racial and sexual minorities. And the abuse carried out in the name of psychiatric healing—forced incarceration, invasive and often painful treatments, forced sterilization, and clitorodectomies, not to mention loss of employment, housing, children, etc.—has been terrible."* (11, Margaret Nichols, 2008)

The view that led to such practices came to an end with the 1973 declaration by the APA that homosexuality was not, after all, a mental disorder. This change did not come about easily. A critical turning point were the Stonewall Riots in New York City in 1969 that led to the birth of the gay rights movement. Consistent protests and lobbying from gay/lesbian activists at annual APA conferences from 1970 to 1973, as well as data from researchers such as Alfred Kinsey and Evelyn Hooker, eventually led to the disappearance of homosexuality from the third edition of the *DSM*.

In 2013 it may be difficult to appreciate the significance of this change in point of view by the APA, but we can get a sense of its importance from remarks of the veteran gay and lesbian advocate in an article commemorating the 30th anniversary of the removal of the mental disorder label: *"The mental illness label for homosexuality was an albatross around our neck ... Yes, we were also viewed as sinners and as lawbreakers, but there was room for legitimate differences of opinion about what should be immoral and what should be illegal.... The sickness label, on the other hand, was supposedly a scientific finding that couldn't be questioned. And that made it tough to argue for our rights. Anything we said on our behalf could be dismissed as 'That's your sickness talking'."* (12)

Not all psychiatrists gave in, however, and attempts were made at various times to incorporate terms such as "sexual orientation disturbance" or "ego-dystonic" homosexuality, terms that persisted until 1987. Vestiges of this refusal to give up on the idea continues in the last version of the DSM *(DSM-IV-TR),* under the category of "sexual disorder not otherwise specified" which may include "persistent and marked distress about one's sexual orientation."

Despite the gradually increasing tolerance and acceptance of homosexuality, it is probably still the case that a portion of the general public, even while accepting and supporting gay rights, tends to view homosexuality as somehow aberrant and troubling. Much of this unease may have a religious basis, but even for those whose views are not religiously based, some sociologists suggest that homosexuality seems to call into question our ingrained and unconscious acceptance of a heterosexually structured world, one that many view as fundamental to our social and sexual existence. It's as if, homosexuality turns our world topsy-turvy, and questions the standard femalemale duality that we imbibe from infancy. In the U.S. those who have the strongest anti-gay sentiments also oppose abortion, pornography, premarital or extramarital sexual relations, divorce, equal rights for women, and sex education in schools, all of which are seen as posing significant threats to the viability and stability of the family in which males and females play complementary supportive roles. The fears for the integrity of the family tend to be felt most keenly by the lower middle classes, for whom a stable family is socially and economically important. It is these groups that respond to the anti-gay teachings of the conservative Christian right. But the antigay sentiments can also come from unexpected sources. Dr. Robert Spitzer from Columbia University, who had a defining role in the 1973 APA decision to remove the mental disorder label was a consistent supporter of gay rights. Nevertheless, even he seemed unable to change his view that homosexuality is not normal or healthy, even if it is not a mental disorder.

The search for the 'cause(s)' of homosexuality

The search for causes is always biased. For example, we typically do not ask for the cause or origin of right-handedness, but we do ask about the cause of left-handedness. In general, we ask about the causes of what is thought to be outside the ordinary pattern of life. We don't ask about the origin(s) or cause(s) of heterosexuality, but we do ask about homosexuality. This question is important to those who think of homosexuality as abnormal or aberrant. In societies in which samesex sexual preference was not considered anomalous (such as the ancient Greek and Roman world), it was not deemed important to ask about its cause.

When homosexuality was considered a mental disorder a search for its origin or cause was justified by thinking that a cure could be discovered. Once homosexuality was removed from the list of mental disorders, there would be no reason, at least no medical reason, to search for its origin. However, the search not only continued but intensified during the 1980's and 1990's. Aside from perhaps the scientific curiosity about what is seen by many, including scientists, as a problematic human trait, many commentators have argued that the primary impetus for the continued search for the cause of homosexuality has been to demonstrate that homosexuality is an in-born trait and hence, the homosexual cannot be blamed for his "affliction", and should not be punished for it either.

The partisans in the battle over the origin of homosexuality are the *biological determinists* and the *social constructionists*. The former argue that the origins of homosexuality lie in an alteration or perturbation in brain function, possibly due, in current models, to genetic mutations. The evidence for this view is weak or nonexistent, but it has still gained adherents among many in the scientific community, in part because it is generally consistent with current ideas about the biological origins of complex behavior. The social constructionists, on the other hand, argue that the biological model ignores the cognitive, social, and contextual aspects of sexuality. Anthropologists, for example, have described a number of non-Western societies in which homosexual practices in the young are a preparation for adult heterosexuality. An impressive diversity in sexual behavior has been described in different societies and periods in time, all of which suggests that sexual behavior is strongly influenced by social imperatives, rather than by biological determinants. Homosexuality, they suggest, is a social construction, a 'conversation' emerging out of the beliefs that people have in a particular time and place in history. In the words of one of the principal proponents of the social constructionist view: ***"No human conversation is free of the time and place in history and culture in which it occurs; this includes whatever activity that is called science in any time and place."*** (13, John H. Gagnon, 2008)

Much effort, money, paper, and ink have been devoted to the search for the biological origins of homosexuality. Because of the importance attached to this effort and the publicity that it has received it may be worthwhile reviewing briefly the history of the search. Three stages in this search can be discerned, and they differ in the type of biological parameter that has been the subject of study.

Hormonal influences

An early model portrayed the male homosexual as an aberrant male, more like a female than a male. There was even a suggestion that the homosexual represented a third sex, in some way intermediate between male and female. It was imagined that male homosexuals would be characterized by female physical traits, such as wider hips, smaller genitalia, and reduced hairiness. Although this simplistic notion was quickly discarded, the idea of a female element embedded in the male homosexual persisted. With the discovery and increased understanding of the role of steroid sex hormones in the reproductive physiology of the female and the male, the femalelike behavior of a male homosexual, that is, the desire for a male, was considered to arise from differences in sex hormone levels, either low androgen or high estrogen levels. Repeated studies, however, have demonstrated that no differences in sex hormone synthesis or levels exist between heterosexual and homosexual males. Homosexuality, then, is not due to a difference in the sex steroid endocrinology in the adult.

But the critics argued: *what about the prenatal period?* It was suggested that individuals born with abnormally formed or developed external genitalia could in principle provide useful information about the effects of elevated or lowered levels of sex steroid hormones on sexual orientation. Much of the focus has been on those XY patients with lower than normal androgen exposure, and XX patients with higher than normal androgen exposure. There is a voluminous literature on this subject, with many contradictory findings. A drawback of these studies is that clear distinctions between sexual identity and sexual orientation (as discussed in the section above) have not been made. An additional complication is that most of these patients are born with abnormally formed external genitalia. The effect that this has on the psychosexual development of the individual has been very difficult to measure. In general then, the studies on pre-natal sex steroid hormonal effects on sexual orientation have not provided meaningful information.

Brain differences

Studies reporting brain morphological differences between

heterosexual and homosexuals began appearing in the 1990s. Some of these studies looked for morphological differences in the human hypothalamus that could be related to sexual orientation. Although some of the differences reported initially made a big splash in the media, none of them have held up in replication studies. In retrospect, it seems highly unlikely that this approach would succeed. Brain morphological differences are too gross a measure for sexual orientation. If there were a biological component to sexual orientation, it would much more likely be found in functional, rather than morphological differences.

Family studies and genetics

Functional brain differences could be due to genetic differences. Different types of observations have been interpreted as suggesting a genetic component to homosexuality. For example, a number of population studies indicate that homosexual males tend to have more homosexual brothers, and homosexual females tend to have more homosexual sisters, compared to heterosexual men or women. In what is called the fraternal birth order effect in males, the risk of being a homosexual increases by around 35% with each older brother. This statistical oddity has generated a huge literature, and a variety of speculative explanations. Although these observations seem at first sight very important, we need to keep in mind that the huge majority of boys late in the birth order do not become homosexual. In addition, no evidence in support of the speculative explanations offered has been presented.

Twin studies have also contributed to the notion of a genetic basis for homosexuality. They have been used to obtain estimates of its heritability – the proportion of the trait's variability that can be accounted for by genes. The reported studies suggest a heritability in the range of 0.25 to 0.50 for males, and somewhat lower for females. For comparison, the heritability for height is 0.84 and 0.95 for head width. Interestingly, the heritability for handedness is 0.32, in the same range as homosexuality. At face value, these studies do suggest a genetic component. But there are complexities in these numbers. For example, the heritability of handedness is 0.32, yet more than 90 percent of the population is right-handed. Why such a large discrepancy? The psychologist, Robert Epstein, suggests that subtle, but powerful cultural influences favors right-handedness, and forces many left-handers in infancy to become right-handed.

In a similar way, he suggests that sexual orientation is influenced greatly by social/cultural forces. Like most other human traits, he suggests that sexual orientation exists in a continuum. At one end of the continuum are the exclusive heterosexuals and at the other the exclusive homosexuals. Societal pressures can have powerful effects on those individuals that are not at the poles of the continuum. Epstein argues that the incidence of homosexuality may be low because of the powerful cultural influences that promote heterosexuality. This reasoning suggests the interesting possibility that in a sexual orientation-neutral society the much larger fraction of the population would be homosexual.

Other studies have suggested a familial concentration. For example, in some of families, male homosexuals have maternal uncles who are also homosexual. Such an inheritance pattern would suggest that homosexuality could be associated with a gene on the X chromosome. Although initial reports of finding a region in the X chromosome linked to male homosexuality in such families made a big splash in the news, replication attempts by other groups have not been successful.

It is interesting to note that no new studies of this type have appeared since the mid 1990s. Numerous attempts to identify distinctive physiological, anatomical, genetic or endocrinological parameters diagnostic for homosexuality have been unsuccessful. In retrospect, the premise of being able to find the magic bullet that would point us to the origin of sexual orientation was highly simplistic given the complexity of the behavior in question.

What can we conclude?

All human behavior is ultimately determined by the activity of the brain. We need a functioning brain and central nervous system to express the diversity of human traits. It is in this sense that we can say that biological processes inform all human sexual behavior. On the other hand, the diversity of sexual behavior across time and space indicates that the biological processes are not deterministic. Social and cultural forces, many of them subtle and difficult to discern, are the sources of differences in sexual behavior and practices. Individual variation or differences in preferences and behavior are to be expected – variation, in fact, is the norm. For example, we all have different preferences in cars, in clothes, in food, in music, in sports, in books, and so on. We don't infer that those differences imply abnormality – we accept the variation as the norm. We also have different preferences in people. Our sexual preferences and behaviors – opposite-sex as well as same-sex preferences and behaviors - span a wide spectrum. Consider opposite-sex preferences: some females may prefer the sports jock, others the nerd, others the extrovert. Males also have different preferences in females based on body type, ethnicity, intelligence. We don't really understand the basis for differences in preferences, but we would never imagine such differences imply an abnormality. The same type of variability goes for same-sex preferences, and behaviors, as well. Many studies have shown that some heterosexuals engage in homosexual acts and that some homosexuals engage in heterosexual acts. The precise basis of this diversity is not yet understood, but the diversity shouldn't be that surprising. Perhaps the most important lesson for us is that it is unreasonable to argue that one type of preference or behavior is in some intrinsic and fundamental sense normal while another is abnormal.

It may be somewhat ironic that much of the current gay and lesbian ideology, while rightly resisting the label of pathological or abnormal, has in general accepted the strict biological deterministic view. An unfortunate consequence of the current tendency by both the pro-gay and antigay groups to polarize sexuality in this way is to partition people into antithetical categories of human beings, which is precisely where we were 100 years ago. The terms gay and lesbian do not reflect a global biological essence that all gays or lesbians share, anymore than we can identify any biological essence that all heterosexuals share. Such terms are more statements of political ideology than statements of biological fact.

Reparative therapy or Sexual Orientation Change Efforts (SOCE)

The 1973 decision of the American Psychiatric Association (APA) to affirm that homosexuality is not a mental disorder did little to change the minds of cultural/religious conservatives and a minority of psychotherapists. For them homosexuality, even if it were shown to be biologically determined, still remains a lifestyle choice. Psychotherapeutic efforts to change sexual orientation – referred to as 'reparative', 'reorientation', or 'conversion' therapy – begun in the 1950s and 1960s continued and expanded in the 1970s, 1980s, and 1990s. These efforts were supported by religiously funded organizations such as Exodus and NARTH (National Association of Research and Therapy of Homosexuality), both of whom promoted views that homosexuality was a developmental defect or a spiritual and moral failing. They published case studies on the successful 'cures' of many homosexuals, that is, the 'reorientation' back to heterosexuality. Dr. Robert Spitzer, the primary mover to remove homosexuality as a mental disorder, nevertheless, initiated his own reorientation study. The concerns of many APA members that the proponents of *Sexual Orientation Change Efforts* (SOCE), most of whom were members of conservative political and religious organizations, were intent on stigmatizing homosexuality led the APA to review the claims of the SOCE proponents. The 2009 Report of the Task Force on Appropriate Therapeutic Responses to Sexual Orientation), whose Abstract reads:

"The APA Task Force on Appropriate Therapeutic Responses to Sexual Orientation conducted a systematic review of the peerreviewed journal literature on sexual orientation change efforts (SOCE) and concluded that efforts to change sexual orientation are unlikely to be successful and involve some risk of harm, contrary to the claims of SOCE practitioners and advocates. Even though the research and clinical literature demonstrate that same-sex sexual and romantic attractions, feelings, and behaviors are normal and positive variations of human sexuality, regardless of sexual orientation identity, the task force concluded that the population that undergoes SOCE tens to have strongly conservative religious views that lead them to seek to change their sexual orientation. Thus, the appropriate application

of affirmative therapeutic interventions for those who seek SOCE involves therapist acceptance, support, and understanding of clients and the facilitation of clients' active coping, social support, and identity exploration and development, without imposing a specific sexual orientation identity outcome." (14)

This SOCE issue came into the news again when Dr. Spitzer, now 80 years old, admitted that he had been wrong in this views on the efficacy of SOCE and issued a public apology: *"I believe I owe the gay community an apology for my study making unproven claims of the efficacy of reparative therapy. I also apologize to any gay person who wasted time and energy undergoing some form of reparative therapy because they believed that I had proven that reparative therapy works with some `highly motivated' individuals."* (15)

And on May 17, 2012, 22 years after the World Health Organization removed homosexuality from its list of disorders, WHO reaffirmed its position on the SOCE controversy:

"Since homosexuality is not a disorder or a disease, it does not require a cure. There is no medical indication for changing sexual orientation," said PAHO Director Dr. Mirta Roses Periago. Practices known as "reparative therapy" or "conversion therapy" represent "a serious threat to the health and well-being—even the lives—of affected people."
"These practices are unjustifiable and should be denounced and subject to sanctions and penalties under national legislation," said Dr. Roses. "These supposed conversion therapies constitute a violation of the ethical principles of health care and violate human rights that are protected by international and regional agreements."(16)

It seems unlikely that this strong statement will convince the fervent SOCE proponents, for many of whom the science is irrelevant: *"Science has nothing to offer that would even remotely constitute persuasive evidence that would compel us to deviate from the historic Christian judgment that full homosexual intimacy, homosexual behavior, is immoral. . . Most of those who agree that a dialogue between science and Christian faith is valid and vital are not defenders of the traditional sexual morality of the church"* ((16)

It may well be worth reflecting on words from a different time and place: *"We can easily reduce our detractors to absurdity and show them their hostility is groundless. But what does it prove? That their hatred is real. When every slander has been rebutted, every misconception cleared up, every false opinion about us overcome, intolerance itself will remain finally irrefutable."* (18, Moritz Goldstein, DeutschJudischer Parnass)

Transgender – *through a glass darkly*

Ignorance works overtime here (19, Wislawa Szymborska, HERE)

A perspective

The term *transgender* was taken from *transgenderist,* a word coined in the 1970s to refer to adult male cross-dressers. Both clinicians and the lay public use *transgender* quite commonly now although not always with a well-defined meaning. Since the 1980s a number of writers have used it as an umbrella term to denote the diverse forms gender/sex incongruence. This incongruence spans a spectrum from simple gender atypical (non-conforming) behaviors to more complex examples of what are known as gender identity conflicts. We will use the term *transgender* in this broad sense.

We have a poor understanding of the origins of the gender non-conforming impulse, or gender identity conflicts. In fact, we know very little about how gender roles and identity develop. What seems clear is that the transgender person experiences a unique type of mind-body dissonance. The origin of this mind-body dissonance has been the subject of many studies, much acrimony and heated debate, but at the present time it remains a mystery. It cannot be correlated with any physiological, anatomical, neuro-endocrinological, or genetic parameter that distinguishes the two sexes. The existence of sex/gender incongruence raises profound questions about the nature of human sexuality. Gender identity presupposes cognition and consciousness. The question of gender identity makes no sense otherwise. This means that animal experiments cannot provide any information about the question of gender identity. Gender identity is a uniquely human trait.

What we do know is that the sex/gender incongruence can express itself in different ways and to different degrees resulting in what we can call a transgender spectrum. At one end of the spectrum are persons who exhibit gender atypical or gender non-conforming behavior. In children, for example, we find girls who prefer boy-like activities (*tomboys*), or boys who prefer girl-like activities. In adults, we find the *cross-dressers,* variously referred to as transvestites, drag queens, drag kings, and the so-called *gender benders/blenders.* These latter categories do not necessarily define distinct entities since there is much fluidity in behavior among the crossdressers and the gender benders, both of which appear to be more common in males than in females. Gender atypical behavior is not a precise term because what we refer to as masculine or feminine traits vary considerably from one society to another, and they also change with time in any given society. In many societies, the demarcations between the masculine and feminine are not absolutely rigid, and generally some variability in behavior and practice is permitted.

At the other end of the transgender spectrum we find people who experience a pronounced discordance between anatomical sex and gender identity, commonly referred to as transsexuality

The German physician and sexologist, Magnus Hirschfeld, coined the term *transsexual* in 1923, although description of patients with features that would likely qualify as transsexual appeared in medical reports as early as the middle of the 19th century.

Consider the poignant testimony of a 30- year-old male patient described by a Baltimore physician, W. Howard, in 1897, as a case of 'psychical hermaphroditism'. Today he would most likely be classified as transsexual.

. . . I can define my disposition no better than to say that I seem to be a female in a perfectly formed male body, for, so far as I know, I am a well-formed man, capable of performing all of man's functions sexually. Yet as far back as I can remember, surely as young as five years, I seemed to have the strongest possible desire to be a girl, and used to wonder if by some peculiar magic I might not be transformed. I played with dolls; girls were my companions; their tastes were my tastes; music, flowers and millinery interested me and do this day.

I have had little sympathy with boys or men. It has always been a topic for thought and speculation, the abnormal development of man. Any such thought or conversation kindles the fire of passion in my brain. My love for a woman is the same that I have for a work of art; for a statue. I believe that Venus herself would not excite a bit of emotion in me. Yet a handsome man throws me into a passionate and emotional fit. In the romances that I draw for myself I always picture myself as a beautiful girl. This is not a forced imagination: such dreams and fancies come uncalled for in my mind." (20)

This one example from the past demonstrates in language that is perfectly understandable to a 21st century audience that sex/gender discordance existed before it was named.

The term transsexuality was introduced into the psychological lexicon in 1949, and was popularized in the 1950s and 1960s by Harry Benjamin, a German endocrinologist transplanted to the United States, particularly with the publication of his book *The Transsexual Phenomenon* in 1966. Benjamin is remembered for his affirmative and sympathetic treatment of transsexual persons of his time.

In the past, the voices of trans people were filtered by psychiatrists in esoteric language full of Latin and Greek terms, a language that was both obscure and titillating at the same time. The famous German sexologist, Krafft-Ebing, in1894 described a form of cross-dressing as "metamorphosis sexualis paranoica" that today would be described as transsexualism. Times have changed. Today trans people are telling their stories in much more direct, often provocative, language.

As Dr. Margaret Nichols, who identifies herself as a 'queer psychologist and sex therapist' puts it:

"Since the early 1990s, there has been a profound paradigm shift among trans people themselves. Whereas before, trans identities were limited, discrete, and categorical, i.e., one was a transvestite, a transsexual, or a drag queen, now there is truly a "transgender continuum" that encompasses a multitude of identities and lifestyles: FTM's and MTF's, part and full-time cross dressers, drag kings and queens, transmen and transwomen, bi-gendered, Two Spirit, gender

benders, femmes, butches, bois, and many more. " (11)

Unfortunately, a significant portion of the public may find itself caught in the middle. The transgender world is still troubling for many and difficult to understand. The provocative language of some transgender activists can have the effect of reinforcing the widespread notion that trans people are freaks, even perverts, and does little to win friends and supporters. It is noteworthy that in 2008 the ENDA legislation passed by the U.S. House of Representatives provided protection for gays, lesbians, and bisexuals, but excluded transsexuals in order to ensure passage.

Nevertheless, in the Western world and the U.S. in particular, the diverse varieties of the transgender experience have received considerable media coverage in the last few years. We mentioned in a previous chapter, the 2003 film *Normal.* Much more noteworthy in a media sense was the 1997 film *Ma Vie En Rose*, a sympathetic, realistic story of a transgender child, or the 1999 film *Boys Don't Cry* about a young trans man, played by Hilary Swank, who was raped and murdered in 1993. She won an Academy Award for her role. Articles in *Time, Saturday Night,* and the New York Times, to name a few, as well as the appearance of trans children and their parents on *The Oprah Winfrey Show,* and ABC's 20/20 broadcast hosted by Barbara Walters. This media coverage has probably had the beneficial effect of humanizing the transgender experience, and may be fostering an increased softening in the general public's attitudes about trans people.

This 'demographic' shift (as sociologists would term it) in attitudes about transgender may also play a role in the upcoming deliberations in reevaluating the status and diagnostic criteria of gender variance for the new DSM. What is needed also is a change (of heart, perhaps) from the psychology/psychiatry community. As one member of this community, a psychologist and trans female puts it:

Psychologists and psychiatrists need to remove transgenderism from the DSM and ICD so that it is studied as objective science instead of as something inherently bad. Once we start treating one another without suspicion and as equals, we can bring our expertise and experiences together to further understand the nature of gender and sexuality. (22)

What we can hope for is that these deliberations may lead to a more civil and less adversarial discourse and lay the groundwork for a true partnership in trying to understand of one of the most mysterious aspects of our sexuality. In the sections that follow we consider the diversity of the transgender experience and ways in which transgender persons and clinicians try to understand that experience.

The transgender spectrum

Cross-gender behavior in children

Gender a typical behavior is not uncommon among children. In the 4-11 year age range different studies carried out in different countries find that 5 - 12 % of girls and 2 – 6 % of boys exhibit behavior patterns typical of the opposite sex. The difference in the rates between girls and boys is generally attributed to the fact that in general we are much more intolerant of boys who behave like girls, than we are of the reverse. Families are fairly quick to suppress any inclination of a boy to behave like a girl at a very young age. Girls are given more freedom to express what are typically seen as masculine traits. The word, *tomboy*, can be traced back to at least the 16th century, when it began to be used for girls who preferred outdoor physical play, appeared more masculine than is usual for girls, and preferred male peers. By and large, the term tomboy is used generally without the strong moral disapproval that would be associated with the term, *sissy*, for example, used for boys who behave like girls. Fathers and older brothers quite often take pride in a girl's tomboy behavior, especially if it involves excellence in sports. On the other hand, mothers may try to emphasize femininity. In general, however, tomboy behavior tends to be tolerated only until around the time of puberty, at which time all of the social mechanisms by which societies enforce gender roles/behavior come into full force for both sexes.

As we might expect, the tomboy experience is varied, but there are common features. Below are partial testimonials of adult women who were tomboys as children.

Example: A bisexual woman who remembers the complex attitudes in her family:

> *I remember my mother's fear, her terror . . . Every year until I was eleven she gave me a doll, and I rejected each of them. I wore handme-down pants and shirts from the boy down the street most of the time, but we had to wear skirts to school. My mother sewed my skirts. I remember begging her to make pockets, low ones, so that I could stick my hands in them. So she did. But I think she was afraid for me if I did not conform, what would happen to me . . . Everyone said you are just like your uncle, and "Shea" was what they called me, not Rebecca . . . This was how my family described the kids: three boys, two girls and Rebecca. I was set apart like that.* (23)

Example: A heterosexual woman describes being compared to males, being different, and being muscular in physique:

> *I would say 90% of my friends were boys, but I never wanted to be one, and I did not become a lesbian. I just liked doing things that boys did. When I was born they said I looked like my grandfather! I was Rrrrr. Like a little bull. I was always just out of place in frilly clothes. I wouldn't have looked right anyway. My sisters had that Princess Diana look. Slender, a longer neck . . . And I have this body type and I'm ok with it.* (23)

Example: A lesbian woman describes a similar paradox in gender expectations:

> *I was actually called Billyboy until I was seven. My father favored me and took me on his little jobs and fishing, leaving my sisters behind. I was like the son my dad never had, but I never actually thought about it or felt it as pressure then . . . I was taunted for being a "tomboy" by my sisters, but I enjoyed playing football and baseball and I guess the trade-offs were worth it for me. My mother said I looked at grownups with a defiance, and so that's why I got into trouble. She said I threw my legs out too far when I walked. I was simply walking how I walked. I didn't understand what she was talking about . . . Funny—she leaned on me to be "the son" as well*

when she needed one. (23)

Example: A 40-year old heterosexual woman replies to the question: "Is there anything about being a tomboy that stays with you as and adult?"

Let me lift it, I can handle it; I was a tomboy. Yeah I wrestled down my son a few days ago and he was shocked I am that strong. I guess I still am a tomboy or whatever. Oh yeah, I think it is that I don't care. I mean if you are not doing your job and it means I have to take up the slack, I am gonna say something. I am not afraid. Because I don't care. I don't care what people think. That's it. It's just who I am. (23)

Many former tomboys have achieved fame in diverse fields as adults. The life histories of seven famous Americans - Marian Anderson, Katherine Hepburn, Margaret Mead, Eleanor Roosevelt, Martha Graham, Dorothy Thompson, and Babe Didrikson Zaharias. – all former tomboys, have been recounted in an engaging book by S.S. Ware. An interesting story is related about Babe Zaharias, renown for her sports accomplishments, and who had given up playing the "feminine" role demanded of women. When asked by a reporter "Is there any sport you don't play?" With perhaps a sly smile, she answered: "Yeah, dolls."

The testimonials presented above and the life histories of many tomboys suggest a couple of conclusions: first, some aspects of tomboy traits persist into adulthood, indicating that they are an integral part of the personality. Second, there is no fixed or predictive correlation between being a tomboy as a child and sexual orientation as an adult. Although we don't have reliable estimates, the majority of tomboys identify as heterosexual in adulthood, and some smaller fraction identify as either homosexual or bisexual. However, irrespective of their sexual orientation, the large majority of tomboys retain a female gender identity.

Gender identity discordance in children

A small fraction of children who exhibit cross-gender behavior also express a strong feeling that they are of the opposite sex, or *gender dysphoria* in the clinical jargon. The identification with the gender that does not correspond to their anatomical sex reveals what we can call a gender identity conflict. Gender identity, the sense of being female or being male, is, when we think about it, a mysterious concept. We normally assume, for example, that a person who is female anatomically will have a female gender identity. So strong is this assumption that when surgical intervention is required in cases of disorders of sexual development, the reconstruction is carried out to normalize the external genitalia as much as possible, and the child will be brought up in a way that is congruent with the external genitalia - the unspoken assumption being that gender identity will be dictated by the anatomical sex. It is only when we are confronted with cases in which that belief does not hold that we begin to raise questions about the nature and origins of gender identity.

Let's consider briefly two examples, both of which were reported in a National Public Radio program in 2008

The boy - Armand; parents – Robert and Danielle This obsession with female clothing had started early, when Armand was around 2. He had found an old Minnie Mouse dress the family had gotten at Disneyland. He put it on and then refused to take it off.

"A lot of times she'd come out and say, 'I'm a girl.' No, at first it was, 'I want to be a girl,' then it's like 'No. I am a girl.' And she'd ask if me if I [thought] she was crazy and I'd say, 'No, honey, you know, it's OK.' And in the front, you know, I'm driving going ... 'Oh my gosh, what is this?'"

The parents tried to steer Armand away from female clothing, fearing their young son would become the object of neighborhood ridicule. But nothing they said or did seemed to make any difference. There was no dissuading him, and so the only-in-the-house rule seemed like reasonable compromise.

Armand agreed — he even seemed comfortable with it. He spent hours in the basement and backyard, playing with his sister's cast-offs.

But one day, Robert came home early and found Armand out front in the middle of their cul-desac. He was wearing a poodle skirt, swaying back and forth, singing. Wanting, Robert says he thought, the whole world to see. (24)

The boy – Bradley; mother - Carol

It wasn't until Halloween when her 2 1/2-yearold son decided to dress as Dorothy from The Wizard of Oz that Carol began to worry.

Bradley had always had a preference for girls' things. From his earliest days he had chosen girls' dolls, identified with female characters and gravitated toward female children. But Carol had never thought to care. As far as she was concerned, it wasn't a loaded gun; it wasn't a lit cigarette. She says it had really never crossed her mind to say, "I'd really rather you played with a truck."

Then, on Halloween, the calculus began to tip. To simulate Dorothy's hair, Carol covered Bradley's blond crew-cut with a brown tea towel. Bradley loved it. In fact, he became obsessed with his tea-towel hair. For months afterward he would wake up every morning and put the towel on his head. When Carol tried to remove it, he would protest.

"It was really obsessive," Carol says. "We really had to negotiate times when he just couldn't wear it anymore. ... He seemed to feel uncomfortable and nervous sometimes when he didn't have this hair, this tea-towel hair."

And as Bradley grew older, his discomfort with things male also grew. He would shun other boys — he played exclusively with girls. Again, this concerned Carol, but she wasn't frantic about it.

It was a single event that transformed her vague sense of worry into something more serious. One day, Bradley came home from an outing at the local playground with his baby sitter. He was covered in blood. A gash on his forehead ran deep into his hairline.

"What had happened was that two 10-year-old boys had thrown him off some playground equipment across the pavement because he'd been playing with a Barbie doll — and they called him a girl," Carol says. "So that sort of struck me, that, you know, if he doesn't learn to socialize with both males and females ... he was going to get hurt.

In particular, there is one typically girl thing — now banned — that her son absolutely cannot resist. "He really struggles with the color pink. He can't even really look at pink," Carol says. "He's like an addict. He's like, 'Mommy, don't take me there! Close my eyes! Cover my eyes! I can't see that stuff; it's all pink!' " (25)

Children like Armand and Bradley who display not only a strong and persistent desire to be of the opposite sex, but also a persistent discomfort with their sex fall in the *Gender Identity Disorder in Children* (GID) category of the current *DSM (DSM-IV-TR)*.

Most of what we have learned about gender identity conflicts in children has come from reports from clinics around that world that specialize in such conflicts. What have we learned from these studies?

First, more boys are referred for gender identity concerns. The reported ratio of boys/girls ranges from 3.8/1 (London) to 4.7/1 (Amsterdam) to 6.6/1(Toronto) in the 3 to 12 year old range. The higher referral rate for boys is attributed to the fact that parents are generally more concerned about their son's gender non-conforming behavior at an earlier age, and hence, more likely to ask for a referral. Cultural factors, such as acceptance of gender atypical behavior may also contribute to the cross-national differences. The boy/girl referral ratio decreases as the children approach adolescence, and ratios close to 1/1 are reported.

Second, for reasons not understood, the gender identity conflicts in childhood diminish as the children approach adolescence. The persistence rate varies slightly from one study to another, but taken together only about 10% are judged to be persistently gender dysphoric, that is, the Gender Identity Disorder designation made in childhood persists into adolescence. The decrease in persistence helps to understand why the referral ratio decreases with age. The persistence rate data indicates strongly that gender identity is probably not inborn, but that it develops over time, and that the length of time required may vary from one child to another. Whatever the ingredients that go into the making of gender identity – genetic, familial, cultural, etc. – most children by the age of 2 to 4 years have integrated them into a stable identity. In a few children, however, a lack of congruence among all the necessary factors persists beyond the 2 to 4 years into late childhood, giving rise to a gender identity conflict, but even in such cases the conflict is in most cases is resolved by adolescence.

Third, the long-term sexual orientation if the gender conflict persists into adolescence and adulthood varies between the two sexes. For boys, the most common outcome is a 'homosexual' orientation; in contrast, a more or less equal distribution between homosexuality and heterosexuality is seen for girls. But let's look at this statistic more closely because it illustrates an important point of contention in defining sexual orientation in transgender cases.

Let's consider the case of a boy in whom the gender identity conflict persists. The boy who thinks of himself as a girl has a high likelihood of preferring men as an adult, that is, this is referred to as a "homosexual" orientation. However, the 'homosexual' label uses as a reference the boy's anatomical sex, and not the preferred female gender identity. If the referent for sexual orientation were gender identity, rather than anatomical sex, such boys would instead have a 'heterosexual' orientation. Hence, the so-called 'homosexual' (anatomical sex as referent) orientation of boys reveals a distinct bias in using anatomical sex, rather than gender identity, as the referent for sexual orientation.

The sexual orientation data for girls with Gender Identity Disorder– roughly half the girls who think of themselves as boys will have a sexual preference for men as adults – is more intriguing because it suggests that the gender identity conflict in these girls has a much stronger effect on their sexual orientation as adults than it does in boys.

What treatment options are available for children like Armand and Bradley? This is the question that weighs most heavily on their parents, troubled and perplexed by their child's behavior, and understandably worried about how the outside world will see or treat them. Unfortunately, there is no simple answer. The experts are still divided with regard to "best practice" in the clinical management of children like Armand or Bradley. Intense disagreements between the therapists reflect their own assumptions about the origin of gender identity conflicts.

At one pole, you find the position taken by Dr. Kenneth Zucker, director of the Toronto clinic, neatly summarized in an NPR interview:

"Suppose you were a clinician and a 4-year-old black kid came into your office and said he wanted to be white. Would you go with that? ... I don't think we would." (24). The analogy of skin color and gender identity may seem facetious perhaps, but Dr. Zucker appears to favor the notion that gender identity is to a great extent socially constructed. He would argue that the fact that gender identity conflicts lessen and disappear in most children supports his contention. His approach then is to work actively with both parents and child through counseling and play therapy to fashion the child's gender identity artificially to bring the child around so that he/she becomes more comfortable with his/her anatomical sex. The hope is that the gender identity conflict will lessen and be resolved.

However, it also seems clear from other studies that some children have much more severe gender identity conflicts than others. Their more extreme scores on a battery of measures of gender identity conflicts suggest to a number of therapists that some children are 'truly' transgendered, and that perhaps in such children the gender identity conflict may have a strong biological component. These are the children whose gender identity conflict will persist into adolescence. For such children, Dr. Diane Ehrensaft, a gender identity therapist based in San Francisco, favors an approach radically different from Dr. Zucker's - to encourage and facilitate the transition to a transgendered role and identity (for example, changing the name of the child, registering the child in school in the transgender role). She remarks: **"If we allow people to unfold and give them the freedom to be who they really are, we engender health. And if we try and constrict it, or bend the twig, we engender poor mental health."** (24) Dr. Ehrensaft is convinced that attempts to mold the gender identity differently in such children are counterproductive and will in the end be more damaging psychologically.

A third approach can be characterized as 'watchful waiting' - no active intervention is undertaken to lessen the cross-gender behavior, nor is cross-gender behavior encouraged. Making essentially no assumptions about the origin of the gender identity conflict, this approach takes the path of least resistance. We don't know yet whether these three approaches will lead to different the long-term psychosexual consequences for the children. Will the persistence rate be lessened? Will these approaches make any difference in the more general psychosocial adjustments and psychological health of the children? We do not have definitive answers to these important questions as yet.

Gender Identity Disorder in the adolescent

Life for the adolescent with a pronounced gender incongruence can be especially harrowing – not only do they have to contend with their gender identity conflicts, but these conflicts are compounded by the pubertal changes that they experience as alienating and agonizing. Consider the case of Bruce, female anatomically, but who considered herself to be male. At age 13 she was so upset with her developing breasts that she tried to stop their growth:

My mother had really large breasts. Nice looking tits. And she would say, "You're going to have breasts just like mine. Look what you have to look forward to." And I'd go, " I'd die if I had to have tits like that." . . . So I would lay on my back and sleep and hope gravity would make my tits not grow. And then it wasn't working so I'd lay on my stomach so that would make them not grow. . . I started binding myself down, even though I had nothing. . . I had T-shirts . . . I had sewn . . . very, very tight . . . or I would pull my undershirt, and just pin it to my pants or a skirt. (26)

Or the case of Mitchell, writing as Madeline, remembering her adolescence:

Puberty destroyed my fantasy that I would just 'become' a girl. It was so horrible. My face starting growing the itchy hair and nobody accidentally called me "miss" anymore. For awhile I just denied the facial hair was growing until some kids made fun of me for long sideburns. Even then I was too embarrassed to ask my dad for help shaving. I just figured it out myself. And I tried so hard to get it all to disappear that my face always bled constantly. My face broke out with acne and I remember going to a dermatologist with mom. They had a sign that said for "electrolysis patient to use the back entrance." I asked my mom what electrolysis was. She said it was to remove facial hair. Wow! A solution! But my mom told me it was just for woman with a little facial hair. Well, I guess that's another solution that wouldn't work? (12)

Many such youngsters have difficulty in adjusting to the demands of school, are prone to use drugs and alcohol, and are often easy targets for harassment or violence. They also are at risk for a variety of psychological problems – depression, anorexia, suicidality, and anti-social behavior.

None of my solutions had worked and I felt like I had nothing to live for. Suicide sounded like a good option. I was going to on many occasions. There was a time when I carefully took one extra pill from various prescriptions in may parent's medicine cabinet. I never found out if it was enough to kill me. . . . All I know by high school was something needed to stop. I was constantly being teased and bullied to the point where socially I was devastated, puberty was destroying my physically. (12)

Because of the severity of the problems faced by many Gender Identity Disorder adolescents, the issue of clinical management is especially acute. Clinicians have been reluctant to consider sex reassignment (hormonal or surgical therapy) for adolescents, deeming it too radical an intervention, given what they consider the uncertainties with the GID diagnosis at a relatively young age. This type of irreversible intervention can only be justified in adulthood when gender identity has been fully consolidated. On the other hand, reports from the clinics that specialize in gender identity problems indicate that the GID designation in adolescents is highly persistent. In many such cases, years of psychotherapy have not been successful in diminishing the gender identity conflict or alleviating the suffering the youngsters experience with the onset of pubertal changes.

It is in response to these 'extreme' cases that the Amsterdam clinic with extensive experience with adolescents with serious gender identity conflicts began in the late 1990s to offer hormonal interventions, often referred to as 'pubertal delay'. As Norman Spack, an endocrinologist at Children's Hospital in Boston, and one of the first in the U.S. to make use of this therapy, explains:

"They decided to see what would happen if they took such a child

that was in such distress over their body, [and stopped their body from] taking the form that they feared. To put off puberty, children -- usually between 10 and 13 — are injected with hormone blockers once a month . . the blockers only affect the gonads, the organs responsible for turning boys into men and girls into women. If you can block the gonads, that is the ovary in women or the testis in men, from making its sex steroids, that being estrogen or testosterone, then you can literally prevent ... almost all the physical differences between the genders. Without testosterone, boys will not grow facial or body hair. Their voices will not deepen. There will be no Adams apple, and height growth will slow. Without estrogen, girls will not develop breasts, fat at the hip, or menstrual periods. And since most growth happens before puberty, if you block estrogen — and therefore puberty — girls will grow taller, closer to a typical male height. (27)

The pubertal delay therapy is a way of 'buying time', permitting the adolescent to explore his/her gender identity more fully without the distress of having to also cope with the pubertal hormonal changes and associated development of the secondary sex characteristics. In all of these cases, clinicians follow the Standards of Care of the World Professional Association for Transgender Health, and for adolescents the guidelines established by the British Royal College of Psychiatrists.

The transgender adult

Cross-gender behavior

In adults, cross-gender behavior is generally manifested in cross-dressing and/or taking on the life of the opposite sex. We don't really think about female cross-dressers anymore because in contemporary Western societies, females cross dress all the time. It is so common place that it is unremarkable. Females are permitted much more freedom in exploring different clothing styles, and cross-dressing by women does not appear to affect their view of themselves as females. That has not been the case for most of recorded history, however. Before the twentieth century female cross-dressing in the Western world was forbidden or strongly discouraged, often punished severely.

Despite the proscription, cross-dressing by females has a long, complex, and even venerable history. The Western historical record contains dozens of stories of females who dressed and lived a good part of their lives as males. We know very little about females living as males in the ancient Greek and Roman world, although tales of femaleto-male sex transformations or of women who tried to live as men have survived, but most of these belong in the category of myths or legends. More reliable perhaps are stories that date from the early Christian centuries and continue to the twentieth century. A number of historians have collected these stories, many of which are based on popular literature, newspaper accounts, court proceedings, rather than medical writings. The few examples presented below illustrate the often audacious, always courageous ways women chose to live as men. In most cases we can only infer their motivations, but if there is a common thread that runs through these stories over the last 2000 years it is women's desire to escape their subordinate status in societies run and ruled by men and for men, and in which women's role was to produce children and keep the household. Women were first ruled by their fathers, later by husbands or brothers, and had no power. The subordinate status was justified by Aristotle in the fourth century BCE, who declared that "the male is by nature superior, and the female inferior; and the one rules and the other is ruled", a view that only began change in the twentieth century.

Many of the early highly venerated female saints – Anastasia Patricia, Athanasia, Dorotheus, Eugenia, Euphrosyne, Marina, Pelagia, Perpetua, Theodora, to name a few - began by disguising themselves as men for the purposes of joining male religious communities. In early Christian theology the female to male transformation was spiritual, rather than anatomical. St. Jerome in the fourth century expressed the prevailing views of the differences between men and women by proclaiming that as *"long as woman is for birth and children, she is different from man as body is from soul. But when she wished to serve Christ more than the world, then she will cease to be a woman and be called a man."* (27) The intriguing idea in this view was that the character of men and women was reflected in their actions and beliefs, rather than in their unchangeable anatomy. Women could elevate themselves to the status of men by devoting themselves entirely to Christ, and those who did so with the most fervor could transform themselves into men.

In medieval Europe the motivation of many women in assuming the role of a man was not so much seeking a spiritual transformation, as it was survival. Joining a monastery disguised as men was an important option for women who lost their source of support because they did not marry or became widowed. Not all women who lived as men were in monasteries. Some would be classified as gender rebels. One of the most famous was Joan of Arc, born a peasant girl in fifteenth century France, who although did not hide her femaleness, lived as a man, and inspired

armies of men.

Beginning in the seventeenth century women began to branch out. The new status allowed women was due to the lessening influence of the church and broadening of economic and social opportunities. Most of these women began their lives as men while young – joining armies, traveling to distant countries, having open love relationships with women. Many never returned to being women, and were discovered to be female only after their deaths. Many lived flagrantly as men even when it was well known that they were females. One who achieved considerable notoriety was Queen Christina of Sweden, who abdicated her throne and left her country in order to live as a man. Because of her fame she couldn't simply disappear as some other woman could. She chose to live openly as a female man and had many love affairs with both men and women. Catalina de Erauso, born in Spain in 1592, grew up in a convent having been placed there by her family while still a child. In her teens and disguised as a man, she escaped from the convent and made her way to Latin America under the name of Alonso Diaz Ramirez de Guzman. Alonso enlisted in the armed forces and distinguished himself in battle, but unfortunately was prone to brawling. After one particularly serious incident where he feared for his death, Alonso confessed to a bishop that he was female. She returned to Spain, but continued to dress as a male. She eventually returned to South America and died in battle in 1645.

Henry Fielding, the eighteenth-century novelist, based his novel *Female Husband*, on a real case in which a woman impersonated a man so successfully that she married another woman who thought she was marrying a man. Fielding had based his story on a newspaper exposé of the time. Many accounts of women living as men have come from newspaper stories. Among them is the case of Charles Durkee Pankhurst, who drove a stagecoach in many of the American western mining towns in the last part of the nineteenth century. No one questioned his masculinity until on his death in 1879 he was found to be a female. A number of women have laid claim to being the famous Mountain Charley, a woman who lived as a man in the western territories in the 1850s.

Cora Anderson who lived successfully as a man known as Ralph Kerwinieo during the early years of the twentieth century made a spirited and poignant defense of her life as a man. Cora's second wife exposed Ralph as a female six months after their marriage. Prior to his second marriage, his first marriage had lasted thirteen years. Cora was ordered to revert to female clothing in the legal proceedings that followed the exposure. Cora, who worked as a nurse, defended her actions with the telling commentary:

" two-thirds of the physicians . . . made a nurse's virtue the price of their influence in getting her steady work. Is it any wonder that I determined to become a member of this privileged sex, if possible? . . . In the future centuries it is possible that woman will be the owner of her own body and the custodian of her own soul . . . [Now] the well cared for woman is a parasite, and the woman who must work is a slave . . . it is still a man-made world – made by men for men . . . Do you blame me for wanting to be a man – free to live as a man in a man-made world? Do you blame me for hating to again resume a woman's clothes and just belong" (26)

Cora Anderson was far ahead of her time. Her explanation would probably apply to many of the women who lived as men. We will never know whether the female cross-dressers of other times would be diagnosed with GI as the term is understood or defined today. Undoubtedly, some would.

The historical record of men living as women is much slimmer. Before the 20th century relatively few stories of men dressing and/or living as women exist. While there are many female saints who lived as men, there are no male saints who lived as women. Of course, because of the development of facial hair, it was much more difficult for men to pass or live as women. Perhaps just as important, for men, in contrast to that of women, dressing or living as a female signified a loss of status. The Western Christian tradition simply assimilated the Greek view that women were inferior to men, a view expressed clearly by the 13th century theologian St. Thomas Aquinas: *"good order would have been wanting the human family if some were not governed by others wiser than themselves. So by such a kind of subjection woman is naturally subject to man, because in men the discretion of reason predominates."* (27) Hence, women wanting to be men made sense, but men wanting to be women made no sense.

One notable exception was in the theater. Until relatively recently, women were not allowed to perform in the theater, and men, especially young men, played the women's roles. This was permitted because the presence of a real woman, even in religious dramas, was considered dangerous or improper, and hence forbidden. According to the historian, Vern Bullough, the Church even tolerated castration so that the impersonation was more realistic, even though technically castration was prohibited. It is possible that some of those who underwent castration might have had transsexual tendencies, but we have no way of knowing that. Despite the difficulties that males acting as women faced, historians have discovered a number of specific cases from medical records or newspaper accounts. The majority of these reports are relatively recent, dating from the 19th and 20th centuries.

One interesting account concerned the case of Jenny Savalette de Lange, who was discovered to be a male when she died in 1858 in Versailles. Apparently, Jenny had been able to get a substitute birth certificate designating himself as a female, and had been engaged to six different men, and even received a pension from the King of France. The famous German sexologist, Krafft-Ebing (1894) reported the case of a physician (no less) who was convinced that he was a woman, and believed that his penis was really a clitoris. In 1937, William Richeson, was discovered to be living as a woman – he/she had been married for over 6 years, and her husband apparently denied that he knew his wife was a male. In 1950 Josephine Montgomery was discovered to be a male when she was sent to a prison for women. He/she maintained that she had lived as a girl all her life, and considered herself a female who just happened to have male sexual organs. In 1951 Georgia Black, married and widowed twice, was discovered during a critical illness to be a male. He/she had normally functioning male organs, but referred to them as "growths", and maintained that she was a woman and had the emotional feelings of a woman. Adele Best lived as a woman for 54 years, married three times, and reported that none of her husbands knew she was a male.

What is the prevalence of transsexuality?

We do not have reliable estimates of the prevalence of transsexuality. Indirect measures have been used to obtain estimates of its prevalence - for example, individuals who seek help from gender identity clinics, individuals who initiate cross-sex hormone therapy in preparation for sexual reassignment surgery (SRS), and individuals who submit to SRS. Estimates beginning in the 1960s and 1970s indicated a prevalence of 1:50,000 (average of male to female (M-t-F) and female to male (F-t-M) transsexuals, while more recent estimates suggest a prevalence of 1:5000. None of these estimates gives us the 'true' prevalence of transsexuality. For a variety of reasons not all individuals who fit the diagnosis seek help, initiate cross-gender hormone therapy, or submit to SRS. Hence, we have to consider these minimum estimates. The increase in these estimates over the last five decades probably indicates not that the inherent prevalence has been increasing but more likely reflects changes in social conditions that make it easier for individuals to seek help or undertake Sex Reassignment Surgery

Brave new worlds emerging

To paraphrase Tolstoy, every transsexual person has his/her own story - sometimes sad, sometimes tragic, often disquieting (for what can be more disconcerting than a doubt about our identity), but always unique.

Consider the case of Hal, born female, who spent 22 years living as a lesbian, during which time she had five major relationships. As a lesbian woman she always felt like a man on the inside, and felt that all of her women lovers related to her as something like a man. Hal and one of her lovers lived together for 14 years, and had two children through donor insemination. But Hal was not happy, but kept putting off starting the surgical transition to become male for several years. Finally, Hal came to this conclusion:

Two salient incidents that clarified my gender for me were, number one, the birth of my first child. I had to come to grips with who I was because I realized I could not fool or lie to a child. And, number two, over a period of a couple of years I gradually realized that I could not see myself becoming an old woman. I had this little boy look. I was a corporate vice president. I felt I needed to grow up, and I could not grow up to be a woman. . . I'd try to imagine myself as a fiftyyear old woman, and there would be nothing there, nothing to see. One day I tried to imagine myself as a fifty-year-old man, and I was amazed to see someone, a man with strong shoulders and graying hair, a neat beard, a handsome face; it was me. And it frightened me. These events meant I should be male because I was male; it was time to make the change, time to grow up. (26)

Or consider Madeline Wyndzen, born male, who finally transitioned into a female, and became a professor of psychology:

That was probably the most profound decision I ever made in my life. My first year of graduate school was also the worst year in my life. My emotions were barely more than an adolescent's since I repressed my feelings from then on. And I acted that way. I fell apart. When one bad thing happened I reacted by being disproportionately upset. I couldn't stop and being so upset made the next minor bad event seem even more disproportionately upsetting and so forth in an escalating cycle of depression and anxiety. But, in addition to feeling out of control I realized how little being a feminine man was what mattered. No matter how feminine of a man I am, I'm still thought of by others as a man. And that's very upsetting. I just don't identify with men. I never have and I probably never could. Being feminine, though something that's very natural for me, just made me more distant from woman because it emphasized how people still feel I'm a guy. By the end of my first year I took the summer off from school. . . You might imagine the hardest part of transitioning is a culture *shock of going from one gendered culture to another? But for me the biggest shock was to my self-concept; I went from being perceived as this really really *really* weird guy to this incredibly *normal* girl!!!!* (21)

Consider the following different narratives taken from six participants in a 2009 study on gay and bisexual identity development among female to male (F-t-M) transsexuals who preferred men. Note that for them sexual orientation is defined with respect to their gender identity and not their birth anatomical sex, in contrast to the way most

gender identity specialists do so. In this sample of 29 persons, 84% were white, 72% were college graduates, 68% had never married, 40% were in committed relationships, and 56% had no religious affiliation. All of the participants had undergone masculinizing hormone therapy and chest surgery. None had undergone a phalloplasty (surgical construction of a penis), but were divided about the desire for it. Adjustment to the absence of a penis takes time, but as the authors comment *"participants (as well as their partners) become more comfortable with their female genital anatomy and were able to put that lack of a penis in perspective."* (21)

Participant #1

I would describe myself first as a guy, then as a gay man, then as an F-t-M, then perhaps, if people are savvy enough, as a queer F-t-M who still has sex with women (usually butch women or M-t-Fs) once in a while.

Participant #2

I do not think being gay and being transsexual are directly related. My awareness of the dissonance between my internal gender identity and my physical body came long before my awareness of sexual orientation. I think for me, it was easier to deal with being homosexual, because I had already dealt with being transsexual.

Participant #3

I think that my identity as an FtM (and not necessarily a "man") often sets me apart from old school tranny men who want to leave their pasts in the closet. I don't have that option due to my visibility as an out FtM, and I use that visibility to educate people and advocate for tranny respect and rights. Those old school trans men who are "real men" like to do manly things and are into stereotypical masculinity really turn me off. I try not to take on people's sexist bullshit about what a man is supposed to be any more than I did about what a woman is supposed to be. I think the concept of masculinity in dominant culture is something that is set up to make sure that by and large, we all pale in comparison. It is an ideal that is never achieved by the majority of men. So how do we as men affirm our identities in the face of such an oppressive stereotype? I chose to maintain my feminist identity and many of my political beliefs that were profoundly influenced by the period in my life I spent as a dyke. I guess I'm really glad that there are those traditional guys out there, because that just frees up a whole lot of room for the rest of us who feel profoundly isolated from those traditional stereotypes to form our own identities and relationships.

Participant #4

I have a queer gender and a queer sexual orientation…I am attracted to people in the same region of the gender galaxy as me regardless of whether they were assigned F or M at birth. Their gender expression matters to me. I like any type of genitalia and birth assigned genders. The only thing that changed was that before reassignment, I was invisible to fags and now I'm invisible to butch dykes. The more transpeople I've known plus the more comfortable I am with myself, the less binary my view has become. The binary gender system doesn't work for me. Neither does a spectrum. For example, it's not a line from female butch women, ftm, male. Many butch women are more butch than many ftms. I'm a sissy tranny fag. I have a friend who's ftm but not male identified who does female drag. I have third gender friends. It's a GENDER GALAXY.

Participant #5

The invisibility of FtMs adds to the problems we face when trying to date other guys. We look like other guys after we've been on hormones long enough. There are many erotic images of MtFs out there, which is just not true for FtMs. There is no FtM section in the porno store... With gay men, many of whom never knew FtMs existed, there is fear of the unknown. If we as FtMs can increase our visibility and voices (not only of ourselves but of the men who love us as well), not only will our dating pool get bigger, but the drama surrounding the issue will cease to be so huge. It takes an exceptional person to deal with a man who has no penis, but a vagina and a clitoris, however hormonally changed they may be. There will also be exceptional men like the few that I have met who can learn to deal with my body and my mind just fine, and not only tolerate my genitals, but love them and me at the same time.

Participant #6

I engage in vaginal intercourse, from behind, while on my stomach. We do vaginal penetration, active oral sex, and mutual manual stimulation. Prior to sex reassignment surgery, and especially hormones, I was rarely tolerant of vaginal penetration. Now I am most pleased with it.

These narratives reveal to us the extensive range and variety of the sex and gender identity experience of each of the participants, and the equanimity with which each person confronts their sex/gender discordance and begin to form their individual personal identity. New identities, no longer limited to the distinct feminine-masculine system that our society imposes, are being forged. We may be distressed by these stories, perhaps even appalled, but they are real and cannot be dismissed as the expressions of weirdoes or perverts. For the transgender community, these stories are old hat – they have been arguing for multi-dimensionality and fluidity of sex and gender for at least two decades. It is only recently that the academic and professional community has begun to give credence and validity to this point of view – in a way they are beginning to come out of the closet and liberating themselves from the straight jacket imposed by the *DSM*.

Sex reassignment surgery (SRS)

The first internationally celebrated case of sex surgery was that of

George Jorgensen, a soldier in the U.S. Army, who in 1953 underwent a male-to-female reconstruction operation in Denmark to become Christine Jorgensen. At the time, this type of operation was not available in the United States. Genital surgery, however, was not new - it had been tried out much earlier in Germany, beginning in the latter part of the 19th century, but the first documented sex reassignment surgery, a female-to-male reconstruction, was performed in Berlin in 1912 under the supervision of Magnus Hirschfeld. This was followed by several male-to-female surgeries (removal of the penis, scrotum and testes, and construction of a 'neo-vagina') during the 1920s and 1930s carried out by the surgeon Felix Abraham. The Jorgensen case, however, struck a chord in the public – not only did Christine Jorgensen become a media celebrity, but her surgeon received requests from 465 men and women to have their sex changed.

On the other hand, the psychiatric profession more or less rejected SRS as an acceptable treatment. Their point of view was expressed by two commentaries criticizing Jorgensen's surgeon ignoring psychotherapy: *"The difficulty of getting the patient into psychiatric treatment should not lead us to compliance with the patient's demands, which are based on his sexual perversion."* A second psychiatrist argued that the only thing that would have helped Jorgensen is not the surgery but *"intensive, prolonged, classic psychotherapy."* (28) The chair of the psychiatry department at Johns Hopkins, P. R. McHugh could not understand how the belief of a man *"that he is a woman trapped in a man's body differs from the feelings of a patient with anorexia nervosa that she is obese despite her emaciated, cachectic state. We don't do liposuction on anorexics. So why amputate the genitals of these patients?"* (30)

For the critics of SRS removal of healthy organs to normalize gender and anatomical sex was clearly a departure from standard medical practice. They argue that transsexual persons who opt for SRS are similar to those rare cases of Body Integrity Identity Disorder (BIID) – a condition in which individuals consider that a part of their body is alien and superfluous, and they desire surgery to remove what they consider an extraneous body part that doesn't belong to them. In some cases if they cannot find a willing surgeon they may mutilate themselves, by cutting off a finger or a toe, shooting into a leg, packing the body part in dry ice to freeze it to death. Everyone except the BIID person would find the amputation of a limb or other body part appalling. Does the desire for amputation of a healthy part of the body by BIID patients differ from the desire of transsexuals for SRS?

It may not, but it doesn't matter anymore, because the Jorgensen case was the point of no return. The dike had been breeched, and a new era of sexual medicine was being born. Since then several thousand persons have undergone what are popularly called "sex change operations". Surgical techniques have improved greatly, and M-to-F sex reassignment surgery has become fairly standardized. F-to-M reconstruction is considerably more difficult, especially for those who desire to have a penis.

By and large, such surgery appears to reconcile body image and identity, and judged by the low percentage of regrets (1-2% from various studies), SRS can be considered quite successful. The success and acceptance of SRS as a medically accepted procedure has been aided greatly by the establishment and periodic revision of guidelines known as the **Standards of Care** (SOC) by the World Professional Association for Transgender Health (WPATH), formerly known as the Harry Benjamin International Gender Dysphoria Association (HBIGDA). The SOC guidelines, implemented by multidisciplinary teams of experts provide a professional consensus about the psychiatric, psychological, medical, and surgical management of a GID patient, is a four-step protocol to be followed for every SRS candidate – diagnostic assessment, real-life experience and psychotherapy, hormone therapy, and surgical reconstruction. The SOC guidelines do not guarantee success, but their continual revision in the light of new information does guarantee that every patient who chooses to follow the SOC protocols will receive the best care possible.

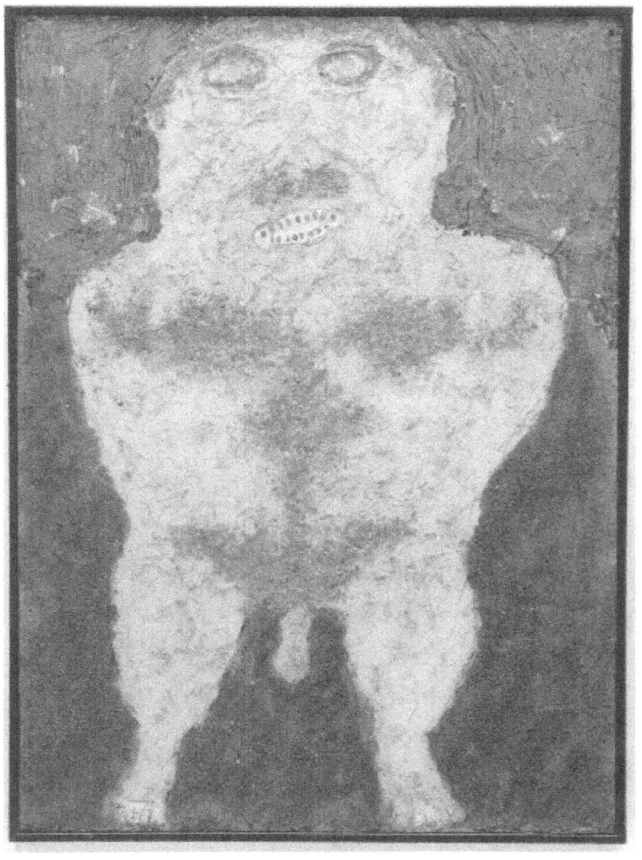

Jean Dubuffer, "Volonte de Puissance (Will to Power), 1946" (c 2013
Arrists Rights Society (ARS), New York/ ADAGP, Paris)

Chapter 6

Our Disturbing Sexual
Corridors

*One need not be a Chamber – to be Haunted – One need not be
a House – The Brain has Corridors – surpassing Material Place* (1,
Emily Dickinson)

Our problematic sexual corridors

*It is important to keep in mind that sexuality is, perhaps more
than any other aspect of human behavior, intertwined with moral
imperatives, conscious fantasy, and unconscious desires, all of which
combine to compromise even the most scientific of observers.* (2, John
H. Gagnon and William Simon)

The *'brain has corridors - surpassing material place'*, in Emily
Dickinson's perceptive phrasing, is a nifty metaphor for the complex and
often obscure passageways in our sexuality that emerge subconsciously,
whose doors we may want to keep locked, and where only we dare enter
sometimes. Were we born with all those corridors, or do they develop,
as many students of human sexual development think, in stages over a
fairly long period of time beginning in infancy and possibly continuing
even into adulthood. We emerge from this long culturing period as
autonomous sexual beings. We know very little about this process other
than it is the result of a continual interplay between factors – genetic,
familial, social, cultural, etc. – that modulate the interaction between
the neurologically developing brain and our environment. Whatever
comes out of this brain-environment interplay is not solely biological or
cultural, but an almost incomprehensible mix of the two.

All human societies have had to contend with sexual practices or behaviors that they consider to fall outside the norm and which therefore are deplorable, immoral, depraved, deviant, or unnatural. Very often, as we saw in the previous chapter, the transgressors of these norms are considered to be a threat to the established order, and have been punished sometimes very severely for their transgressions. But we also know that what is considered immoral or deviant changes with time. Consider adultery, once punishable, according to Mosaic law, by stoning (for the woman, not the man). Although still considered a sin by some religious groups, adultery is no longer a punishable offense, at least in most parts of the world. And certainly no religious group in the Western world would condone stoning. A few decades ago masturbation, pre-marital sex, oral sex, and homosexuality were considered immoral or deviant behaviors. Although some religious groups continue their strong disapproval and even vehement hostility, the widespread strong cultural and even legal proscriptions against these practices in the Western countries have disappeared or diminished greatly.

In this chapter we focus on two categories of sexual practices or behaviors that in contemporary society are considered deviant, troubling, and/or dangerous. First, the *paraphilias,* a psychiatric term used to label sexual desires that may be thought of as deviant or perverse. More specifically, the term, as used today, designates sexual desires or interests involving non-human objects, children or other non-consenting persons, or the suffering or humiliation of oneself or someone else. Perhaps the most problematic of the paraphilias and the one that commands most of our attention is *pedophilia* – a strong and pervasive sexual interest in children. Once relegated to the margins of our public discourse, pedophilia has become an important public policy concern in many Western countries, perhaps triggered in part by the pedophilia scandals of the Roman Catholic Church, and the increasing attention devoted to child sexual molestation.

Second, sexual violence – rape and child sexual abuse (CSA) - both of which in the eyes of many investigators have reached crisis levels worldwide. The general tendency has been to attribute all cases of CSA to pedophiles. However, it is important to keep in mind that many, perhaps most, pedophiles (overwhelmingly male) never act out their desires. The ones that command the headlines are those that do carry over their desire into sexual abuse. Non-pedophiles are responsible for a significant fraction of CSA.

The huge numbers of victims and ruined lives from both child sexual abuse and rape cry out for explanations that may aid in prevention. We struggle to understand the origin of these problematic and dangerous desires and behaviors. At the same time, as our society gains in understanding in these complex matters, we realize that not all sexual behaviors that we might consider deviant or problematic are equally horrific or equally dangerous. Our strategy as a society in dealing with or coming to terms with them should be based on making rational distinctions between the behaviors that are consensual, voluntary, and harmless, and those that are coerced, violent, or dangerous.

Arousal in the margins – *unresolved questions*

My partner dressed in uniform – it would really turn me on (3, Bret Kahr)

Less traveled byways

Human beings in their long history have probably explored the vast reaches of our sexual universe. Daniel Bergner, a staff writer for The New York Times Magazine in his fascinating book *The Other Side of Desire: Four Journeys Into the Far Realms of Lust and Longing (2009)* tells the stories of four outwardly normal individuals with unusual erotic interests: a shy salesman devoted to his wife, but tormented and obsessed by women's feet; a man who becomes consumed by his passion for his 12 year old stepdaughter; an art director in an advertising firm who is turned on by females with missing limbs; and a woman who runs New York's longest-running fetish party catering to sadomasochists.

Or consider a man who has a fetish about his roommate's underwear:

I like to dress up in my flatmate's underwear. He's good looking and a stud He has no idea how much I fancy him. I will sometimes take his undies out of the laundry basket, have a good sniff, and then wear them to work. I have a hardon all fucking day long, and then when I come home at night, I have a fantastic wank in his pants. Then I put them back in the laundry basket and pretend that he knows. (3, p.196)

And then there are the 'dirty old men', enthralled by young girls. Humbert Humbert, the middle-aged man in Vladimir Nabokov's novel *Lolita* (1955) becomes infatuated with a 12-year old girl Dolores Haze (Lolita). He describes his first sexual encounter with Lolita: ***"I had thought that months, perhaps years, would elapse before I dared to reveal myself to Dolores Haze, but by six she was awake, and by 6:15 we were technically lovers. I am going to tell you something strange: it was she*** who seduced me." (4) Or Yoshio Eguchi, the protagonist of Yasunari Kawabata's novella House of the Sleeping Beauties (1961), a frequent visitor to a procuress who provides drugged girls for aging men, as he contemplates the young body lying next to him: ***"The ugly senility of the sad men who came to this house was not many years away for Eguchi himself. The immeasurable expanse of sex, its bottomless depth – what part of it had Eguchi known in his sixty-seven years? And around the old men, new flesh, young flesh, beautiful flesh was forever being born. Were not the longing of the sad old men for the unfinished dream, the regret for days lost without ever being had, concealed in the secret of this house?"*** (5)

We no longer have to rely on books or stories for accounts of unusual sexual desires. The Internet abounds with sites that cater to almost any imaginable and even unimaginable sexual taste. How do we understand such 'far out' desires in otherwise normal people? Are they mentally ill? Or, more generally, where do such sexual desires come from? Are they inborn, present in a latent form even when we are very young, and then appear after puberty? Or are they learned, emerging out of the turmoil of our life history? How do we decide when a sexual desire or practice is beyond the pale, when it becomes deviant, or abnormal? And who decides?

The paraphilias - the DSM classification

We commonly use the term perversions to label 'unusual' sexual practices or desires, especially if we disapprove of them. Agreeing on what constitutes a perversion is another story. To help us decide, we generally turn to the 'experts' – psychiatrists and psychologists. Psychiatrists assumed custodial rights of our sexuality at the end of the

19th and beginning of the 20th centuries when they began to branch away from the mental asylums and become community based. An important part of their work as they saw it was to codify in ostensibly more scientific ways 'deviant' sexual practices and desires presumably because this would aid in their diagnosis and possible therapy.

The German psychiatrist, von Krafft-Ebing, a pioneer in the study of human sexuality and best known for his principal work *Psychopathia Sexualis* (1886), compiled sexual case histories based on his patients' reports of their sexual practices. The book popularized the terms *sadism* (derived from the novels of the Marquis de Sade which described brutal sexual practices), *masochism* (derived from a novel by Leopold von Sacher-Masoch whose protagonist requires flogging by a beautiful woman to achieve sexual satisfaction), and the terms homosexual and heterosexual. von Krafft-Ebing gave the term *perversion* a definition that had far-reaching repercussions: ***"every expression of sexual instinct that does not correspond with the purpose of nature, i.e., propagation"***. (6) This definition was not based on any scientific finding in any sense of the term. Rather, von Krafft-Ebing, as a man of his time, was expressing the prevailing belief in the medical and psychiatric professions of that era. The conviction that essentially any sexual activity other than penile-vaginal intercourse, for example, oral sex, was a perversion persisted through the first half of the 20th century. It is a point of view that unfortunately continues in many sectors of our own society to this day. Perhaps the most regrettable consequence of this belief was that it led, with the complicity of the psychiatric community, to laws punishing sodomy, homosexuality, and other so-called perverse sexual practices. Prejudice and value judgments masquerading as science has unfortunately been a characteristic of much of psychiatric literature since then, a legacy that has been very difficult to shake off.

The term perversion is not a medicalpsychiatric term anymore. Homosexuality, masturbation, or oral sex, are not considered perversions. Nevertheless, some psychiatrists do continue to use the term, but only in very specific instances. For the noted American psychiatrist, Robert Stoller, a perversion was an erotic form of hatred, an exercise of domination and power, reserving the term to an act in which a person derives erotic pleasure from hurting someone else or even oneself. Certain types of sadistic or masochistic practices, rape, violent child sexual abuse would be considered perverse acts.

There are those who fuck from desire, and those who fuck from intent, the latter are the perverts. Because intent, by definition, implies the exercise of will and power to achieve its ends, whereas desire entails mutuality and reciprocity for its gratification (7, M. Khan)

The term that replaced perversion was *paraphilia*, a term coined in the 1920s, and later adopted to refer to sexual desires or interests that were considered 'deviant'. It was first incorporated into the American Psychiatric Association's (APA) third edition of the *Diagnostic and Statistical Manual of Mental Disorders (DSM-III)* in 1980. In the previous two *DSM* editions the sexual practices now included under the paraphilia rubric were designated as 'sexual deviancy'. Sexual deviancy was understood to be sexual preferences *"directed primarily toward objects other than people of the opposite sex, toward sexual acts not usually associated with coitus, or toward coitus performed under bizarre circumstances."*

Note the term 'bizarre' appearing in what purports to be a scientific definition. Like von Krafft-Ebing's definition of perversion, this definition of sexual deviancy was not grounded on any empirical evidence, but was a statement of belief held by the membership of the APA at that time. Several types of sexual deviation were listed: homosexuality, fetishism, pedophilia, transvestism, exhibitionism, voyeurism, sadism, and masochism (*DSM*-II, 1968). Homosexuality was removed from this list in 1973, and one other type not listed in the previous editions – frotteurism (see below for the definition)– was added later. Inclusion in the *DSM* meant that these practices or behaviors were considered mental disorders. The latest *DSM* (*DSM*-IV-TR) lists the following paraphilias:

Exhibitionism: the recurrent urge or behavior to expose one's genitals to an unsuspecting person, or to perform sexual acts that can be watched by others. There are different forms of exhibitionism, some fairly innocuous: *flashing* – typically the momentary display of the bare female breast, and quite popular during the spring break festivals of university students; *mooning* – the display of the bare buttocks; and *streaking*.

More serious are the cases of males (almost exclusively) displaying themselves to children or young girls, and usually considered a criminal offence. Although first described in 1877 by the French physician and psychiatrist Charles Lasègue (1809–1883), exhibitionism has an ancient history. The second book of Samuel describes the exuberant dance that Kind David performs as he accompanies the Ark in a procession, and because of his short tunic displays his genitals. His wife, Michal, is furious and greets David when he comes home:

And Michal the daughter of Saul came out to meet David, and said, How glorious was the king of Israel today, who uncovered himself today in the eyes of the handmaids of his servants, as one of the vain fellows shamelessly uncovereth himself. (II Samuel 6:20)

Fetishism: the use of inanimate objects to gain sexual excitement. Included in this category is *partialism* – fetishes specifically involving nonsexual parts of the body. Almost any item can have sexually arousing qualities. A recent Internet survey involving about 5000 respondents revealed that about 30% had body part fetishes, and 36% had fetishes about objects associated with body parts. A few tend to be the most popular: rubber, leather, boots, high heels, ribbons, fur, women's panties or bras. Male fetishists greatly outnumber female fetishists. The foot fetish is by far the most common of the fetishes that focus on the nonsexual parts of the body. Men have always found the female foot attractive and arousing, which perhaps explains why the female foot has been the recipient of an extraordinary amount of attention all through human history. The different ways decorating the feet – painting the toe nails, toe rings, ankle bracelets, pedicures; different ways of dressing the feet – high heels, moccasins, sandals, flip flops, ballet flats, boots – can enhance the various degrees of arousal caused by the foot. Tickling, massaging, kissing, licking, sucking the toes have been common practices throughout human history. The sexual arousal value of the foot varies from one individual to another – some men may climax from touching or massaging the foot, or even observing the foot.

Another form of fetishism, although listed separately is *Transvestic fetishism* (simply transvestism in previous DSM editions): arousal from wearing clothing associated with members of the opposite sex.

Frotteurism: recurrent urges of behavior of touching or rubbing against a non-consenting person. A person who practices frotteurism is known as a *frotteur*. The majority of frotteurs are male and the majority of victims are female. This activity is often done in circumstances where the victim cannot easily respond, such as a crowded train or concert. In most cases such nonconsensual sexual contact is considered a criminal offense: a type of sexual assault generally classified as a misdemeanor. The British psychiatrist, Anthony Storr, considered 'liberal' in his views of sexual deviancy, in his 1964 book Sexual Deviation had an interesting comment about frotteurism: *"There can be few men who have not experienced something of the same urge in crowded lifts. Such advances, though distasteful to many women, are not always repelled"* (8), implying of course that some women enjoyed the advances.

Pedophilia: strong sexual attraction to prepubescent children. We will consider pedophilia in more detail in the next section.

Sexual masochism: the recurrent urge or behavior of wanting to be humiliated, beaten, bound, or otherwise made to suffer for sexual pleasure.

Sexual sadism: the recurrent urge or behavior involving acts in which the pain or humiliation of a person is sexually exciting.

Sexual sadism and sexual masochism are generally considered together and referred to as SadoMasochism (SM), and also known as S/M, BDSM, D/S, and Leather. For many of us, SadoMasochism may at first glance not make sense: how can sexual pleasure be derived from physical and psychological pain? Havelock Ellis, British psychologist and student of human sexuality, working around the turn of the 20th century, recognized the import of the question:

The relation of love to pain is one of the most difficult problems, and yet one of the most fundamental, in the whole range of sexual psychology. . . . [I]f we succeed in answering it . . . we shall have made clear the normal basis on which rest the extreme aberrations of love. (9)

Perhaps because it has been studied the least, Sado-Masochism is probably one of the least understood of the paraphilias. The standard psychiatric and psychological view is that sexual pleasure obtained through bondage, pain, and humiliation is indicative of psychopathology and mental disorder. It is not unusual in psychiatric literature to find SM linked with criminal activities such as rape and murder. However, recent research, which has focused on the perspectives that SM participants provide about their activities, suggests that it is more appropriate to think of SM as a complex social behavior phenomenon involving a large number of people of both sexes who consent to SM practices. Although no reliable estimates are available, some psychiatrists on the basis of their experience with the SM community suggest that as many as 10% of people in the U. S. participate in consensual SM activities. The Internet abounds with sites dedicated to SM activities and associations. This new research suggests that the *Diagnostic and Statistical Manual of Mental Disorders (DSM)* view in which pain is the defining criteria of SM is not a particularly useful way of understanding SM. A 2006 study of the SM communities concludes as follows:

> *Sadomasochists in this research reported having had more sex partners and a greater likelihood of having explored non-heterosexual experiences. They were also more likely to be sexually active relative to non-sadomasochists. One might wonder, on the basis of these findings, whether sadomasochists are simply individuals for whom sex and sexuality play a relatively important role. One might wonder whether SM ought to be understood best as a game explored by the sexually sophisticated and adventurous, involving the manipulation of power for erotic purposes. Further research is needed to determine whether these preliminary impressions are in fact accurate.* (10).

Voyeurism: the recurrent urge or behavior to observe an unsuspecting person who is naked, or disrobing, or engaging in sexual activities, or who is engaging in activities usually considered to be of a private nature. King David may have had voyeuristic tendencies, for as the book of Samuel indicates, one evening David spied a very attractive woman bathing. David sent someone to find out who the woman was. The messenger came back to report that the woman was Bathsheba, the wife of Uriah the Hittite, one of the generals in David's army. *"And David sent messengers, and took her; and she came in unto him, and he lay* *with her.*"

Finally, there is another category, **Paraphilias NOS** (not otherwise specified), added perhaps for completeness sake, provides a nonexhaustive list of other paraphilias - **scatalogia** (obscene phone calls), **necrophilia** (corpses), **zoophilia** (animals), **coprophilia** (feces), and others. In fact, the list of known paraphilias is very long - a 2009 publication lists as many as 547 paraphilias, which gives us an idea of how many of our sexual corridors humans have explored. We may be reminded of Winston Churchill's reflection of France: 'how can you govern a country that produces over 400 different kinds of cheese?' Is it possible to make sense of 547 paraphilias?

Sexual violence – an ancient scourge

The Brain, within its Groove

Runs evenly – and trueBut let a Splinter swerve –

'Twere easier for You –

To put a Current back –

When Floods have slit the Hills –

And scooped a Turnpike for Themselves –

And trodden out the Mills

(11, Emily Dickinson)

What price sex?

We seem to be living through an epidemic of sexual violence. Almost daily we read about horrible incidents of sexual violence, almost all of it directed against women and girls – acid throwing, bride burning, dowry death, honor killing, female genital mutilation, forced abortion, forced pregnancy, domestic violence, marital rape, date rape, child and teen sexual abuse, child pornography, the rape and mutilation of women in countries racked by civil wars, a world wide network of female sexual slavery - so much pain and tragedy that after a while we may become insensitive to it. It is difficult to know with certainty whether the level of sexual violence is greater now then in the past. Perhaps we are much more aware of it now than we were before. But it is important that we try to understand the origins of sexual violence. Perhaps only then can we begin to find ways to help prevent it.

Sexual violence can take many different forms. The World Health Organization (WHO) defines sexual violence as

any sexual act, attempt to obtain a sexual act, unwanted sexual comments or advances, or acts to traffic, or otherwise directed, against a person's sexuality using coercion, by any person regardless of their relationship to the victim, in any setting, including but not limited to home and work. (12, WHO, 2002)

Defined in this way sexual violence encompasses not only rape and child sexual abuse (CSA) but other forms of sexually violent acts, such as systematic rape during armed conflicts, forced marriages, forced prostitution and trafficking of women and children for sexual exploitation, and female genital mutilation.

Surveys of rape and CSA, which are the focus of this chapter, indicate that in the U.S., for example, approximately 12% of adolescent girls and 20% of adult women have been raped. About 15% of female college students in the U.S. have been raped by force or while intoxicated. Similar prevalence rates are found in other Western countries, and much higher rates have been reported in many developing countries. With respect to child sexual abuse (CSA), estimates suggest that 20% of women and 5 to 10% of men have been sexually abused as children. Since many, perhaps a majority of cases of rape or CSA are not reported to the authorities, the true prevalence rates may be significantly higher than these data indicate. The studies also tell us that

- *The large majority of victims are female and most perpetrators are male.*

- *In most cases of rape or CSA, the perpetrator is someone the victim knows, and perhaps knows well, such as a current or former intimate partner, friend, or close relative.*

- *Both rape and CSA have significant, sometimes devastating, physical and psychological effects on health and wellbeing. In many cases the victims remain scarred for the rest of their lives. The health consequences of, and the responses to, rape or CSA vary markedly between individuals and according to the nature of the abuse (e.g. frequency, severity, perpetrator).*

By any measure we may care to use, these statistics are extremely disturbing and disheartening. They also raise many questions, questions that have been argued and debated for several decades. Consider rape, for example: what is the meaning of rape? What is the motivation for rape – sex or violence? Has the nature of rape or its meaning changed with time? Is rape interpreted in the same way in different societies? What is the connection between sex and violence? Why is it that males are the perpetrators? Are they condemned to always be the perpetrators? Is it biology? Is rape a social phenomenon? Is rape preventable?

We will consider these questions in the following two sections.

Rape – an intractable problem?
A moral injury

But it is striking to me and others who look at the history of crimes against women is that they were not perceived as wrong until quite recently, and that the failure of people to understand them as wrong was intimately connected to a view of women as lower, inferior, lesser in value. (13, jean Hampton, p. 134)

The publication of *Against Our Will: Men, Woman, and Rape* (1975) by Susan Brownmiller brought the subject of rape out of the closet and into widespread public discourse. Her provocative language: *"From prehistoric times to the present, I believe, rape has played a critical function. It is nothing more or less than a conscious process of intimidation by which all men keep all women in a state of fear".* (14), guaranteed that rape would now be seen through very different lens. Before that rape had generally been seen as the act of a mentally disturbed man, or the act of an evil man. In other words, rape was seen as an act of one individual against another, and not as Brownmiller now conceived it – as an institution whose purpose was to keep women in their place. Her work and others that followed by the early feminist writers inspired a vast literature on sexual violence and the status of women. The questions and issues raised by these early works are still with us today, seemingly resistant to satisfactory resolution. The most important message from these early works and confirmed by many others that followed was that rape was not simply a rare individual act, but was part of an extensive system of sexual dominance and power, maintained by mythology, religion, and legal precedents, that permitted males to control and exploit almost every aspect of a female's life. In crude terms this system ensures that the sexual, emotional, and economic needs of males are to be met at the expense of females. Sharon Block in her book *Rape and Sexual Power in Early America* (2006) makes the point that during the 18th century *"individual men seemed to assume that they might sexually overpower women as a matter of course. Such attitudes appear in court documents, diaries, and private recollection from the first decades of the century."* (15, p. 21) Rape was part of the fabric of early American racial and gender policies that used women's bodies to satisfy white men's prerogatives. Even an independent thinker such as Benjamin Franklin accepted the sexual norms of the time: women *"were designed to gratify our Passions".* (15, p. 19)

Kathleen Barry, in her study *Female Sexual Slavery* (1979) summarizes in strong language

Considering the arrested sexual development that is understood to be normal in the male population, and considering the numbers of men who are pimps, procurers, members of slavery gangs, corrupt officials participating in this traffic, owners, operators, employees of brothels, and lodging and entertainment facilities, pornography purveyors, associated with prostitution, wife beaters, child molesters, incest perpetrators, Johns (tricks), and rapists, one cannot but be momentarily stunned by the enormous male population engaging female sexual slavery. The huge number of men engaged in these practices should be cause for declaration of an international emergency, a crisis in sexual violence. But what should be cause for alarm is instead accepted as normal sexual intercourse. (16, p. 120)

Sexual dominance applies not only to the obvious examples of female sexual slavery, but also to the ordinary, day-to-day relationships between men and women. For many women the possibility of rape is ever present. The overriding implicit and explicit message for women is – *you are always a target, so be cautious.* Women can imagine themselves as rape victims, while men in general do not (the exception are men in prison). Perhaps this is why women and men perceive rape and their response to it differently. When a woman is assaulted or raped a man's first response is likely to scold the woman, "Well, why was she dressed the way she was, just asking for it" or "She was egging him on, she should have known what was going to happen", or "why did she put herself in a dangerous situation, she should know better". Men may not clearly understand that rape is an act that terrorizes and humiliates the female, or may dismiss the trauma of the rape victim – 'get over it'. The feminist writer Catherine MacKinnon captures the dilemma of the victim:

If a woman has ever been raped, does she ever fully regain the feeling of physical integrity, of self-respect, of having what she wants count somewhere, of being able to make herself clear to those who have not gone through what she has gone through, of living in a fair society, of equality. (17)

For MacKinnon and other feminist writers, rape is not just an offense against one woman, it is also a transgression against all women. The philosopher, Jean Hampton, argues that rape is a moral injury, that is, *"damage to the realization of a victim's value, or damage to the acknowledgment of the victim's value, accomplished through behavior whose meaning is such that the victim is diminished in value."* (21, p. 132) Rape is a *"moral injury to all women because it is part of a pattern of response of many men toward many women that aims to establish their mastery as male over a woman as female."* (13, p 132) Rape, in this sense, is an institution, much like the Jim Crow segregation system in the American South, in that it was not only an affront to one individual, but also to an entire community.

The difficult question that we struggle with today is how we replace the sexually inequitable system we have now with a new standard of freedom that protects women from sexual violence and promotes their creativity and aspirations. What is required is a national social transformation similar in scope to that which ended racial segregation.

The past is always with us

The term *rape* is derived from the Latin *raptus,* which had two general meanings: the most common one referred to non-contractual marriage by abduction; the secondary meaning was 'forced coitus', or rape in the modern sense. In Roman law, raptus in the first sense was a serious crime, and applied to the abduction of a virgin with a dowry. Raptus represented the theft of valuable property, brought dishonor to the father, and incurred severe penalties, even death. Raptus of a widow, prostitute, slave, servant, or even a married woman was not considered a crime because none of them were considered valuable property.

The early Church retained for the most part the Roman juridical views of raptus. Forced coitus was not a crime in church law because it was not considered a canonical problem. The canonical issue that concerned the church was sexual behavior in marriage. While church (canon) law was full of regulations specifying the days, times, circumstances, and positions that lawfully married couples could have intercourse, it ignored completely forced coitus. In the early 12th century, Gratian, a noted scholar of canon law and jurist, compiled a comprehensive juridical system for the Church that defined canon law until the late 19th century. In his *Decretum* (1140 CE) he focuses specifically on what we would now refer to as sexual violence. He first appealed to the civil courts to temper rape prosecutions in the name of Christian love, and removed the death penalty for raptus (abduction of a virgin), and recommended excommunication for one to two years. Raptus was now defined not only as abduction of a virgin from her father's house, but it specified that unlawful coitus must have taken place at the same time as the abduction. The revised raptus law clearly was concerned with the protection of the father's rights, not those of the daughter. Rape, then, was a crime against the father, and not against the person of the daughter. Forced coitus in other cases, such as rape of non-virgins, rape in which coitus was not completed, rape in isolated places, sexual assault other than vaginal penetration were all sins of fornication, but not crimes. According to the historian Kathryn Gravdal, *"the softening influence of Christian love appears to temper only the fate of the ravisher.*" (18).

Despite the official canonical silence regarding non-consensual intercourse, stories of rape and its consequences were of great interest to people during the Middle Ages. It may not be generally appreciated that our contemporary views of rape and much of the rhetoric surrounding rape can be traced to ancient Greek and Roman mythical stories of rape and the way these stories were analyzed and interpreted during the early and latter periods of the Middle Ages. The widely held view that rape is non-consensual sex, or sex against a woman's will, rests on concepts that were developed by St. Augustine in his refutations of pagan views of rape. Medieval writers used Greek and Roman tales of rape to explore legal, theological, and cultural notions, such as the significance of the loss of virginity, abduction of women, the nature of female sexuality, the consequences for the rape victim, and punishment for the rapist. Perhaps because these are issues that we still struggle with today, these stories and their interpretations have left their imprint in modern mentality. We consider briefly three of these – the rapes of Lucretia, Philomela, and Chiomara – all three of which have relevance for us today.

Lucretia. The legend of Lucretia, with its heartrending story, struck a deep responsive chord all through the Middle Ages. The story, originally recounted by the Roman historian, Livy (ca 59 BCE – 17 CE), and Roman poet, Ovid (43 BCE – 18 CE) was celebrated in painting and drama. Writers such as St. Augustine, Chaucer, Boccaccio, and Shakespeare, while keeping the basic elements, embellished it with their own versions. Lucretia was the wife of a Roman nobleman, Collatinus, who bragged to his fellow soldiers about the beauty and fidelity of his wife. Sextus Tarquinius, the son of the tyrant and ruler of Rome during the 6th century BCE, and friend of Collatinus lusted after Lucretia after he met her. Sextus returned to the household when Collatinus was absent, and Lucretia welcomes him as her husband's friend. After they retire for the night, Sextus breaks into her bedchamber, sword in hand, and demands sex. Lucretia refuses. He threatens to kill her and a slave, strip them, entangle the bodies, and tell Collatinus that he found them so. Rather than disgrace Collatinus, Lucretia gives in, and Sextus rapes her, and leaves.

The next morning Lucretia summons her father and husband, and in a moving speech recounts what had happened:

"In your bed, Collatinus, is the impress of another man. My body only has been violated. My heart is innocent, and death will be my witness. Give me your solemn vow that the adulterer shall be punished-he is Sextus Tarquinius. He it is who last night came as my enemy disguised as my guest, and took his pleasure of me. That pleasure will be my deathand his, too, if you are men.... As for me I am innocent of fault, but I will take my punishment. Never shall Lucretia provide a precedent for unchaste women to escape what they deserve" (Livy, History of Rome, I, 27)

She then stabs herself with a concealed dagger.

According to Roman law, Lucretia's violation by Sextus would have been considered adultery or 'fornication achieved by force'. In either case, the violation was wrong not because it injured Lucretia, but because it brought shame and dishonor to her family. Lucretia's suicide was motivated by shame, rather than guilt. Her final extremely moving statement reveals that she was concerned about how her behavior would be seen if she lived, that is, she worried that people might think that she had consented to the violation. In her mind, the only way she could prove her innocence was to take her life. According to the standards of the time for a woman of her class, Lucretia died an honorable and heroic death. She was venerated throughout the classical pagan and even during the early Christian world as a symbol of purity and chastity.

St. Augustine took up Lucretia's story in his book *City of God Against the Pagans,* in which he explains and develops his view of Christian values in contrast to pagan impiety. The Lucretia story is the background for his radical view of chastity. Christian writers before Augustine, such as St. Ambrose and St. Jerome, had written that women should die rather than submit to rape. Augustine, in contrast, defended the honor of 300 nuns who had been raped during the sack of Rome in 400 CE by the Visigoths, none of whom had taken their own lives. *". . . the holy and religiously chaste women who were criminally attacked by an enemy in such a way as to grieve their modesty, although they lost nothing of their unshaken chastity. "* (19, Augustine, City of God 1) Chastity is a quality of the mind, not of the body; it is internal, not external. *". . .*

the body becomes holy through the exercise of the holy will, and while such a will remains unshaken and steadfast, no matter what anyone else does with the body or in the body that a person has no power to avoid without sin on his own part, no blame attaches to the one who suffers it." (20, Augustine, I, p. 249). In contrast to the prevailing view that a violated woman is polluted or impure, St. Augustine argues that a woman who is violated against her will remains chaste.

Lucretia's suicide, therefore, had a different meaning for Augustine. He begins his discussion of Lucretia:

What are we to say of her? Is she to be judged adulterous or chaste? ... Someone put the truth well in a declamation on this subject: 'A paradox! there were two persons involved, and only one committed adultery.' Finely and truly said. The speaker observed in the union of two bodies the disgusting lechery of the one, the chaste intention of the other, and he saw in that act not the conjunction of their bodies but the diversity of their minds. ... But how is it that she who did not commit adultery received the heavier punishment? For the adulterer was driven from his country, with his father; his victim suffered the supreme penalty. If there is no unchastity when a woman is ravished against her will, then there is no justice in the punishment of the chaste"(19, Augustine, 1)

Augustine then proceeds to dissect the meaning of Lucretia's suicide. For him suicide was a mortal sin, because it was equivalent to murder. Lucretia's suicide, rather than being viewed according to the pagan tradition as a heroic act, becomes for St. Augustine a reason to question her innocence. Perhaps, he suggests, Lucretia did not take her life because of shame, but because of guilt: "*. . . What if – but she herself alone could know – she was seduced by her own lust and, though the man violently attacked her, consented, and in punishing that act of hers was so remorseful that death seemed to be due expiation?*" (20, Augustine I; p. 250) Here, Augustine was expressing the widely held view, presented in medical and theological writings, that women were inherently sexual, and that they would experience pleasure even in rape. This was the female's punishment for her participation in the Fall and the expulsion from Eden. "William of Conches writing much later in 1547 states: "*And if in rape the act is at first distressing, in the end,* *however, as a result of the weakness of the flesh, it is pleasing."* (20, p.246) These attitudes sound completely contemporary.

Augustine's logic is relentless and merciless – a raped woman is always suspect, because even if she resists the violation, she may have obtained some pleasure from it. Rape, in fact, serves a divine purpose – it serves to counter existing pride in their virginity and the potential pride at not having suffered a violation. He argues: *"The former were treated for a tumor already swollen; the latter for tumor all ready to swell."* (20, Augustine I, p. 247). Assuming the role of a Hebrew prophet he addresses all women: *"If you have not consented in the sin, divine aid has been added to divine grace, to prevent your losing that grace, while men's reproach has come in place of men's praise, to prevent your loving that praise. Accept this twofold consolation, you fainthearted creatures. On the one hand there is your probation, on the other your chastisement; on the one side your justification, on the other, your correction."* (19, Augustine, 1)

The poor female – the faint-hearted creature - is condemned by her sexuality – her sexuality is the inescapable tragedy of the female sex. The historian, Jennifer Thompson, argues that Augustine's views widely accepted throughout the Middle Ages continues to inflict its damage today:

Contemporary discourse about rape - from media coverage to second-wave feminist theory - owes both its concepts and its rhetoric to a crucial shift in the definition of rape. In 410 C.E., Augustine of Hippo set out to redefine rape from a pagan concept of stuprum or sexual misconduct to a chastity-based and specifically Christian notion. Augustine's definition of rape as sex against a woman's will persists to this day, with serious consequences;. . .it continues to set a damaging precedent followed unknowingly by feminists and media outlets alike. . . his definition of rape holds up an ideal of chastity at the very moment that it asserts that our fallen state and the nature of our genitals renders any pure will to chastity impossible. As a result, rather than focus on the guilt of perpetrators, Augustine obsessively probes the consciences of victims, suggesting that they deserve and indeed solicit their own abuse. (19)

Philomela. Several versions of the legend of Philomela exist, but the core of the story is that Procne, the wife of Tereus, King of Thrace, sends for Philomela, her sister, who lives in Athens. Tereus, who lusts after the virginal Philomela, agrees to escort Philomela from Athens to Thrace. Along the way, he forces her into a cabin in the woods, and rapes Philomela. The scene in the cabin as told by Chaucer in his Legend of Good Women is heartrending: when Philomela realizes what is to happen:

And at that she wept tenderly, and trembled with fear, pale and piteous just like the lamb that is bitten by the wolf; or like the dove stricken by the eagle, that escapes from his claws, yet is dazed and afraid lest it be seized again, even so she sat. But it could not be otherwise, this was all: by force this betrayer did his deed, all in spite of her. Lo! Here was a manly deed, and a righteous one! She cried, "Sister!"' with a loud voice, and "Father dear!" and "God in heaven, help me!" All of these did not avail her. And this false thief did this lady still more harm, out of fear lest she should cry out his shame and openly disgrace him, and he cut off her tongue with his sword; and in a castle he put her secretly in prison for evermore and kept her in possession, so that she could never escape him. (21)

Tereus continues on to Thrace and makes up a tearful story that Philomela died along the way. Chaucer returns to Philomela and continues:

This woeful lady had learned in her youth to make embroidery, and in her frame weave tapestry, as women have long been accustomed to do. And, to tell it briefly, she had her fill of food and drink, and clothing at her desire, and could also read and compose a thing well enough, but truly she could not write with a pen; but she knew how to weave letters back and forth, so that by the time the year was all gone, she had woven on a large woolen cloth how she had been brought in a ship from Athens, and taken into a cave; and well she wove all that Tereus had done and composed the story on the top, how she had been treated because she loved her sister. (21)

Ovid's version of the tapestry is shorter and more poetic:

Mute and imprisoned, Philomena cannot reveal the wrong she has suffered: "Speechless lips can give no token of her wrongs. But grief has sharp wits, and in trouble cunning comes. She hangs a Thracian web oher loom, and skillfully weaving purple signs on a white background, she thus tells the story of her wrongs" (22)

Philomela bribes her page to go to Thrace and tell Procne what had happened. Procne returns to look for Philomela

And in a little while she found her mute sister sitting weeping all by herself in the castle. Alas, for the woe, lament, and moan that Procne voiced over her dumb sister! Each took the other in her arms; and thus I leave them in their sorrow. (21)

Philomela's tapestry allows her, even if she cannot speak, to tell her story. The tapestry becomes a powerful symbol of a raped woman's resilience and of her creativity in finding a new feminine voice. What is most interesting about Chaucer's retelling of the Philomela legend is that he leaves out the last part in which Philomela and Procne take revenge on Tereus: Procne kills Tereus' son, cuts him up, and serves him as dinner to Tereus. Before Tereus can exact his revenge on Procne, the gods turn Procne and Philomela into nightingales. Chaucer doesn't tell us why he ignores the revenge part of the story, but by leaving it out Philomela remains *"the victim figure rather than the image of vengeful woman once wronged. Instead of following the male example of violence in order to seek revenge, Chaucer's Philomela lives our her womanhood and its traits of truth, cleanness, and steadfastness, finding a new and alternative language."* (20, p.251)

Chiomara. Chiomara was another ancient woman who exacted their own justice. Her story is one of 106 that are recounted in Giovanni Boccacio's On Famous Women. Chiomara, the wife of a Galatian chieftain, was captured by the Romans in the Galatian War (189 BCE), and placed under the guard of a Roman centurion. The centurion assaulted and raped her, although she resisted fiercely. To get Chiomara back the Galatians had to pay a ransom. Chiomara's servants brought the money, and while the centurion was counting the gold, Chiomara signaled the servants in the Galatian language to overpower the centurion. They killed him and cut off his head. Chiomara wrapped the head in her garments and delivered it to her husband, declaring that only one living man could be intimate with her. Her body may have been defiled, but she remained chaste in her mind. According to Boccaccio, the delivery of the rapist's head ".. was the price of her dishonor and womanly shame." (23)

What is striking about these legends from long ago is how current they are. Women are still at the mercy of men, and to a large extent they are effectively silenced when they are violated. The stories of Lucretia, Philomela, and Chiomara, are exceptional, since they are examples of women who found ways to find justice. Few women can make that claim. Augustine's argument that rape is 'sex against a woman's will', rather than a stain on family honor, is now widely accepted, and seems self-evident to us today. We think of it as a significant advance because we believe that it recognizes the rights of women and that it works for their benefit. Yet, that view places huge burdens on violated women because to protest means that their motivation will be questioned, and that they will expose themselves to mistaken and pernicious notions of female sexuality, that are carryovers from long ago.

Rape myths. Unfortunately, ignorance and misinformation continue to perpetuate the rape myths that seem so ingrained in the public consciousness. It is worth stating these myths that so often lead to injustice:

Women have unconscious desire to be raped; they provoke rape by appearance or behavior; Most charges of rape are exaggerated or unfounded; Most rapists are oversexed, and they lose control; Only certain types of women get raped

In probably no other type of criminal offense is the victim's conduct and state of mind put on trial. Unfortunately, the police and the judicial system, and even the public, continue in many instances to blame the victim partially, if not fully, for the sexual assault. While the victim cannot displace her responsibility, the perpetrator can often mitigate his behavior by attributing it to alcohol or drugs. Rape stories always seem to end the same – a victim left with physical and psychological scars for the rest of her life, and by comparison the rapist with a slap on the wrist and free to rape again.

Perhaps this is why some feminist writers have sought to remove the sex from rape. Susan Brownmiller's memorable phrase "rape is a crime of violence", from her 1975 polemical history, *Against Our Will. Men, Women and Rape,* was a way of shifting the focus away from a view of rape that somehow always ended up blaming the victim for being violated. With rape, however, nothing is that simple. In contrast to other forms of violence, sex is an inseparable component of rape.

Can rape be understood?

Men rape women because men are men and women are women, in other words, rape obtains it meaning above all within the domain of sexual politics and sexual relations. (24, p.3)

Males are overwhelmingly responsible for violence in general and sexual violence, in particular. Does this mean that males are innately predisposed to the different forms of violence? Is there something about the biology of males – the Y chromosome, the testosterone levels, for example – that is the source of their aggressive and violent tendencies? We may be tempted to answer in the affirmative until we realize that most men are not violent at all times and that most men are not rapists. Non-violence is as much a part of human nature as is violence. It would seem then that the roots and sources of sexual violence must lie therefore not in male biology but in the values and traditions of societies in which they are raised.

Not everyone accepts this conclusion. The notion that male aggression is rooted in biology has a long history. Freud's view that the male sexual drive is inherently aggressive continues to have wide appeal, even among some scientists:

The sexuality of most men shows an admixture of aggression, of a propensity to subdue, the biological significance of which lies in the necessity for overcoming the resistance of the sexual object by actions other than mere courting (25)

The self-described 'dissident feminist', teacher and social critic, Camille Paglia, has long argued that males have a powerful sex drive, which often gets out of control.

Aggression and eroticism are deeply intertwined. Hunt, pursuit, and capture are biologically programmed into male sexuality. . . I see in the simple, swaggering masculinity of the jock and in the noisy posturing of the heavymetal guitarist certain fundamental, unchangeable truths about sex. . . There are sexual differences based in biology. Academic feminism is lost in a fog of social constructionism. (26)

Paglia is convinced that feminists have overestimated the dangers of rape, especially date rape. Part of the thrill for women, she argues, is the danger of it. *"I'm encouraging women to accept the adventure, accept the danger. You have to accept the fact that part of the sizzle of sex comes from the danger of sex. You can be overpowered."* (26) In date rape, the female brings it on herself because she goes with a male due to the thrill that she might be risking rape. For Paglia, women derive part of their pleasure from sex by submitting to the power of the male, and they can't complain if they get hurt. Those who agree with Paglia's views can point to the rape fantasies so common in women as evidence that females derive pleasure in being overpowered. Consider the following fantasy – it has all the classic stereotypes of the uncontrollable male sexual drive overpowering the initial apparent resistance of the female:

This friend of mine comes over and immediately shoves me against the wall, pinning my hands over my head and kisses me passionately. The guy in my fantasy is my current boyfriend but I started having this dream last year when we were good friends but both dating other people. But he doesn't look as sweet as he normally does; he looks hungry for me. He does all the initiating. I tell him to stop, that it's wrong and we can't do this. He says he doesn't care; he cannot wait another minute. He's thinking that he has to have me immediately. His motivation is satisfying his own sexual hunger. I am thinking that this is wrong but it feels so good. While my hands are still pinned over my head he uses his other hand to tear off my clothes not caring if they rip. He undresses himself and shoves his body against mine shoving his tongue into my mouth. He tells me he finds me irresistible and that he doesn't care if we are both with other people. I tell him it's wrong and we can't do this. He tells me he knows I want him; he can tell from the way I look at him and touch him when we're together.

We're both naked and he kisses me all over my body. He is still only motivated with fulfilling his desire. I am begging him to stop, telling him it's wrong and that we can get caught any minute. He picks me up and screws me against the wall. At first it hurts but it feels so good that I can't help but enjoy it. When we're done he leaves because he knows my boyfriend is going to be over soon. He tells me how much he loves my body and how I please him like no woman ever has before and that he would give anything to be with me. I am torn between the pleasure and knowing that it's morally wrong. (27)

We don't really know how to interpret the meaning or significance of such powerful fantasies, but it is easy to see that, if taken literally, they support Paglia's views on the nature of male and female sexuality.

Given such notions, what is the source of male's aggressive sexual drive? Testosterone has often been proposed, but although testosterone is necessary for male sexual function, clear and compelling evidence that it is responsible for aggression and violence is lacking. For some scientists our genes and our evolutionary inheritance are the keys to understanding not only our sexuality, but also many other aspects of our lives. According to some evolutionary psychologists, rape is an evolutionary and biological necessity, a consequence of the different reproductive strategies of males and females in evolution. Rape is favored by evolution because it promotes the spread of the male's genes. Males can't help it – they are rapists because of evolution. Women just have to accept it. The violence that accompanies rape and the physical and psychological consequences to the victims of rape – 'collateral damage' - are minimized or ignored. These evolutionary scenarios appeal to those who look for biological causes for our social problems, but as scientific hypotheses they are based on pure speculation, and lack any evidence to support them.

Some geneticists, for their part, are promoting views that there is a direct causal connection between genes and behavior. Gays are gays because of a 'gay' gene; a depressed person has a 'depression' gene; an alcoholic has a gene 'for' alcoholism; aggression, violence and criminality are the products of 'aggression', 'violent' and 'criminal' genes; and so it goes. These ideas may be appealing because many of us are at heart biological determinists – that is, we believe that biology plays a big role in our behavior. We would like to think that we might be able to reduce or eliminate troubling social problems by modifying the genes responsible for problematic behaviors. This also gets us off the hook because we won't have to invest money and energy in curing our social problems by social means – a pill may be all we need. This is the implicit message when a researcher announces, amidst an extensive publicity campaign, the discovery of a 'new' gene for behavior X. In none of the studies published so far has any causality been demonstrated – only correlations – and none of these studies has yielded any important insights into complex human behaviors.

According to neuroscientist Steven Rose, the most worrying aspect of the 'gene-behavior' mindset, what he calls 'neurogenetic determinism', is that it can lead to governmental programs such as the Federal Violence Initiative, whose purpose was to study the origins of violence in U.S. society by looking for biochemical and genetic defects in 100,000 inner city blacks and whites. He comments: ***"But as an approach to diminishing the violence of city streets it would seem unlikely to achieve as significant an impact as would measures to reduce the estimated 280 million handguns currently in personal possession in the U. S."*** (28)

It is highly unlikely that any behavior can be explained by one gene in isolation. Knowing how an internal combustion engine works doesn't help us in understanding the difference between a Cadillac, a Mercedes-Benz, or a Volkswagen Beetle. Understanding any human behavior, especially one as complex as rape, requires that we understand the social context in which it takes place.

Feminist writers beginning in the 1970s discarded the view of biology as the determinant of aggressive male sexuality, and instead proposed an alternative explanation - that sexual violence was a product of a male-privileged society. The best evidence we have that rape and other forms of sexual violence are socially constructed, and not biologically determined, are the cross-cultural studies that demonstrate that sexual violence is most common in cultures characterized by male dominance. The cross-cultural record does not support the notion that male violence against women is universal.

Although few in number, societies relatively free of gender-based violence (particularly rape and wife-abuse) exist or have existed, indicating that male biology in itself does not lead to sexual violence. Rather, it is the 'indoctrination' of males that matters. Although cultures differ in their views of what it means to be male, a masculine mystique appears to be common in many societies. The anthropologist, David Gilmore, notes that in many peasant and urban societies *"there is a constantly recurring notion that real manhood is different from simple anatomical maleness, that it is not a neutral condition that comes about spontaneously through biological maturation but rather is a precarious or artificial state that boys must win against powerful odds".* (29)

On the other hand, *"femininity usually involves questions of body ornament or sexual allure, or other essentially cosmetic behaviors that enhance, rather than create, and inherent quality of character. An authentic femininity rarely involves tests or proofs of action."* (29)

Manhood is an earned status, which is probably why many societies have elaborate rituals and rites of passage to transform boys into men. But manhood also has to be continually demonstrated by some type of action and this requirement promotes insecurity in men that can only be overcome by their behavior toward women. The social theorist John Stolenberg notes:

Most people born with a penis between their legs grow up aspiring to feel and act unambiguously male, longing to belong to the sex that is male and daring not to belong to the sex that is not, and feeling the urgency for a visceral and constant verification of their male sexual identity – for a fleshy connection to manhood – as the driving force of their life. The drive does not originate in the anatomy. The sensations derive from the idea. The idea gives the feelings social meaning; the idea determines which sensations shall be sought. (30, p. 31)

Maleness develops in opposition to femaleness – hence, the focus on sex and sexuality

The male confirms and proves his maleness, his virility, through his sexuality. It becomes the core, the very essence around which he

consciously and unconsciously forms his ideas about himself as a man. The female sexual identity has not been formed in relationship to sexuality, but in the need to be chosen by a man .
. .By being chosen the woman receives the necessary proof of her values as a woman – both in her own eyes and in others. (31, p. 73)

The extent to which men need to demonstrate power as males is a reliable indicator of the levels of violence against women. High rates of sexual violence are found in societies characterized by violent interpersonal conflict resolution, economic inequality between men and women, masculine ideal of male dominance, toughness, and honor, and male economic and decision-making authority in the family.

Lawrence Kramer in his evocative, *After the Lovedeath. Sexual Violence and the Making of Culture,* states the case for the social foundations of rape in no uncertain terms:

. . . the forms of selfhood mandated as normal in modern Western culture both promote and rationalize violence against women. Even if unacted, the possibility of sexual violence ripples in the air like rising heat, visible and invisible at the same time. Far from being haunted or threatened by this possibility, normal selfhood is permeated by it. Both men and women alike are enjoined to construct heterosexual gender identities based on a mercurial love-hate relationship to whatever is understood as femininity. Violence simply transcribes this attitude as action. Virtually everyone regrets it, including those who inflict it. Yet it persists, indifferent to social distinctions and impervious to sociologically inspired remedies—sensitivity training, better role models, more ideal media images—that try to promote less tolerance in women and less aggressiveness in men. The tendency to sexual violence seems lodged in the very core of ordinary subjectivity like a bone in the throat. (32)

That 'indifference to social distinctions' applies as well to social scientists who study human behavior and who certainly should know better. It is captured by Martha McCaughey, a sociologist attending a scientific meeting:

"If you were stranded on a deserted island with a woman, would

you rape her?" This dilemma was put forward by a male scholar attending the second annual conference of the Human Behavior and Evolution Society. . . I wondered if I was the only woman in the room uncomfortable with the question, with the way male scholars talked to one another as men, and with the presumptuousness that raping a woman is a man's choice. . . what got me was the gall of these male scholars to assume that they could rape if they wanted to or were driven to. This astonished me, as did their understanding of the human female as the passive object of the aggressive behaviors men have presumably evolved to dish out. (33)

What is striking about McCaughey's observation of the male scholar's cavalier view of the male's prerogatives with respect to women (written in 2008) is how it coincides with the views of the radical feminist Andrea Dworkin writing 21 years before:

The act – Intercourse – is the possession . . .The normal fuck by a normal man is taken to be an act of invasion and ownership undertaken in a mode of predation: colonizing, forceful (manly) or nearly violent; the sexual act that by its nature makes her his. (34, p. 22)

There is a deep recognition in culture and in experience that intercourse is the normal use of a woman, her human potentiality affirmed by it, and a violative abuse, her privacy irredeemably compromised, her selfhood changed in a way that is irrevocable, unrecoverable. (34, p, 122)

For Dworkin, it is not only rape but sexual intercourse itself that renders the woman inferior. The act of penetration defines the relationship between men and women. The female: *"She is defined by how she is made, that hole, which is synonymous with entry . . . when he enters her, he confirms for himself and for her what she is: that is something, not someone; certainly not someone equal."* (34, p.123) In her intensely argued and harrowing study, *Intercourse*, Dworkin paints a dark picture of what most of us would call normal sexual intercourse. The male always seeks to master the female, to make her subordinate to him. The male is the exploiter, and female is always the victim. Enjoyment, tenderness, playfulness, even real pleasure is absent.

Lest we imagine that Dworkin's views of the male psyche are so extreme as to be unbelievable, consider the following examples of misogyny in writers and artists that we might admire: their potential for sexual violence is palpable

The muralist, Diego Rivera:

If I loved a woman, the more I loved her, the more I wanted to hurt her. Frida was only the most obvious target of this disgusting trait. (34, p181)

The poet W.H. Auden:

The greater the love, the more false to its object, Not to be born is the best for man; After the kiss comes the impulse to throttle, Break the embraces, dance while you can. (35)

The poet T.S. Eliot:

I knew a man once did a girl in Any man might do a girl in Any man has to, needs to, wants to Once in a lifetime, do a girl in. (36)

William Shakespeare (after he learns he has syphilis):

Down from the waist they are Centaurs, Though women all above: But to the girdle do the Gods inherit, Beneath is all the fiend's: there's hell, there's darkness, There is the sulphurous pit – burning, scalding, Stench, consumption; fie, fie, fie!. pah! (37)

Frank Chambers, the drifter who narrates James M. Cain's first novel, *The Postman Always Rings Twice* (1934), (later made into a film noir starring John Garfield and Lana Turner) says to himself when he first sees Cora, the cook at the tavern where he gets a job *"Except for the shape, she really wasn't any raving beauty, but she had a sulky look to her, and her lips stuck out in a way that made me want to mash them in for her."*

What then?

Chaucer (c1343 – 1400 CE) may have been unusual for his time in recognizing that the heart of the problem of rape lies in the perfidy of men. Consider the last few lines of *The Legend of Lucrece and The Legend of Philomela*:

And as for men, look what tyrannical deeds they do every day. Test them who may wish: the truest is entirely fickle to trust. (21)

The rest of the story it matters not to tell, for this is the sum of it, that she who never merited the wickedness of this cruel man, nor caused him any harm that she knew of, was treated this way. May you beware of man, if you wish. For albeit he wishes not for shame to act as Tereus did, lest he lose his fair reputation, or treat you as a villain or murderer, yet you shall find him true for only a short time. This I say, even if he ere now my own brother--unless it should happen that he can find no new love. (21, The Legend of Philomela)

Or consider a passage from Dante's *Purgatory* related by the soul of a slain woman that Dante encounters in his visit to purgatory:

I am La Pia, murdered on The orders of my husband; locked away And dealt with so that he might, with me gone, Marry again. He's still up there today. He knows about it, he who with his jewel Pledged love, and faith, and wed me, and was cruel. (38)

This desire to hurt and violate expressed so vividly and unexpectedly in the passages above may help us understand why rape seems such an intractable problem. Despite dozens of studies, changes in the legal system that make rape easier to prosecute, numerous projects aimed at prevention, the prevalence of intimate partner abuse, marital rape, date rape does not appear to decrease.

Feminists have worked steadily and heroically to expose the political nature of rape. We have passed legislation and prosecuted rapists; we have published scholarly studies and memoirs; we have founded and staffed rape crisis centers and battered women's shelters; we have learned to speak up, to fight, and to shoot; we have consoled victims, and many of us have served as midwives at our own rebirth after suffering this crime. (19)

But in the plaintive song of W. B. Yeats:

`What then?' sang Plato's ghost.  `What then? (39)

Child Sexual Abuse (CSA) – a major social concern

Definition

Individually and collectively we would have no qualms in saying that 'child sexual abuse' is wrong, immoral, and should be illegal. But, what is the basis for our conviction? At one level it seems self-evident, but a devil's advocate might point out that from a legal perspective we would need to define 'child' (when does a person cease being a child?); or 'sexual' (do we mean kissing and fondling, genital touching, oral sex, vaginal or anal penetration?); or 'abuse' (when does an act become abusive; if consent is given, is the act abusive?). Then there is the question of the 'offender' – does the age of the 'offender' or the relationship of the offender to the child matter? It shouldn't surprise us then that defining child sexual abuse in a concise and legally workable way is problematic. The American Psychological Association (APA) in 2001 acknowledged the difficulty but proposed the following definition

There is no universal definition of child sexual abuse. However, a central characteristic of any abuse is the dominant position of an adult that allows him or her to force or coerce a child into sexual activity. Child sexual abuse may include fondling a child's genitals, masturbation, oralgenital contact, digital penetration, and vaginal and anal intercourse Child sexual abuse is not solely restricted to physical contact; such abuse could include noncontact abuse, such as exposure, voyeurism, and child pornography. Abuse by peers also occurs. (40)

Note that the age limits are not specified. And what about the last sentence – 'abuse by peers' – how is that dealt with? What if there is no coercion? Anthropologists tell us that adult-child sex has been common and accepted in different parts of the world. The 18th century explorer, James Cook, reported that in the Hawaiian Islands and Polynesia the copulation of adult men and very young girls often took place in public

"without the least sense of being improper or indecent." (41, cited in Green, p. 467) To us these practices are abhorrent and unacceptable. In our own society, however, most cases of adult-child sexual contact take place in a relationship in which the child, because she or he knows, trusts, and maybe even loves the offender, appears to be a willing participant. The acts don't take place in public, but are they intrinsically different from those that Cook reported on?

Most psychologists recognize that most children younger than 16 are interested in sex. However, as a society we find a child's sexual curiosity disturbing and threatening. But we are also very schizophrenic: *"As a society, we seem to be intensely uncomfortable discussing the fact that our children may be sexually curious or may masturbate, even as we allow pornography to become increasingly visible to children on highstreet shelves or television channels, and as we encourage our little daughters to dress in bikinis, thongs and high-heeled shoes and to parade around using the sexualized body language of majorettes or pop stars."* (41, p. 171)

The journalist Judith Levine, author of *Harmful to Minors: The Perils of Protecting Children from Sex,* argues *"sex is not in itself harmful to minors. Rather, the real potential for harm lies in circumstances under which some children and teens have sex . . . these are the same conditions that set children up to suffer many other miseries"*. (42, p.xxxiii) There are many groups around the world who maintain that adult-child sex (referred to variously as 'man-boy love', 'intergenerational intimacy', 'age-discrepant relationships', or child-adult sexual contact') is harmless and may even beneficial, just as in the societies that Cook mentioned, adult-child sex was considered to benefit the child by preparing them for marriage. The radical feminist, Shulamith Firestone, went so far as to hope that in the future adult relations with children *"would include as much genital sex as they were capable of – probably considerably more than we now believe"*. (41, p. 173)

Perhaps because different groups and individuals might propose legitimacy to adult- child sexual contact, it is all the more important and necessary that we formulate a clear understanding of why child sexual abuse is wrong and unacceptable. The core of this understanding has to be based on the recognition of the psychological and neurophysiological immaturity of the child. In 1978 the psychologists Ruth Kempe and C. Henry Kempe stated this concept quite clearly: ***"child sexual abuse is the involvement of dependent, developmentally immature children and adolescents in sexual activities that they do not fully comprehend, to which they are unable to give informed consent, or that violate the social taboos of the family roles"***. (41, p. 175).

In Sarah Goode's view child sexual abuse is (a) not context-dependent, and (b) does not require an element of coercion. **Child sexual abuse is wrong and unacceptable because it is intrinsically harmful to the child irrespective of the circumstance or whether it is culturally acceptable or not.** Even if the child appears to consent, we need to keep in mind that:
"Children cannot technically consent to having sex with adults. For consent to truly occur, two conditions must prevail: a child must know what he/she is consenting to and have the freedom to say yes or no. . . They rarely resist, run, scream for help, or report the perpetrator. As adults we cannot fault them for making the choice they do." (43, p. 73)

A brief historical perspective

The recognition of the intrinsic harm of child sexual abuse has been long in coming. In the U.S. and Western Europe practices troubling to contemporary sensibilities existed until the 20th century without much public outcry. In 18th century London court records show that 25% of rape prosecutions between 1730 and 1789 involved females younger than 10 – the apparent justification was that sexual intercourse with a child would cure venereal disease. In France, between 1858 and 1869, 75% of men charged with rape were accused of raping young children. Domestic servants, many of whom were children were easy targets for the male members of the family. In the American South slave girls were routinely raped, and sometimes used for forced breeding, and even after the Civil War during the Jim Crow era, young black girls were raped with impunity.

Beginning around the middle of the 19th century a diverse collection of reformers – churchmen, the first generation feminists (although that term had not yet been coined), and others in Western Europe and U. S. – began to expose the extent of child abuse and the sexual victimization of children in many sectors of the society, and to press for changes in the legal structures that permitted such practices. In the U.S. the Society for the Prevention of Cruelty to Children (SPCC) founded in 1874 in New York focused its efforts on child neglect and the sexual abuse of children among the immigrant poor and working class families. Other reformers argued that incest and child sexual abuse were crimes that occurred in all social classes. In Great Britain, British feminists were responsible for raising the age of consent from 10 to 13 in 1875, and to 16 in 1885. Incest became a crime in 1908, and the severity of sentences for sexual assaults on female children was increased (petty theft entailed longer jail terms than did assaults on girls). The persistent effort of generations of reformers over more than a century has transformed our social and legal landscape with respect to the sexual victimization of children in ways that we take so much for granted that we may not appreciate how difficult it was.

During these turbulent times the ideology of 'male privilege', especially if the male belonged to the middle or upper classes, made it difficult to bring charges against men for child sexual abuse. For many in the legal and psychiatric professions it was considered inconceivable that a married man with a family and a secure profession – a socalled 'respectable man' - would be guilty of child sexual abuse. In fact, there was plenty of evidence to the contrary, but this evidence was largely ignored. In France, for example, during the latter half of the 19th century, French physicians documented tens of thousands of cases of child sexual abuse and rape. These reports showed that sexual assaults against children were frequent, that children's reports were largely truthful, that fathers and brothers were often the molesters, and that high status and education did not inhibit men from committing such acts. These findings, although well known around the beginning of the 20th century in the medical community of Western Europe, appeared to have little influence on the views of many in the legal and psychiatric professions. A lawyer writing in 1904 expressed the 'male defensive' notion of the legal and medical community in no uncertain terms:

Modern psychiatrists have amply studied the behavior of errant young

girls and women coming before the courts in all sorts of cases. Their psychic complexes are multifarious, distorted partly by inherited defects, partly by diseased derangements or abnormal instincts, partly by bad social environments, partly by temporary physiological or emotional conditions. One form taken by these complexes is that of contriving false charges of sexual offenses by men. (44)

Thirty years later, these notions had not changed. Dr. Lauretta Bender, an eminent researcher in the child sexual abuse field wrote in 1937, referring to children who were brave enough to accuse a man of molestation:

"These children undoubtedly do not deserve completely the cloak of innocence with which they have been endowed by moralists, social reformists, and legislation. Frequently we consider the possibility that the child might have been the actual seducer rather than the one innocently seduced" (43, p.165).

Not all psychiatrists held these views, however. The Hungarian psychiatrist, Sandor Ferenczi, a contemporary of Sigmund Freud, expressed views that are very modern:

. . .trauma, especially the sexual trauma, as the pathogenic factor cannot be valued highly enough. Even children of very respectable, sincerely puritanical families fall victim to real violence or rape much more often than one had dared to suppose. . . These children feel physically and morally helpless, their personalities are not sufficiently consolidated in order to be able to protest, even if only in thought, for the overwhelming force and authority of the adult silences them and rob them of their senses. (44, p. 7; Sandor Ferenczi, 1955, first published 1933)

Freud himself was aware of the French findings and in his early years stated that incest was more common than suspected, even in respectable families, understood the imbalance between the child and the adult – the child who "is at the mercy of the arbitrary use of power", and appreciated that the frequency of 'hysteria' in adult women stemmed from the fact that as girls they had been sexually assaulted, in many cases by their fathers. However, thirty years later, for reasons that remain unclear, he changed his mind completely and adopted the view that the children who report abuse were suffering from fantasies, referring to such accounts as 'imaginary', 'fictitious', or made up. Apparently he was so convinced of the validity of his new views that he was instrumental in not only suppressing the publication of Ferenczi's work, but also in destroying existing copies. Fortunately, an English translation survived but was not discovered until decades later.

The strong influence of Freud and other psychiatrists who held the same views continued to give life to the notion of respectable men falling victim to the sexual whims of young girls. This widespread bias continued until rather late into the 20th century, and complicated attempts to prosecute sexual offenders. The influential British psychiatrist Anthony Storr, in his book *Sexual Deviance* (1964) commented on child sexual abuse: *"an act which in itself is dreadful, but which might be committed by many of us if the provocation was sufficient.* The distress caused was *"more the result of adult horror than of anything intrinsically dreadful in the sexual contact itself."* (8)

Florence Rush, in her book *Freud and the Sexual Abuse of Children* (1977), writes:

"As a consequence of existing professional theories, surrounded by scientific aura, victims are being effectively silenced . . .Any attempt on the part of the child to expose the violator also exposes her own alleged innate sexual motives and shames her more than the offender . . . The dilemma of the sexual abuse of children has provided a system of foolproof emotional blackmail: if the victim incriminates the abuser, she also incriminates herself. The child is offered no protection, while the offender is permitted to further indulge his predilection for children." (43, p 176)

Pedophilia – reality and dilemma

The reality

Pedophiles exist and we must learn to live with them in full awareness (41, p. 168)

The child sexual abuse scandals of the Roman Catholic Church as well as media coverage of the abduction and assault of many young girls during the last few years have made 'pedophilia' and 'pedophile' into household terms. Probably almost every adult and adolescent in the U.S. has heard or knows about pedophilia. All these stories have imprinted in our minds images of pedophiles as creepy, evil, sinister men. The English sociologist and occupational therapist, Sarah Goode, in her highly informative study of pedophilia, *Understanding and Addressing Adult Sexual Attraction to Children,* confessed to a feeling that many people would share:

I hated paedophiles as much as anyone. I thought if I ever met a paedophile I would want to kill them (even though I'm generally a pretty tolerant, pacifist Christian sort of person). (41, p. ix)

As a sociologist she also understood that pedophiles come in all colors and stripes, that is, they are as diverse as non-pedophiles. She continues: *"But at the same time I could see that the images of deviant, cunning monsters being portrayed by the news stories just could not be correct."*

What is pedophilia? The German physician von Krafft-Ebing coined the term 'pedophilia' in the late 19th century. He considered 'pedophilia erotica', as he referred to the disorder, a form of sexual deviancy (a category that also included homosexuality, sadism, masochism, and fetishism) that was in-born and should be viewed as a medical, rather than a legal problem. Since then defining pedophilias has proven to be a contentious issue.

Features of pedophilia. Most, if not all, pedophiles are male. The noted German physician, Peer Briken, from the Institute for Sexual Research and Forensic Psychiatry in Hamburg, Germany has studied pedophilia for many years comments: *"Although it is true that women are capable of and have committed child sex abuse, there is no such thing as a pedophile woman. At least I have never seen or heard of a single case over the course of my career."* (45) We don't really know why pedophilia is confined to males. Those who favor biological explanations suggest that a disorder in brain chemistry/anatomy in male embryos during the early stages of pregnancy results in a 'reduced masculinization' of the brain. Brain chemistry alterations have been proposed also for the causes of homosexuality, gender identity disorders, and paraphilias in general. What these presumptive brain chemistry alterations are specifically remains unknown. Others have looked for environmental/social conditions that might be correlated with pedophilia, but as yet none have been found that could be validated empirically.

Although probably most pedophiles have an exclusive attraction to children, some are also attracted to adults. Pedophiles may or may not act on their sexual impulses with respect to children, and this means that pedophilia, an involuntary desire, is conceptually different from child sexual abuse, a voluntary action. Pedophilia is generally thought to be a sexual orientation distinct from homosexuality or heterosexuality, and that it can develop in a person who is homosexual or heterosexual. Like heterosexuality or homosexuality, pedophiles discover, rather than choose, their pedophilic tendencies. Pedophiles can have gender preferences in children, and may be classified as heterosexual, homosexual, or bisexual in their pedophilic preferences. Studies suggest that 9% to 40% of pedophiles are homosexual in their gender preferences in children, but that does not mean they are homosexual. It is important to keep in mind that homosexual adults are no more likely than heterosexuals to abuse children.

Unfortunately, the clergy abuse scandal of the Catholic Church reinforced the opposite notion, that is, *homosexuality equals pedophilia equals child sexual abuse.* In fact, as studies have shown the majority of priest offenders were not pedophiles, and most of their victims were not prepubescent. Sadly, the erroneous equating of homosexuality and pedophilia still exists in the minds of many, especially in those who already have strong anti-homosexual attitudes. By focusing on homosexuals as being the principal danger to children, all the cases of child sexual abuse perpetrated by fathers, brothers, uncles, other relatives and friends of the victim tend to be forgotten or ignored.

In most cases of child sexual abuse the perpetrator is a relative, neighbor, family friend, teacher, coach, clergyman, or someone else in regular contact with the child.

Pedophiles exist. This is a scary thought and something many people

find difficult to accept. . .that we know them and often are very fond of them; they live in our communities and are members of our family, our friends, our work colleagues. They are in our churches and other religious settings, they are in positions of authority and trust. Quite often they may be involved in looking after our children. (41, p. 168)

Precisely because the victim knows and trusts them, the pedophile can manipulate the child, gradually introducing them to inappropriate behavior. A common tactic used by pedophiles is to take advantage of a child's normal need to feel loved and cared for. They may seek out those children who might be especially vulnerable, those, for example, who lack close parental supervision, or who feel emotionally or physically neglected. One victim reports: *"I think it happened because I was needy, because I didn't have anything."* (45, p.37). Another one: *"Well, once I realized I got fucked with by the prick . . . then I was thinking that I had something to do with it; maybe it was my fault."* (43, p. 129)

How many pedophiles are there in the population?

We don't have a reliable way of providing an answer. What we have instead are the results of studies that assess the sexual attraction of men in the adult male population – men who are not defined in any way as 'pedophile' – to prepubescent children. Two types of studies have been carried out. The first, which we refer to as the clinical studies, measures the penile response – using an instrument called a 'penile plethysmography' - to images of young children and adolescents, and the second are surveys using questionnaires designed to explore adult sexual arousal to children, such as having sexual fantasies about children, masturbating to sexual fantasies of children, desire to have sex with a child if not caught.

The results are quite surprising. Five clinical studies indicate that between 17 and 58 per cent of a presumably 'normal' population of adult men (who do not think of themselves as pedophile) are capable of being sexually aroused by children under the age of 12 years old. The latest of the questionnaire surveys found that 7% of men admitted sexual attraction to children, 18% had sexual fantasies about children, 8% admitted to masturbating the sexual fantasies of children, and

4% indicating that they would have sex with a child if no one knew. Given the nature of the questions asked in these questionnaires it is highly likely that these figures represent minimum estimates. The questionnaire studies agree in general with the clinical findings and suggest that about 20% of 'normal' men have some degree of sexual attraction to children. These numbers unfortunately don't tell us what fraction of men are pedophiles as defined by DSM-IV, nor do they tells us what fraction would act on their urges and impulses, but they suggest that the prevalence of pedophilia is much higher than is indicated by the reported cases of child sexual abuse. The experts estimate that only about 5% of child abuse cases (some of which are committed by pedophiles) are reported to the authorities.

Faces of the pedophile.

Before the advent of the Internet information about pedophilia and pedophiles was the province of psychiatrists who specialized in sexual deviancy disorders and hence was generally difficult to obtain. The revolutionary aspect of the Internet is that it has opened up the previously secret and underground world of the pedophile to public view. The diverse online pedophilic communities that have appeared provide information, discussion, debate, and advocacy on issues that are of interest to pedophiles. At the same time these opinions and points of view are challenged and attacked by online anti-pedophile communities. These dynamic give-and-take online conversations and debates are probably one of the most important sources of information about the contemporary pedophilia world.

For many people the proliferation of and easy access to pedophilic sites are disturbing and cause for concern. The child pornographic (virtual) images and the pro-pedophilic sites that advocate pedophilia as a lifestyle are alarming to those who feel that susceptible young people may be lured into the pedophilic world, or worse, that they are encouraging child sexual abuse. Others argue that the online communities make surveillance of potential offenders easier for law enforcement officials and help prevent child sexual abuse. What seems clear in any case is that for those interested in fully understanding contemporary pedophilia a full awareness of the complex and continually changing online pedophilia culture is a necessity.

One important aspect of the online pedophilic sites is that they give us a more comprehensive view of the diversity of pedophiles – such as how they view themselves, for some their struggles with their affliction, their search for their identity and coming to terms with who they are. If we are of a mind to, we can get a glimpse of them as people, rather than as distorted mental images. They also reveal that pedophiles are diverse in their views, which range from acceptance of terrible acts of sexual abuse to controlling their impulses and imposing on themselves a celibate and law-abiding life style. A few examples provided by moderators of online sites:

This forum provides the means for a community to develop, for paedophiles to interact with each other, question each other, discuss ideas, form bonds, provide mutual support . . . we operate scrupulously within the law. Law enforcement agencies are fully aware of the existence of our sites and doubtless monitor their content closely. Strictly speaking, every poster on this site is 'noncontact' – because no poster is having illegal sexual contact with underage girls. (41, p. 136)

'Pro-contact' means to take the view that, while a person wisely obeys the law, in principle, laws aside, there is nothing wrong with loving and consensual sexual contact, and therefore to argue for changes to the law. . . There are others who are 'anti-contact', to differing degrees. These are a smaller section of the community, but they feel that it could never be right for children and adults to act sexually with each other. Of course they may express that to different degrees and with different shades of emphasis. (41, p. 137)

Regarding the pro-contact sites:

People on there that are obviously pro-contact, have not reason not to have sexual contact with children, and obviously do not care about the welfare of children. . . It's the BS (bullshit) factor . . . it's obvious to me that some posters have sex with children, but of course would never admit it and would deny it or skirt the question if asked. I hate superficiality and lying so that's one part of (the online paedophile community) I don't like. (41, p. 13)

Sarah Goode reports many individual pedophile commentaries. We list a few of these below.

Sources that helped constructing their identity in more positive terms:

These websites have helped me to understand my attractions to a greater extent, and to understand my place as an Minor-Attracted Adult (MAA) in modern society. (41, Ed, aged 17; p. 84)

[Websites} have certainly helped me crystallize my identity as an MAA. . .My thinking has been changed by reading articles and research relating to pedophilia, and links to many of thse have been discovered on line. Also, I have clarified my own attitudes to many things, such as sexual activity with children, child pornography and so on, through discovering what other MAAs think about these issue. (41, Tim; p. 91)

W*ikipedia helped me discover that there were people who believed that attraction to children was not evil, and that the predatory paedophiles in popular culture were not necessarily accurate descriptions.* (41, Kristof: p. 90)

Struggling with who they were:

The secret shame of paedophilia is a pervasively crippling experience, and it does not just make a person feel broken and divided, it makes them act that way. . . I felt my life would be over if I ever shared my secret with anyone, and I was very afraid that one day I would be 'found out'. That was a terrible way to live, as you might imagine. (41, Tim; p. 38)

I experience the apparently congenital condition described as 'sexual attraction to children'. . . I believe that there is a significant risk of harm to children who are involved in sexual relationships with adults, and do not support changing age of consent types of laws. I believe that child pornography is harmful to my community, as well as to the public at large. I believe that the repression this community of people live under forces our public efforts to extreme political views. . . Outside of the issue of orientation, I am indistinguishable from larger society. I am conservative, Christian, and Republican; I voted for George Bush and support Tony Blair. . . I am married and a parent. . . I am human, and at times others do not realize that I share the same concerns and ambitions as they in society. (41, Darren; p. 42)

Night after night alone in my bedroom fear was growing and growing, I could feel it. There was such hatred for paedophiles being expressed by every newspaper and the thing about it was, they were right to feel that way about Father Smith and people like him. People like me. I suddenly realized at this point, that everyone in this life, my friends, my family, my mum and dad, all hate me too, it's just that they don't know it yet! I started to feel isolated from everyone around me. To feel alone in this world, to face a battle with a cancer I might never win. . . Is it right for me to continue to live knowing what I'll end up doing to boys in the future? I felt the answer but didn't say it. Suicide brought with it the absolute, guaranteed and undisputable fact that I would never be in this life harm even one boy ever. (41, David; p. 7)

Views on having sex with adults:

Unappealing. I have attempted it a couple of times but was never aroused and this unable to ejaculate. There was simple no chemistry at all. (41, Gary; p. 86)

I find the idea of sex with females to be very distasteful, even nauseating, adult females particularly so. (41, Louis; p. 87)

To me, the idea of sex, erotic love or romantic relations with a woman just feels as though it is in the 'wrong category". (41, William; p. 87)

I have had sex with adults (my ex-wife mainly). . . Sex with my wife was usually good, often very good. I almost always fantasied that she was a child, and she often helped me by dressing as a schoolgirl. (41, Lenny; p. 87)

I'm really lucky, as while my preference is for girls aged eight to thirteen years old, I am also sexually attracted to adult women. (41,

Bill; p. 87)

Expression of support or non-support from family and friends:

The fact that my mum has accepted me for who I am even though I am attracted to minors has helped me a lot. I know I would hurt her a lot if I acted out on my fantasies, which by the way I have already promised her I will never do. I would feel I am letting my family down if my selfcontrol fails, they have been real understanding with me and I can't fail (41, p. 115)

The first person I told was my father, and he was always supportive. [After arrest for child sexual abuse] members of my family learned about the news, some have rejected me totally and don't want to see me. One of my two families rejected me out of it, while the other one does not know. The friends who know are okay with it in general. However, I have recently lost friends, just because they found out I told a seventeenyear-old girl I liked her, without even asking her anything. People are in a state of hysteria right now and it's not healthy. (41, Carl; p. 121)

My family and friends have totally rejected me and no longer maintain any relationship with me. I generally turn for support to other minorattracted adults whom I know in real life. (41, Clive; p. 122)

I keep these feelings secret from my family and friends, so I don't think they know. The only support I know of is within online discussion boards where other Adults Who Are Sexually Attracted to Children hang out If any other support resources exit, I would be reluctant to use them, out of fear that I would be reported for being attracted to children, even though I've never actually touched any child inappropriately, and don't' consider myself to pose any danger to any child. (41, Ken; p. 123)

I can't say they approve, but they have been supportive. My arrest made it impossible to keep that particular cat in the bag. My parents were there for my trial (1,500 miles away from their home). I have a warm relationship with my parents as well as my sister and brother and their kids. (41, Jerry; p.127)

My friends/family are disturbed by the nature of my sexuality, they don't like to hear much details, but they have always trusted me to be dealing with it and as one of my friends said to me, 'I know you and you are not a predator'. . . I have a number of support networks in place. First, I have God and my church family. . . .I have my online MAA community. . . Through them I've come to better understand and accept myself and my sexuality. It was such a relief just to discover that I was not alone in loving boys but have no desire to do anything socially/sexually harmful to them. (41, Louis; p. 130)

There's really no one from my life that I'd like to tell. I wouldn't tell my family since I could not see anything positive coming out from that, and unlike some others, keeping it a secret isn't hard or stressful for me. (41, Ben; p. 123)

The dilemma

Can pedophiles be cured? Pedophilia, like any other type of sexual orientation, cannot be changed or reoriented. Blaming the pedophile for his sexual fantasies and involuntary desires is counterproductive, and certainly won't protect children. On the other hand, it is possible to help the pedophile to recognize that he is responsible for his behavior, and to help him develop strategies for avoiding sexual situations with children, and to learn how to control his impulses. Different forms of psychotherapy and drug treatment programs are available, but the success rate is mixed. Outcomes are better when the pedophile is motivated and committed to controlling his behavior. Family and other forms of social support groups can be extremely helpful in enhancing the benefits of therapy and medication. For the pedophile coming to terms with his affliction and learning how to control his desires is a life long effort.

It is easy demonize pedophiles as monstrous strangers ready to pounce on our children. This is why we drive our children everywhere, always trying to keep them in our sights. We resist accepting what all the studies tell us – the greatest danger to our children is not the stranger, but those that our children and we know – relatives and friends. At some deep level, we as a society do know that this is the case. Otherwise it would be difficult to explain why the majority of cases of child sexual abuse are not reported. To report them would mean that we would have to face the uncomfortable truth that relatives or friends we love and trust sexually abuse children. To expose them means that we risk destroying the normal relationships within the family, the networks which are essential to family cohesion and solidarity. We greet the child's accusation (if in fact the child does make an accusation) by denying it, blaming the child, and minimizing the abuse. As one victim reports after telling her mother that her father had sexually abused her: *"First she said it did not happen; I was making it up. . .Then after she thought about it for a while she said if it did happen she would have known. . .Then she came back at me and said what did I do to encourage it, that he was a good man, what did I do? Then she said, 'Well, you seem fine to me. It must not have been that bad. Let's not talk about it again."* (43, p. 175)

Even the abusing adults have difficulty in understanding the harm they cause. Fran Henry, the founder of Stop It Now!, was sexually abused by her father from the age of 12 to 16 writes when she confronted him many years later:

> *"I found my father did not understand how much damage he did to me when he abused me . . .Ignorance, not evil, lies at the heart of this devastation wrought on us and on our sexuality. Ignorance and a good measure of human greed and fear. As I witnessed my father's ignorance, I realized the he was caught in a a great trap of how society dealt with sexuality and sexual abuse – through silence and evasion"* (41, p. 181)

E. Olafson, D.L. Corwin, and R.C. Summit in their article *Modern History of Child Sexual Abuse Awareness: Cycles of Discovery and Suppression* state the dilemma of pedophilia:

> *The truth gets suppressed not because it is peripheral to major social interests, but because it is so central that as a society we choose to reject our knowledge of it rather than make the changes in our*

thinking and our institutions and our daily lives that sustained awareness of child sexual abuse demands. (44, p. 24)

The scope and nature of Child Sexual Abuse

Epidemiology: The sexual victimization of children covers a wide spectrum of sexual offenses and crimes, ranging from sexual fondling, exhibitionism, sexual intercourse, to using children in pornography, not all of which are always included under the term child sexual abuse. Nevertheless, all studies indicate that CSA in its various forms is a social problem of major proportions. Surveys of adults in the U. S. indicate that 25 – 40% of women and 8 – 13% of men report a history of sexual abuse. In a population study of sexual behaviors in the U.S., 12% of men and 17% of women reported being touched sexually by an older person. One recent survey estimated that 3.2% of children between 2 and 17 were sexually molested in 2002. Child protection authorities reported 78,000 cases of sexual abuse nationally in 2006. Surveys of the international literature indicate that 20% of women and 8% of men experienced some form of sexual abuse as children. In 2007 in the United Kingdom 10-11% of boys and 21-25% of girls under the age of 16 experienced forced sexual intercourse. The World Health Organization reports that on a global scale 150 million girls and women and 73 million boys have been victims of forced sexual intercourse.

Girls outnumber boys as victims. The risk for girls increases with age, while the risks for boys peak around puberty. Offenders are overwhelmingly male, ranging from adolescents to the elderly. Life stages at which offenses peak are adolescence (coincides with peak in delinquent behavior), and then during the thirties (presumably because access to children is greater). Other risk factors for CSA: not living with both parents, families characterized by separation, divorce, violence, substance abuse, lack of proper supervision.

Complexity of CSA: Sex offenders include adults, adolescents, or children related or unrelated to the victims. Most sex offenders do not conform to the stereotype prevalent in the media, that is, exclusively adult men sexually attracted to prepubescent children (pedophiles), who prey on children in public environments, highly resistant to treatment, and likely to continue offending. Most offenders are never caught, arrested, and convicted. Among those who are caught, most are not pedophiles. At least a third or more of adults who abuse children under 13 do not qualify as pedophiles, that is, they are not sexually attracted to children. Half of all victims are post-pubescent and range in age 12 – 17. About a third of offenders against adolescents are themselves adolescents. The adolescent offenders are not pedophiles but belong to groups of generally delinquent juveniles.

Two other data sources in the U.S. – the Third National Incidence Study of Child Abuse and Neglect (NIS-3) and the FBI's National IncidentBased Reporting System - give us a revealing picture of the offender population. During the period from 1986 to 1993 the NCIS-3 reported that natural parents accounted for 29%, other parents for 25%, and others in the caretaking role for 40% of the offenders; about 89% of the children were abused by a male, and 12% were abused by a female. The FBI data, compiled from reports from 12 states from 1991 to 1996, indicates that 67% of sexual assaults that came to the attention of law enforcement agencies involved victims, of whom 1 of every 7 was younger than 6 years, and a third were younger than 12 years. Eighty three percent (83%) of those younger than 12 years were female. Adults were the offenders in 60% of sexual abuse on children younger than 12 years, and 5 out of every 6 assaults took place in a residence. Almost all of the offenders were male, although females accounted for sexual abuse on children younger than 6 years. Strangers (persons unknown to the victim) accounted for less than 5% of the offenders, family members 42%, and family friends or acquaintances for 53% of the offenders.

To complicate matters, about a third of adult offenses against juveniles are characterized as "compliant victim" or "statutory sex offenses". These involve teenagers who have voluntary or semi-voluntary sexual relationships with adults, which can range from seduction by the adult to initiation by the teen. A number of them have made the national headlines. One recent case was that of Mary Kay Letourneau, the teacher who was sent to prison for having sex with an underage boy, nevertheless eventually married the youth and had children with him. Such cases present police, prosecutors, judges, psychiatrists, teachers, and families with questions that are different from the usual cases of CSA, and for which there are as yet no adequate responses.

The term 'statutory' refers to a relationship between an adult and juvenile that is illegal under the consent statutes of a given state (typically varying between 16 and 18), and which is characterized by the absence of coercion or force. Since the age of consent varies from one state to another, a particular relationship may be illegal in one state, but legal in another. Four types of these relationships have been studied: adolescent female/adult male (the most common and most studied), adolescent male/adult female (96% of adults who have sexual relationships with adolescent males are female), adolescent male/adult male (6% of adults who have sexual relationships with adolescent males are male), and adolescent female/adult female. The dynamics and motivations of the two participants in these relationships are quite diverse and complex, ranging from true affection, to sexual initiation, and exploitation.

Violent versus non-violent CSA. In 1927 the German physician Karl Abraham identified two categories of sexual abuse of minors. The first he called 'traumatic' – the offender is a stranger, the victim is clearly aware that it is wrong, reacts strongly, negatively, and reports the abusive act to the authorities. The assault is violent and it often ends with the victim's death, and the offender is usually not caught. This type is depressingly familiar to us – we read and hear about these cases with regularity. The sexual offender in these cases (some of whom are pedophiles) is the archetype of the pedophile as an evil monster that is portrayed in the media. Referring to this type of sexual abuse as 'traumatic' was completely understandable.

The second category Abraham called 'participant' - the abuse is non-violent, the victim knows the offender (very often a relative or trusted friend of the family) and especially if younger than 12 years old does not interpret the abuse as wrong, often has more than one experience with the offender, and keeps it a secret for many years. The offender exploits a child's normal need to feel loved, valued, and cared for, and seeks out and woos children who might be particularly vulnerable to his attentions. And since the offender is usually someone the child knows and trusts, the child acquiesces. Many victims recount that the abuse was not traumatic when it took place. Even in Abraham's day it was known that this type of abuse was much more common than the first, but was very often not reported to the authorities. Yet, in contrast to the 'traumatic' type of abuse, society's reaction to 'participant' cases when they came to light was more muted and ambivalent. Calling the abusive act 'participant' implied that the child was consenting to the abuse. The child therefore was partly to blame.

We may be baffled by the child's acquiescence. Why did the child not say no? Why did it happen multiple times? Why did the child not tell anyone right after it happened the first time? Why did the child continue in many cases to care about the offender? We ask ourselves these questions because we are seeing the abuse through adult eyes, projecting our own repulsion and horror on to the child, assuming that the child would react to the abuse as we would. We forget, however, that the child is not an adult, and that the child does not have the developmental maturity to understand what is happening. If the child has a close relationship to the offender, as is often the case, it is very difficult to say 'Stop, I don't like it.'

Most victims, especially if they were quite young when the abuse took place, do not understand the nature or meaning of what has happened to them until some time later in life. The harm or damage to the victim comes not from the abuse itself, but how the victim comes to feel about themselves and others much later. It is only then that they begin to understand the full import of their violation – and they react with shame, anger, a sense of betrayal, guilt, and very often blame themselves.

". . .on the good side people believed me . . .But the bad part was that they were also mad at me. They were saying 'Why would you have allowed that? How could you not have told anyone and had it gone on for so long. . .They didn't actually come out and say it, but it was clear that they thought I deserved some degree of the blame too". (43, p. 129)

"What did I do? What signal did I send that made him do that to me?" (43, p. 29)

"I think it happened because I was damaged. . .This is why he [a stepfather] sought me out; this is why I responded the way I did. I know what he did was wrong, but I cannot escape feeling that there

is something wrong with me." (43, p. 130)

"I have been in therapy for this for a long time and it is still difficult for me to come to terms with what happened and to accept that it is not my fault. . .The way I understand abuse is that it is something done to you against your will. But the way it happened to me, I guess I allowed it. So in that way I very much feel like it was my fault." (43, p. 132)

"They said if it happened I must have done something to encourage it. . .I was, like, what could I have done? I was eight . . .They said I was always after him for attention, following him around like a puppy." (43, p. 129)

The unfortunate tragedy for so many victims is that they feel they were complicit in their abuse. They *"blame themselves inappropriately for situations over which they had no control. Oddly, it is less painful to think you brought tragedy upon yourself than to face your vulnerability to mistreatment."* (47)

Are child sex molesters incorrigible?

Contrary to public perceptions, studies show that the overall re-offense rate for child molesters is lower than that for other criminals. Data from the state of Washington indicate that 2.8% of child sex abusers recommitted a sexual offense, and that 24.5% recommitted any (non-sexual) offense over a period of five years. In contrast, other types of felony offenders had a re-offense rate of 48% for all crimes. Analyses that combine data from many studies indicate that 14% of sex offenders recommit a sex offense after 5 years, and 24% after 15 years. The recidivism rates for juvenile abusers and family offenders are considerably lower than the overall rates. Researchers suggest that the lower recidivism rates for child sex abusers is partly due to the fact that in general child molesters are more likely to be educated and employed. The child sex abuser population is very diverse – at one end is a small group with very serious pathology and high recidivism rate, and at the other a much larger group that exhibits transitory sex offenses and much lower recidivism risk.

Vulnerability and resilience.

Recent studies link Child Sexual Abuse to a wide spectrum of serious mental and physical health problems, ranging from posttraumatic stress disorder to sexual dysfunctions, and even criminality in adulthood. However, there is little uniformity in responses either short or long term -the consequences and severity of the problems linked to CSA vary significantly from one person to another. The variables – whether genetic or familial - that influence or determine the diversity in responses are not well understood. Obvious factors that may be important are the child's age and level of developmental maturity at the time of the abuse, the duration of the abuse, the type of physical acts the abuse involved, the child's relationship to the offender, fear of retribution, or the sense of guilt or blame that the victim feels.

In one disturbing finding a significant proportion of cases, the sexual abuse victim may repeat the abuse later on other victims. For example, in a study published in 2003 investigators in England followed 224 male victims of sexual abuse, up to the age of 18 – 32 years, and assessed whether they had committed sexual offenses. A surprising 11.6% of the male victims became sexual perpetrators in later life, despite the fact that most of them had been under therapy for different periods of their life after being victimized. The authors report that intra-familial violence and neglect were associated with the repetition of sexual abuse, indicating that familial and social factors can be crucially important in determining the whether the CSA victims become repeat offenders, but also suggesting that familial and social conditions may play important roles in the long term outcome of CSA.

On a much more positive note are recent observations that 10% to 25% of CSA victims report no psychological problems in childhood, and that 20% to 40% of CSA victims report little or no detrimental symptoms as adults. These figures, while surprising, are not unexpected, since recent literature indicates that resilience is the most common response to trauma. Understanding the characteristics of resilient individuals and identifying the coping mechanisms used by them should help in developing resilience strategies in the more vulnerable victims of CSA.

While prevention of CSA seems like a hopeless enterprise, David Finkelhor, a noted expert on Child Sexual Abuse sounds a hopeful note:

Sexual abuse is a special challenge, different in many of its dimensions from other types of child maltreatment, crime, and child welfare problems. But enormous strides have been made to understand the problem, educate the public, and mobilize resources to address it. With additional research and program development, there is every reason to believe much more can be accomplished. (48, p. 188)

Colleen Patricia Williams, "Cracks in my Façade: Resentment"
14 x12" painted on galvanized metal with encaustin c 2013 Colleen
Patricia Williams Damage to a person and relationship of hidden
resentments

Chapter 7

Sexual Discontent and Its Origins

The tragedy of the bedroom

Man survives earthquakes, epidemics, the horrors of disease, and agonies of the soul, but all the time his most tormenting tragedy has been, is, and will always be, the tragedy of the bedroom (1, Leo Tolstoy)

We can surmise that what Tolstoy had in mind by the tragedy of the bedroom is sexual dissatisfaction. 'Tragedy' may be an exaggeration perhaps, but for individuals like Tolstoy for whom sex was very important, the adjective seems appropriate. Our sexual concerns and problems are different from the physical ailments, afflictions, and diseases that have plagued humankind since time immemorial. They are, in a real sense, spiritual ailments. The toll they take is on our spirit. It seems quite likely that people have always worried and wondered about the causes of their sexual problems, and if possible, to resolve them. We do know that men have complained about impotence consistently for many centuries. Women by comparison have remained conspicuously silent, and it is only beginning in the latter half of the 20th century that we have begun to hear their voices and their stories.

What about today? What types of sexual complaints are being reported currently? The Global Study of Sexual Attitudes and Behavior (GSSAB), the largest multinational, crosssectional study of sexual behavior to date, gives us a rough idea. In the survey standard questionnaire was administered to 27,500 men and women ages 40-80 years in 29 countries. Respondents rated the severity of the reported problem by indicating the frequency of occurrence – occasionally, sometimes, or frequently. Sampling was not uniform and this limits meaningful cross-cultural comparisons. In males the two most commonly reported problems were Early Ejaculation (sometimes or frequently, 13% in the U.S., 15.7 in the non-European West) and Erectile Difficulties (sometimes or frequently, 10% in the U. S., 11.2 % in the non-European West). In females the most frequent problems were Lack of Sexual Interest (sometimes or frequently, 12% in the U. S., 19.6% in the non-European West) and Orgasm difficulties (sometimes or frequently, 12% in the U. S., 18.7% in the non-European West). From this and other surveys we learn that sexual complaints are fairly common, but most occur occasionally and for the most part are transitory. Females have more sexual complaints than males, and female complaints of lack of lubrication and male complaints of erectile problems increase with age.

While the findings of these mass surveys give us a bird's eye view of the forest, we know little about the individual trees. In particular, they fail to give us a complete picture of the complexity of the origins and history of our sexual problems. Unlike many of our physical ailments, the 'tragedy of the bedroom' quite often can be traced to the 'problems of living' – difficulties, dilemmas, and predicaments that arise from our personal, familial, or cultural circumstances. Despite the huge amount of sex information (and unfortunately misinformation) available today, sexual problems resist easy or facile solutions. The absence of valid and reliable diagnostic criteria and the difficulty in integrating the medical and psychological or social determinants effectively pose special problems for psychiatrists and other mental health professionals.

Sexual discontent – a *perspective*

Great is the force of imagination, and much more ought the cause of melancholy to be ascribed to this alone, than to the distemperature of the body. (2, Robert Burton, The Anatomy of Melancholy)

The ancients, according to Michel de Montaigne, believed that *'a strong imagination brings on the event'*, a shrewd recognition of the power, both positive and negative, that the imagination has on our lives. Filtered through the prism of personal circumstance, family, religion, culture and mythology, our imagination contributes to many of our ailments, vexations, and complaints. It is probably the source of many of our sexual problems and our sexual discontent – the 'love melancholy' and 'anguish of the mind' – that can so often disturb our emotional well-being.

Masculinity and its discontents

We have reason to remake the intractable liberties taken by this member, which intrudes so tiresomely when we do not require it and fails us so annoyingly when we need it most, imperiously pitting its authority against that of the will, and most proudly and obstinately refusing our solicitations both mental and manual. (3, Michel de Montaigne)

In our popular mythology males are more interested in sex and have a stronger sex drive than females, and by and large, population surveys taken at face value support these views. In a large 1994 survey, while 33% of women reported being uninterested sex, only 16.5% of men reported the same; and 20% of women said sex was not pleasurable, but only 10% of men found no pleasure in sex. Males are also assumed to have uncomplicated views of sex: *". . . there is little or nothing to be learned or said about men and sex. The males after all, are so simple and quite content as long as they're getting enough"* (4, Paula Nicolson and Jennifer Burt). Women also tend to have the view that sex is easier and less problematic for men than for women. In response to the question: *"Do you think there's a difference between men and women's sexuality?"* a female responded: *"Yes, I think basically for men, it is a lot more of a physical thing. As a general rule, it appears to be that they are more easily excitable and have an orgasm. For women it's a lot slower. Women don't get turned on as easily or have orgasms easily."* (4, Paula Nicolson and Jennifer Burt)

Some would maintain that the readiness for sex is what being masculine implies. The historian Thomas Laqueur points out that "masculinity" entered the English language in 1748, suggesting "a new self-consciousness about what it meant to be a man." (5, p. 97) Unfortunately, we still struggle to define it – we have yet to agree on what masculinity means. For many, masculinity means 'potency', the ability to get and maintain an erection. Potency is a sign of competence, of virility. Perhaps men have sex not only for pleasure, but to prove they are competent. Before the modern world, proof of virility was having children. In the modern world having children doesn't have the importance it did before, and we have less tangible evidence of potency. Males may be particularly vulnerable to the power of their sexual imagination because so much of being a man is tied to potency. But potency – manhood - is inherently unstable, liable to be lost. The penis is unreliable, sometimes failing to respond when circumstances warrant, and its unreliability is a continual source of anxiety for men.

It is no wonder that the most common male sexual concern is impotence, or the inability to get and maintain an erection (the preferred term currently is erectile dysfunction, or erectile disorder, terms adopted because they sound more 'medical' and seems less psychologically stigmatizing). We don't know how prevalent erection problems were in previous historical periods. All we have is anecdotal information that men have complained about erection problems at least since ancient Egyptian times, and the preoccupation with potency and impotence has remained constant since then.

In some cases impotence anxiety can take the form of a mass delusion, an epidemic referred to as a 'penis panic' that can affect hundreds of men. In the 1980's an epidemic of 'penis snatchers' swept through West Africa, and according to the victims, sorcerers had shrunk their penises as a form of blackmail. Perhaps the best known of these mass delusions is the *koro* syndrome, a morbid belief that the penis is retracting into the abdomen, and that this could be fatal. Men may be so afraid of losing their penis that they may hold on to it continuously or attach weights to it to prevent it from disappearing. *Koro* appears predominately in China, Hong Kong, Singapore, Taiwan, and the Chinese in Malaysia. In India and Sri Lanka loss of semen syndromes (referred to as *Dhat* in India), characterized by the belief that semen is being lost through the urine. The symptoms include fatigue, weakness, headache, depression, impotence, and even loss of memory.

Although impotence is primarily an individual problem, in some societies it often had wider legal and political implications. Family fortunes, political stability, transfer of power in many societies depended on the potency of the ruler and ability to produce male heirs. Hence, potency, especially of the ruler, was a public concern during most of medieval Europe.

According to the jurist, Hincmar of Rheims writing in the 9th century, impotence, if attributed to witchcraft, or if found to be incurable by prayer or confession, was grounds for dissolution of a marriage, and this allowed both parties to remarry. Some men desiring to divorce their wives, were suspected of feigning impotence with their wife (but not with other women), claiming that the impotence was the wife's fault. Situational impotence (situational ED in technical language), or impotence under some circumstances, has been known for a long time. The Roman poet, Marcus Valerius Martiallis, known in English as Martial (40 – 104 CE) comments about a man who now desired the same woman he had spurned when she was his wife: **"Is it that when secure you lack appetite"** (5)

The English writer, William Byre, left a detailed account of his sexual adventures, both his successes as well as his failures. A woman **'could provoke me to do nothing because my roger would not stand with all she could do. About ten, I want home and said my prayers"** (6, p.97) In 18th century England, impotence and premature ejaculation were considered so important that its causes were debated in the English parliament in 1714. This is how the debate began:

There are many Men whose Penis very readily rises, nay lifts its self up in a most proud and ostentatious manner; but then its Fury is soon spent; like a Fire made of Straw, the Moment it approaches its Mistress's Door, it basely falls down at the very threshold, and piteously vomits out its frothy soul. . . For tho' he appears to be a Man, he is not presently to be concluded such, because there are some whose Ensignia of Manhood is a mere Cheat, gives mighty Hopes, but performs nothing.(6, p.72)

By the 19th and most of the 20th century, impotence became a private matter, but in the late 20th century, especially with the introduction of the so-called 'wonder drug' - Viagra – impotence reentered the public realm again. The popular media, especially newspapers, books, and magazine, is full of ads promoting products or therapies for treating impotence.

Impotence has always evoked ambivalent and contradictory feelings in men. According to historian Angus McLaren, *"Western culture has simultaneously regarded impotence as life's greatest tragedy and life's greatest joke"* (6, p.xiv).

Laments over the loss of potency are common in many classical writings. In *The Love Poems,* the Roman poet Ovid (43 BCE - 18 CE) describes his loss of potency (7)

Yes, she was beautiful and well turned out, The girl that I'd so often dreamed about. Yet I lay with her limp as if I loved not, A shameful burden on the bed that moved not. Though both of us were sure of our intent, Yet could I not cast anchor where I meant

The U. S. Army surgeon William A. Hammond wrote in 1883 *"no cause is . . .so destructive to the happiness of the average man as the loss of his virile power . . .his peace of mind is interfered with to an extent that no other disease is capable of causing."* (8)

In Ernest Hemingway's The Sun Also Rises, set in post World War I Italy, France and Spain, the protagonist Jake Barnes, recovering in a hospital from a war wound that has left him impotent (the wound itself is never described) receives a visit from an Italian officer:

Well, it was a rotten way to be wounded and flying on a joke front like the Italian. In the Italian hospital we were going to form a society. It had a funny name in Italian. I wonder what became of the others, the Italians. That was in the Ospedale Maggiore in Milano, Padiglione Ponte. The next building was the Padiglione Zonda. There was a statue of Ponte, or maybe it was Zonda. That was where the liaison colonel came to visit me. That was funny. That was about the first funny thing. I was all bandaged up. But they had told him about it. Then he made that wonderful speech: "You, a foreigner, an Englishman" (any foreigner was an Englishman) "have given more than your life." What a speech! I would like to have it illuminated to hang in the office. He never laughed. He was putting himself in my place, I guess. "Che mala fortuna! Che mala fortuna!" (9)

Consider the lament of a contemporary physician after the surgical removal of his testes (orchidectomy) to treat his prostate cancer:

After the orchidectomy I was still physically able to do almost all that I wanted. But I was impotent, and despite considering all the possibilities, from penile implants to pumps, I remained in a state of despair. As a consequence of trying to sort out this complex emotional tangle, I gradually became aware of how deep my gender socialization had been. Not only had I a sense of having been mutilated, I had also lost the very capacities that were symbolically associated with manhood in American society. I no longer had a prostate, I was incapable of an erection, and I had no testicles. More fundamentally, I had lost the capacity to experience desire. The sudden loss of libido produced forms of suffering I had not anticipated. The initial forms were stimulated by my context: I taught at a university each day; on campus and elsewhere, I encountered young people caught in the throes of raging hormones. Because I had lost the capacity to experience desire did not mean that I was not tormented by memories of desire. (10)

At the same time, songs and ballads have often made fun of men unable to satisfy their exigent wives.

Tom Farthing, or The Married Woman's Complaint:

Tom Farthing, Tom Farthing, thou mak'st me mad, Tom Farthing

'Twas not for this I did thee wed, nor brought thee to my marriage bed. But 'twas to lose my maiden head, of which I'm wondrous weary (6, p.62)

Or in *The Forced Marriage; or Unfortunate Celia,* Celia sings

When my fumbler's in bed,

and has laid down his head

he lies with closed eyes

just as though he was dead.

(6, p.62)

Accusations of impotence were a popular form of insulting other men. Martial, known for his witty poems, was particularly adept at such insults:

You no longer rise, Marius, except in your sleep, and your penis begins to piss onto the middle of your feet, your shriveled cock is stirred by your weary fingers, thus solicited, does not lift its useless head (6)

For many males the main lament about aging has been the decline in sexual drive and activity. We read in the King James translation of the Hebrew Bible (Kings I:1–4) that King David, a prodigious womanizer all of his life, in his seventies *"gat no heat."* The young woman sent to arouse him *"cherished the king and ministered to him: but the king knew her not."*

Stories of old men married to young, demanding wives were a staple in medieval literature:

She was young and he was old, And therefore he feared to be a cuckold. And how should it otherwise be? old age is a disease of itself, loathsome, full of suspicion and fear; when it is at best, unable, unfit for such matters. (2)

Or consider Mark Twain in his laconic, unsparing, and unsentimental commentary about the aging male:

But man is only briefly competent; and only then in the moderate measure applicable to the word in his sex's case. He is competent from the age of sixteen or seventeen thenceforward for thirty-five years. After fifty his performance is of poor quality, the intervals are wide, and its satisfactions of no great value to either party; whereas his great-grandmother is as good as new. There is nothing the matter with her plant. Her candlestick is as firm as ever, whereas his candle is increasingly softened and weakened by the weather of age, as the years go by, until at last it can no longer stand, and is mournfully laid to rest into the hope of a blessed resurrection which is never to come. (11)

Or the lament of a woman who although of advanced age wanted to remain sexually active:

I have gone through at least six men in the past 13 years since my husband died. The first one talked nothing but sex, and he was certainly handsome, and though his penis was the most glorious work of art ever created, with a lot of work, we could manage to get it to stand up for a few minutes, but when it came to actually performing, it would collapse at the thought of what it was expected to do. I have a TV in the bedroom, so we got to see a lot of late night television. (12)

Not all men, however, see their diminishing loss of sexual vigor with dismay:

Greet impotence with a sense of relief, like getting off a wild horse.(13)

It is particularly interesting to note that in the Kinsey study, *Sexual Behavior in the Human Male* (1948), American men, especially young men, rarely reported impotence problems. Transitory erectile problems occurred but they were considered to be due to mental or emotional preoccupation and not of major concern. Kinsey devoted less than four pages to a section entitled "Old Age and Impotence" since presumably it was not of any special import. It was simply considered to be a common outcome of old age. Many men at that time apparently accepted the loss of sexual vigor with advancing age with equanimity. In the 21st century this is no longer the case.

The causes of and cures for impotence have a complex and tortuous history. Different cultures in different eras assigned different causes and cures for impotence. In earlier times impotence was blamed on revenge of the gods, magic, sorcery, curses by a supernatural force such as a ghost, or imbalance in the bodily humors. Michel de Montaigne relates the story of one Amasis, King of Egypt:

Amasis, king of Egypt, married a very beautiful Greek girl called Laodice; but though he had shown himself a regular gallant everywhere else, he found himself unable to enjoy her. Believing that there was some sorcery in this, he threatened to kill her. But she, considering his trouble to be of the imagination, sent him to his devotions. He made his vows and promises to Venus, and on the first night after the performance of his oblations and sacrifices found his potency divinely restored. (3, p.41)

In the 18th century diet and lack of exercise were to blame; in the 19th, masturbation or sexual deviancy was the culprit. The physician William H. King in his book Spermatorrhea, Impotence and Sterility (1897) wrote that *"true (physical) impotence . . . will always present the history of masturbation."* (6). The U.S. Army surgeon William Hammond (1883), on the other hand, argued that those who practiced deviant sexual behavior were impotent because they failed to be aroused by heterosexual intercourse.

In the 20th century different causes were proposed depending on who was consulted. The psychiatrist Wilhelm Stekel in his two-volume text *Impotence in the Male* (1927), maintained that "impotence is a social disorder". For him all impotence was "psychic impotence". (6). For the Freudians, repressed sexuality and unconscious conflicts were the cause of impotence, and only psychoanalysis could bring about a cure. On the other hand, Edwin Hirsch in his *Impotence and Frigidity* (1966) dismissed psychoanalysis as an ineffective cure. Instead he argued that it contributed to impotence because it reinforced men's passive acceptance of women's liberation, hence giving rise to a 'culture of wishy-washy men'. The urologist Leonard Wershub in his book *Sexual Impotence in the Male* (1959), although accepting the notion current at that time that only 10% of impotence had an organic cause, nevertheless maintained that urologists would do a much better job of treating the remaining 90% of impotent males than psychiatrists or psychoanalysts.

Times have changed. In the 21st century urologists assure us that impotence is really a plumbing problem – vascular blockage – one that can be treated easily and successfully with a class of drugs known as phosphodiesterase type 5 (PDE5) inhibitors, much better known by their trade names *Viagra*, *Cialis*, and *Levitra*. The introduction of *Viagra* in 1998 promised eternally youthful sexual vigor for all men and, probably because of that, was a financial blockbuster for its maker, Pfizer Pharmaceuticals. *Viagra* also made more evident the disparity in the way societies view male and female sexuality. It took 34 years for the birth control pill to be approved in Japan, but only six months to approve the sale of *Viagra*. In the U. S., after almost 60 years since the first birth control pill was approved, contraception for women continues to be a divisive and contentious issue, while *Viagra* and its cousins are advertised widely on television without public or religious protest. This is a reminder that men see themselves as the final arbiters of sexual behavior and practices for both sexes, while women should remain silent and acquiesce. Not all women remain silent, however. Many women did not view *Viagra* with the same acclaim as men and they registered their complaints. One example of the thousands of letters to the editor of Newsweek read: '*We don't need more virile senior male citizens thinking they are virile teenagers. We have enough of that already. What about birth control for men, that's what we really want!*' (12)

The female also rises

Sexual boredom is the most pandemic dysfunction in this country

(Judith Seifer, former president of the American Association of Sex Educators, Counselors, and Therapists)

Female sexuality has always been viewed as problematic. Two opposing images of the female have persisted through Western history – the seductive *femme fatale* and the asexual Madonna – the temptress and the mother. In the classical Greek and Roman world, women were seen as highly sexed creatures, and their pleasure in intercourse was thought to be greater than that of men. *Aphrodite*, the Greek goddess of love and beauty, was the archetype of a robust female sexuality; she embodied seduction, sexual energy, and pleasure. According to legend, the other gods were jealous of her beauty and feared that she would ignite a war between them. They appealed to Zeus, who married her to Hephaestus, the lame god of metallurgy and sculptors, and not considered a threat to the other gods. Aphrodite's seductive power was deemed too dangerous by the Greek patriarchal society that managed to channel seduction and pleasure to one class of women. An Athenian could thus declare:

We have courtesans for pleasure, concubines to look after the day-to-day needs of the body, wives that we may breed legitimate children and have a trusty warden of what we have in the house (6, p.6)

The classification of women into these categories revealed the ambivalent view of the sexual potential of the female – attraction, fascination, denial, and fear, all at the same time – always mysterious and enigmatic. The historian, Elaine Pagels, comments on a long poem dating back to the first century of the Christian era. The poem titled Thunder, Perfect Mind, found in 1945 among many texts in the buried Coptic library of Nag Hammadi, gives us a vision of the eternal female principle in a series of antitheses astounding for its time, and probably bewildering in our time.

I am the whore and the holy one. I am the wife and the virgin. I am the mother and the daughter. I am the members of my mother. I am the barren one and many are her sons. I am she whose wedding is great, and I not taken a husband. I am the midwife and she who does not bear. I am the solace of my labor pains. I am the bride and the bridegroom. Why, you who hate me, do you love me, and hate those who love me? You who deny me, and confess me, and you who confess me, deny me. You who tell the truth about me, lie about me, And you who lied about me, tell the truth about me. (14)

Three centuries later St. Augustine saw the female in the same way and set the tone for what became the predominant Western view of the female for many centuries: *"What is the difference whether it is a wife or mother, it is still Eve, the temptress that we must beware of in any woman."* (15) The woman's sexual urges were the undoing of men. Chastity, modesty, and fidelity, rather than lust, desire and seduction, became the models of feminine behavior, qualities that not only suppressed the female's sexuality, but also confirmed her powerlessness. Her sexuality was submerged under the demands of maternity and the responsibilities of attending to the home. In the U.S., the view that women are (or should be) less sexed than men can be traced to physicians in the 19th century who maintained that women were maternal, rather than carnal creatures. The eminent Victorian physician William Acton (1857) summarized the prevailing notion in polite society: *"I should say that the majority of women, happily for them, are not very much troubled with sexual feelings of any kind"*. (16) Even in our post sexual-revolution times these biases still permeate much of the idealized view of women: women should not appear to be as sexual as men.

Excessive sexual desire in a woman is considered dangerous and anxiety-producing, especially in men. Ironically, as we shall see below, the lack of sexual feelings is now seen as a type of female sexual disorder that requires medical treatment. What used to be considered sexual virtue has become a mental disorder.

Sharp distinctions between acceptable behaviors and pleasures of men and women, were imposed, perhaps as a way to deal with male anxiety about female sexuality. Male superiority was assumed without question, and the woman's role was to reflect that superiority. To be sure, there were exceptions – free spirits who contravened the cultural and religious norms of their time. One example that comes to mind is Mary Ann Evans, better known as George Eliot, the pen name of the English novelist during the Victorian era, and who lived with a married man for over 20 years. In general, however, the female free spirits, at least in novels, plays, and operas of the 18th and 19th century, always ended up badly. Anna Karenina, in Tolstoy's novel, to appease her readers and pay for her sin of adultery, jumps in front of a train. Emma Bovary, in Flaubert's novel, dies a gruesome death.

In the main, however, the female's subservient sexual role was accepted by the wider society. Professor Shoshana Felman, who has written extensively about this topic summarizes the male – female relationship through most of Western history: **"Women have served all these centuries as looking glasses possessing the magic and delicious power of reflecting the figure of man at twice its natural size."** (17)

Far reaching social, economic, educational, religious, and political transformations beginning in the 19th century led to profound changes in society, female – male relations and marriage itself. In particular, marital sexuality began to expand beyond its procreative role to include sexual pleasure, for the woman especially. Not all women were receptive to this change initially, for it required them to assume a sexual role that had been reserved for prostitutes. The young protagonist in an 1897 Parisian play *Les trois filles de M. Dupont* (Mr. Dupont's Three Daughters) by Eugene Brieux reacts angrily to what she considers her husband's outrageous bedroom behavior: *"They used to say about us: housewife or harlot. Now it's all changed. There's been progress— you need both in the same woman: housewife and harlot."* (18).

The last quarter of the 19th century also saw the birth of psychiatry, which with its focus on sexual deviance, perversions, and unusual sexual behaviors – homosexuality, transsexuality, masochism, sadism, fetishism – tended to paint a dark picture of sexuality. In the case of women, there was a strong focus on frigidity and nymphomania. Too little (frigidity), or too much (nymphomania), sexual desire, were seen as symptoms of developmental mental disorders. According to the Freudian psychoanalytic school, female sexuality developed in the transfer of erotic zones from the clitoris as a child to the vagina as an adult. The vaginal orgasm was the 'mature' form of sexuality in that it prepared the woman for reproduction and heterosexuality. Frigidity was defined as the failure to experience a vaginal orgasm, and would if untreated, lead to irritability or hysteria.

On the other hand, women who sought sexual satisfaction (that is, desired clitoral stimulation) were like men, and liable to become lesbians or worse, nymphomaniacs, a condition that could lead to neurosis, personal, and social disintegration. Interestingly, a decidedly different view was provided in the marital advice manuals that began to find a receptive audience among the middle classes in both Europe and the United States in the late 19th and the early decades of the 20th century. The overall message of many of these manuals was clear: a happy and successful marriage now depended on sexual pleasure and fulfillment for both the woman and the man.

But there were problems. Helena Wright, British pioneer in family planning and contraception, argued that the impediments to sexual fulfillment for women were due to differences between the two sexes. *"A man's sex feelings are easily and quickly aroused, and quickly satisfied, and the actual sensations are limited to the relatively small area of the skin of the penis. A woman's desires, on the contrary, are neither quickly aroused nor quickly satisfied"* (19).

The wedding night was critically important for the future conjugal life of the couple, for a wife traumatized by what she might see as the brutality of her husband, could forever limit her potential for sexual happiness. The woman had the "potential of a keen sexual appetite" and it was the husband's responsibility to "arouse and maintain it" with special care and tenderness. The husband's role was to bring about his bride's transformation from girlhood to womanhood. Honoré de Balzac, author of the classic 19th French work, *La Commedie Humaine,* and who also wrote a marriage manual (Physiology of Marriage, 1829) gave the following advice: ***"Never begin marriage with a rape. . . Skillfully grasping the subtleties of pleasure, developing them, finding novel ways to practice them, giving them original expression, that is what constitutes the genius of the lover or the husband."*** (20).

Frigidity, instead of being due to abnormal erotic development from child to adult, was now interpreted as the failure of the husband to elicit and develop the latent sexuality of the wife. The consequence if he failed, discontent, irritability, or hysteria that could lead to chronic nervous and mental illness for his poor wife. But the husband had to be very careful because if he was too successful in awakening his wife's sexuality, she might veer off into nymphomania, which could land the poor wife in an insane asylum.

What is perhaps most striking about these prescriptions for a happy conjugal life is the complete passivity assumed for women before marriage – she is an empty vessel that has to be shaped and decorated by the skill of her husband. This is a striking perception: in contrast to the Freudian view, where the woman is instead seen as innately asexual. At the same time, however, once her sexuality has been awakened, it becomes a formidable force, difficult to control, acquiring a life of its own. Female sexuality once awakened was a problem for men. Balzac expressed this unease very emphatically:

> *The art of governing a woman is even less well known than that of choosing one. Nevertheless, marital politics involves no more than the steady application of three principles which must lie at the heart of your conduct. The first is never to believe in what a woman says; the second, always to look for the intention behind her actions rather than focus on the surface; and the third, not to forget that a woman is never so talkative as when she is silent, never so energetic as when she is at rest. (20)*

The male perception of the female as cryptic and enigmatic may have been the source of Freud's classic statement:

Despite my 30 years of research into the feminine soul, I have not been able to answer the great question that has never been answered: what does a woman want? (21)

A very early response to this question, even before it was asked in the rhetorical way Freud did was from Medb, legendary Irish queen and warrior who set high standards for her husband: *"For I asked a harder wedding gift than any woman ever asked before from a man in Ireland - the absence of meanness and jealousy and fear"* (22)

What was Freud driving at? His question may seem disparaging, facetious, and even misogynist, but it does underscore a real dilemma. For the feminists of three or four decades ago the widely accepted assumption, perhaps in reaction to the centuries of male sexual domination, was that the female erotic drive was innate, powered from within, and that it did not depend on being initiated by someone else, especially a male.

Consider comments supporting this view:

There is the thing going round that men have this uncontrollable desire. I don't think it is much different for women. There are people in both sexes who look for a relationship where sex is the most important thing. I don't think it really applies only to the men. (4)

In terms of pleasure I find it very difficult to associate emotion and sex together. Because I have a problem now, a serious relationship has ended, almost a year ago. If I were to just have a physical relationship I would feel absolutely fine, utterly in control. I can manipulate the situation however I want. If I want to have sex with somebody I can. I don't say 'no'. I feel totally in control. In an arrogant type of way, maybe that is a defense mechanism. But tying emotion with sex I find very difficult, because it becomes dangerous, because somebody has got an emotional hold on you and you can be judged by your behavior. (4)

My husband doesn't want sex and I need it so bad. His new job has created stress and is developing into a work anxiety meanwhile I am so horny and have developed a sexual anxiety which is causing me to be stressed out and frustrated. I'm not quite sure what to do as I struggle through my evenings feeling very unloved and unwanted. My girlfriends have told me to find someone on the side but I couldn't do that. I married my husband for better or worse and that's a promise I have to keep. (23)

However, reality is much more complex. An assembly of new qualitative studies dispense with statistical surveys, and focus on in-depth personal, detailed interviews or on clinical experience. They provide important insights into the complexities of the nature and diversity of the erotic drive of the female. In particular, they may lead us to understand why lack of sexual drive is one of the most common sexual complaints that contemporary women have.

Consider the work of Lisa Diamond, professor of psychology and gender studies at the University of Utah. Her studies suggest that sexual desire in the female is determined by a search for intimacy and emotional connection. She begins her book, Sexual Fluidity: Understanding Women's Love and Desire as follows:

"In 1997, the actress Anne Heche began a widely publicized romantic relationship with the openly lesbian comedian Ellen DeGeneres after having had no prior same-sex attractions or relationships. The relationship with DeGeneres ended after two years, and Heche went on to marry a man. Julie Cypher left a heterosexual marriage for the musician Melissa Etheridge in 1988. After 12 years together, the pair separated and Cypher – like Heche – has returned to heterosexual relationships. . . . What's going on?" (24)

From her close study of nearly 100 young women and the many shifts they made between sexual identities and detailed descriptions of their erotic lives, Diamond concludes that for the participants in her study, and perhaps for all women, sexual desire is fluid and malleable, dictated by the search for emotional closeness that can override any innate sexual orientation. Sexual desire often emerges when a woman develops a strong emotional connection to another person, whether male or female. Changing partners reflects the search for a relationship that restores the emotional connection and intimacy. The lack of sexual desire may be simply due to the absence of a partner, or, if partnered, the loss of intimacy or emotional closeness.

Consider an interview participant commenting on her emotional response to sex:

"The fundamental thing about caring and feeling something for a person—the fact that you have someone who does care for you as a person—not for your body. To have a stable relationship where the basis is one of love. It is important for me to have physical contact with them. I am physical I like to hug and hold hands and have that comforting relationship. I wouldn't say that orgasms come anywhere near the top of the list." (4)

A woman's motivation for sex and ease of feeling sexual arousal often depends on her partner. In a recent study exploring the criteria for female sexual arousal disorder (FSAD), the authors conclude

Among women who found it difficult to get sexually aroused, the majority reported they would have liked to receive more effective physical stimulation from a sexual partner. Importantly, even in the subsample of partnered women who easily became sexually aroused, 56% reported the same wish. It is possible, therefore, that in the vast majority of cases in which a clinician would administer a diagnosis of FSAD, that if more effective stimulation were applied, arousal may not be impaired, and the FSAD diagnosis would not be given. These data reinforce that adequate and sufficient sexual stimulation is required and very important to women's sexual experience. More importantly, diagnosing a sexual dysfunction in a woman when the etiology is related to poor technique or (perhaps) partner-dependent factors seems illogical. (25)

That's not the whole story, however. Marta Meana, professor of psychology at the University of Nevada, Las Vegas, argues on the basis of her studies that female desire is not always relational, but narcissistic. Bad relationships may kill desire, but good ones do not necessarily spark it. A participant in one of her studies relates: *"We kiss. We hug. I tell him, 'I don't know what it is.' We have a great relationship. It's just that one area".* (26) Meana notes that women's erotic fantasies focus on getting, rather than giving pleasure. Meana notes, for women, "being desired is the orgasm" Meana comments. In long term relationships women are more likely than men to lose interest in sex.

A study of the waning of desire in women in outwardly happy relationships finds that for many of the women an important measure of their desirability, and therefore their feeling sexual desire, was external validation from other men (27)

I don't feel sexy—It's not like when you walk by a construction site and all these men are whistling—getting the attention of another person just to get a compliment or just a glance makes you feel good. (34 year old)

Now it is the same guy and there is no novelty anymore. Would I be tempted if another man initiated it? Perhaps. I don't know . . . perhaps feeling beautiful again, feeling attractive to somebody else, desirable to somebody else. (33 year old)

He's such a good guy, like kind of wholesome . . . sometimes I wish he had a little more bad boy in him. Like those are the types of guys I really liked, but I knew it wouldn't be the type of guy I should marry. (33 year old)

Meana does not dismiss the relational aspect of female sexuality. Intimacy and stability are important, but just as the woman above wishes that her partner had "a little bad boy in him", Meana comments: *". . .it is wrong to think that because relationships are what women choose they're the primary source of women's desire"* (28)

Meana concludes her study with the following comment:

There is likely a wide diversity of psychosocial factors that impact on different women's sexual desire and a good chance that the very relational conditions many women strive for and value may not, in and of themselves, be conducive to the facilitation of desire. . .Despite self-reportedly happy marriages, they (the participants in her study) frequently referred to the excitement sparked from the attention of other men. Some felt certain that their desire would return if they experienced a new partner. We have long associated the link between sexual excitement and novelty to men's sexual desire, but rarely do we associate it to women's desire. In our sample, closeness had led to familiarity which had too often led to efficient but boring sex. (27)

The narcissistic aspect of female sexual desire is evident in the recent movie The Kids Are Alright. The character Jules in a long term relationship with Nic and with two children fathered by artificial insemination, has a fling with Paul (played by Mark Ruffalo), who happens to have been the sperm donor for the children. As portrayed in the movie, Jules desire for Paul is driven by his intense desire to have sex with her at all costs.

Or consider the reflection of the female protagonist, Kathie Jones, in a short story by the English writer Margaret Drabble. Kathie is thrilled by the aggressive sexual attentions of a womanizing American playwright:

"She thought of his face, looking at her, heavy, drunk, sexy, battered, knowing, and wanting her, however idly: and it gave her a permanent satisfaction that she'd been able to do that to him, that she'd been able to make a man like that look at her in that way. It was better than words, better than friendship. " . . .It's an awful thing to say, but that's how some women are. Even nice, sensible, fulfilled, happy women like Kathie Jones. . . What ever can one do about it?" (29)

Or consider the heroine Christine in Theodore Fontane's novel On Tangled Paths, speaking of her marriage that has shifted under her feet:

"In spite of having the best of husbands whom she loved as much as he loved her, she yet did not possess that peace for which she longed; in spite of all their love, his easy-going temperament was no longer in harmony with her melancholy. " (30)

Sexual discontent - origins

The way in which we attempt to manage our sexual tribulations depends to a large extent on how the origin of the sexual problem is imagined. Roughly speaking there have been two models for understanding the origin of our sexual problems. One model – call this the *biological origins model* – proposes that they arise from an organic defect, an intrinsic pathology, a physiological abnormality, a genetic defect or some as yet undefined 'chemical imbalance' in the brain. Our personal circumstances or personal relationships may exacerbate our problem, but they are not the cause. Biologically oriented psychiatry favors this model, and it is easy to see why. The great success of modern medicine and the pharmaceutical industry in their collaboration in the development of antibiotics and the triumph over infectious diseases has conditioned us to expect, even believe, that most, if not all, of our ills and afflictions have an organic cause, and that they can be relieved or cured with a pill. A visit to a doctor more often than not results in a prescription for some medication – we probably would be disappointed if it didn't. We still hold on to that belief even when confronted with the serious difficulties in treating the chronic, complex diseases, such as heart disease, diabetes, dementia, and cancer, all without a clear causal agent, and for which no entirely successful therapy is available. We argue, of course, that it is only a matter of time before suitable pharmacological therapies will be discovered.

The alternative view – for ease of reference, the *social origins model* - proposes that our sexual problems arise from vicissitudes of our life histories, a repressive sexual upbringing, cultural or religious teachings, ignorance of sexual matters, behavioral maladjustments, a history of physical or sexual abuse, abusive or problematic personal relationships, unfulfilled sexual expectations. Simply put – the complexity of the problems of living contribute to our sexual tribulations; no simple pill can cure or resolve them. Let's consider each in turn.

Biological causes – the medical solutions

Conceptualization of the etiology of sexual disorders has been shifting in various ways: from an interpersonal to an individual model, and from a psychodynamic to a biological model. (31)

Psychiatry is increasingly emphasizing a biological interpretation of mental illness and sexual problems. With a sense of lament a prominent psychiatrist comments:

"The goal of contemporary bio-psychiatry . . . is not the achievement of deep insight into one's personality but symptom relief, accomplished by breaking down and classifying all of the various diseases of the brain and nervous system; identifying criteria that allow the psychiatrist to diagnose the proper disease; and prescribing psychotropic drugs . . to

eliminate debilitating symptoms" (32)

In this perspective, personal relationships, familial circumstances, cultural and/or religious issues are less likely to be seen as important or relevant by many psychiatrists. The shift from a 'psychodynamic' to a 'biological' focus is due in part to significant changes in the health care landscape in the U. S.: the dominance of managed care organizations that place a premium on straightforward diagnoses, their focus short-term treatment and presumed cost-effectiveness. Add to that the pharmaceutical industry's aggressive interest in redefining sexual function norms, using direct-to-consumer advertising, promotion of offlabel prescribing, and promising simple drug treatments for sexual problems.

The therapeutic success of Viagra in the treatment of impotence has reinforced the notion not only that our sexual problems can be treated like medical problems amenable to pharmacological intervention, but has also fueled an expectation that a pharmaceutical solution to all of our sexual problems is just around the corner. Before the 1960s, for example, impotence was generally considered to be psychogenic in origin and treatment came under the purview of psychiatrists. But now in the 21st century urologists assure us that impotence is really a hormonal (low testosterone) and/or vascular problem (blockage of blood to the penis). Hormonal and vascular problems are frequently mentioned as the causes of decrease in sexual drive and increase in erectile problems as men age. Despite this general trend, men differ considerably in how quickly they age sexually. The Baltimore Longitudinal Aging Study in the 1970s found that men who reported the highest frequency of sexual activity when they were young had the slowest decline in sexuality as they aged.

This finding has been ignored when focusing on the great success of drugs like *Viagra,* first available in 1998, in promoting erections. *Viagra, and Cialis and Levitra,* introduced later, belong to a class of compounds known as phosphodiesterase type 5 (PDE5) inhibitors that exert their effects by inducing the relaxation of the smooth muscle of the penis, thereby allowing blood to accumulate and thus leading to the erection. PDE5 inhibitors are just the latest in a long line of treatments for impotence that date back to ancient Egyptian times. The ingenuity of some of these treatments (as well as the sense of desperation that led to them) is quite impressive: electrocautery of the penis, hydrotherapy, surgical removal of tight foreskins, removal of 'irritable' rectums, rest, abstinence, application of herbal extracts to the penis, the use of the first oral drug – yohimbine, an extract from the African yohimbe tree, considered to have aphrodisiac effects (1900), diverse forms of androgen therapies – ingestion or injection of testicular extracts from animals, or transplantation of testes from animals or executed criminals. A radical shift in the management of impotence from psychiatrists to urologists took place with the introduction of penile prosthetic devices, such as inflatable penile implants (1973), vacuum erection device therapy (1983), intracavernosal penile injection therapy (1995), medicated urethral system for erections (MUSE) (1997).

PDE5 inhibitors have become the most prevalent form of oral therapy especially for non-persistent impotence. Occasional impotence is probably quite common and no cause for concern, but for men particularly sensitive to what they regard as the ultimate sign of masculinity, even a few instances of impotence will be very troubling. Young males will very likely be more troubled by instances of impotence than older males, many of whom have accepted perhaps with reluctant equanimity that erectile problems tend to increase with age. PDE5 inhibitors are an easy and quick fix for most cases of occasional impotence. Once PDE5 inhibitors became available, the urologists, in turn, lost control of the game to primary care physicians, and with the advent of Internet pharmacies the procurement of these types of drugs has turned into a virtual free for all, where now anyone whether they suffer from erectile problems or not can obtain them.

There is no doubt that from an individual perspective the discovery of the PDE5 inhibitors has been a boon to millions of men. Less well known, perhaps, is that PDE5 inhibitors are not the hoped-for universal therapy for erectile problems: they are effective in only about 70% of men; they are not a long term cure, but a temporary remedy; long term use does not decrease the individual's need for the drug; studies with *Viagra* indicate that its effects diminish with use and time, perhaps accounting in part for the low continuance rates (another factor could be the high cost). All of which reminds us that the causes of impotence are complex. Simple, fast, and permanent cures in the form of a pill are not always available. Nevertheless, a clinic in San Diego specializing in erectile disorder and premature ejaculation promises in its advertisement *"we will resolve your problem in one visit."*

The financial bonanza for pharmaceutical companies that came with the PDE5 inhibitors has stimulated the industry to broaden its search for market opportunities by developing 'sexuo-pharmaceuticals' for enhancing sexual function in targeted populations. Part of the focus of this development effort is in redefining the 'norms' for sexual function. Consider the ageing male, a new and promising target. During the 19th century physicians considered sex after 60 to be injurious to health. Nature's plan was that sex was reserved for the reproductive years, after which a quieter, sexless phase of life would begin. In contrast, continued sexual function is now seen as necessary for a healthy old age, and the waning of sexual function with age is now seen as a sign of deteriorating health and possible pathology. The press release for the 2007 North American Congress on the Aging Male was headlined *"Failure to treat sexual dysfunction can pose serious risk for aging males" and warned that "leading research scientists and clinicians from around the world are reaching the consensus that failure to treat decreased sexual function in aging males may actually put them at greater risk for heart disease and cancer"* (33).

Despite the lack of evidence showing a causal connection between the two, a new cultural ideal for sexual function in the aging male – sexual potency and virility at any age - is being defined and promoted under the guise of preventing heart disease and cancer. What was once considered a normal part of aging is now being seen as 'dysfunctional'. A new disease entity is being manufactured, but the good news – we are told - is that it is treatable, opening up a huge potential market of patients as the population ages.

Critics within and outside the psychiatric profession have been pointing out that the biological interpretation of mental illness and sexual problems, in particular, has led to an increasingly disturbing relationship between the pharmaceutical industry and the American Psychiatric Association, one whose primary beneficiary has been the pharmaceutical industry. Increased industry funding of psychiatric and sexual function research and their sponsorship of and ubiquitous presence at professional meetings and conferences has facilitated the creation, definition, and promotion of new disorders for the benefit of the industry. The intrusion of the industry into medicine has led to an unhealthy medicalization of sex, or as some of the harshest critics would say, 'disease mongering' - turning ordinary sexual problems or complaints into serious medical problems, treating personal problems as mental disorders that require medication. Arnold Relman, former editor of the New England Journal of Medicine, has lamented that *'the medical profession is being bought by the pharmaceutical industry, not only in terms of the practice of medicine, but also in terms of teaching and research.'* (34)

The emergence of *Female Sexual Dysfunction* in the late 90s is a good example of this trend. The female became the center of attention in 1997 when a new disorder, *Female Sexual Dysfunction* (FSD) was discussed in the pharmaceutical industry-sponsored Cape Cod conference 'Sexual Function Assessment in Clinical Trials'. At the time it wasn't clear what Female Sexual Dysfunction meant. The introduction to the supplement of the issue of the *International Journal of Impotence Research* in which the proceedings of the conference were published stated unambiguously:

In the area of female sexual dysfunction, there is widespread lack of agreement about the definition of sexual dysfunction, its pathophysiology or clinical manifestations, and the optimal approach for research or clinical assessment (35).

Despite these uncertainties, Pfizer, the maker of *Viagra,* tried to have it (labeled the 'red' Viagra in the media) approved to treat one presumed form of Female Sexual Dysfunction, 'female sexual arousal disorder', in the absence of evidence that the drug had any effect on stimulating arousal in men. Pfizer abandoned the effort in 2003 when clinical trials showed the drug had no effects on women. John Bancroft, director of the Kinsey Institute, in his critique of the trial stated: *"The recent history of the study of female sexual dysfunction is a classic example of starting with some preconceived, and nonevidence based diagnostic categorization for women's sexual dysfunction, based on the male model, and then requiring further research to be based on that structure. Increasingly it is becoming evident that women's sexual problems are not usefully conceptualized in that way.*" (36) Despite the trial results, *Viagra* continues to be prescribed off-label for women, a practice allowed by the FDA Modernization Act (1997), which permitted off-label prescribing and directto-consumer advertising. Procter & Gamble took over the reins from Pfizer when they began investing heavily in 2004 in a testosterone patch (brand name *Intrinsa*) to treat a new FSD entity, 'hypoactive sexual desire disorder' (HSDD). Given that low sexual desire is one of the most common sexual complaints that women report, finding a drug to stimulate desire might equal *Viagra's* financial payoff. Just as the alchemists of old tried to transform base metals into gold, the quest for love potions to transform indifference into passion and desire is an ancient one and the stuff of many stories.

Fetch me that flower; the herb I show'd thee once. The juice of it, on sleeping eyelids laid, Will make or man or women madly dote Upon the next live creature that it sees. (37)

Unfortunately for Proctor & Gamble, the FDA withheld its approval of *Intrinsa*, – lack of clinical significance and absence of long-term safety data were the reasons cited. Nevertheless, it is estimated that one-fifth of all testosterone products approved for men are actually written for women off-label. In another flagrant stab-in-thedark ploy similar to 'red' Viagra, the German pharmaceutical giant Boehringer Ingelheim sought approval for an experimental drug flibanserin that had failed in trials as an antidepressant to treat female HSDD. Finding evidence of significant harm, the FDA did not grant approval. HSDD remains a controversial diagnosis. Critics argue that it is not clear what hypoactive sexual desire disorder is, how it should be defined, and whether it needs treatment. But for the pharmaceutical industry, HSDD is still alive and well: in 2005 two dozen companies were known to be developing drugs to treat women for HSDD.

With the exception of PDE5 inhibitors, effective drug options for treating sexual problems as defined in the *DSM* are not available. This rather bleak situation is summarized in a recent text *Clinical Manual of Sexual Disorders* by two prominent psychiatrists

Solid evidence beyond case reports or case series for using these [medications] strategies is usually weak or nonexistent. The best

existing evidence supports the use of PDE5 inhibitors for erectile dysfunction and bupropion for low libido. (31)

Estrogen supplementation for lost genital sensitivity, reduced elasticity and vaginal lubrication, are sometimes effective in treating Genito/Pelvic Pain Disorder (pain during intercourse). Other types of pharmaceutical adjuncts remain investigational. The safety and effectiveness of testosterone supplementation for treating low sexual desire remains problematic and controversial.

On the other hand, there are many examples of medications with significant negative sexual effects, including anti-hypertensives, serotonergic anti-depressants, anti-convulsants, anti-psychotics, narcotics, anti-androgens, alcohol, cocaine, oral contraceptives and oral estrogen therapy.

Social causes – the unavoidable problems of living

Sex became very important in Europe in the 20th century, more important than religion and almost as important as money, and everyone wanted to have sexual intercourse in different ways and some men rubbed their sexual organ with cocaine to prolong their erection even though cocaine was banned in all circumstances. . And women wanted to have orgasm all the time and that made men nervous and they had problems with erections and tried various aphrodisiacs and attend psychoanalysis to discover where the problem lay, such as whether they might have suffered some childhood trauma that they were unaware of. (38)

Patrik Ourednik's dead-pan and droll description of sex in the 20th century may sound facetious and simplistic but it does serve to remind us that our sexual life, its pleasures and its problems, are quite often dependent on influences beyond our control. The sexual ethos of a given period in history can shape our sexual behavior and our perceptions of our sexual problems. The widespread sexual liberation that accompanied the arrival of the 20th century brought with it changing demands and expectations for both women and men, demands that have increased with time. Whereas in prior decades the sex-advice experts emphasized sexual moderation – for example, sexual intercourse once a week - the sex advice experts today recommend frequent orgasms. We live, to the dismay of many, in a highly eroticized society and we are continually bombarded by sexualized images. The Internet and print media are replete with information telling us how to increase and intensify our sexual pleasure. The cover of a recent issue of Cosmopolitan magazine announced 100 different ways to improve our sex life.

An active sexual life, generally meaning frequent intercourse and orgasms, appears to have become a necessary requirement for a happy and fulfilling life. Disinterest in sex, abstinence (for adults), and celibacy are now seen as the new deviancy. This new emphasis on sexual fulfillment at all ages has quite likely had an unintended consequence: increased anxiety and frustration when our expectations for sexual gratification are not fulfilled. It seems plausible that the increased focus on sexual fulfillment may account in part for findings from several population surveys during the last two decades indicating that sexual discontent is fairly prevalent.

In the social origins model, the nature of our sexual problems and discontent emerge from personal circumstances that in different ways lead to a disturbance or maladjustment in our sexual functioning. Sexual problems do not arise only or simply because of sexual organ difficulties, but also from complications or dilemmas in our lives. Although each life history is unique, the disturbances that affect sexual functioning fall into distinguishable patterns or classes that reveal the nature of the underlying problem. Proper therapeutic management then entails recognizing and understanding that the different natures of sexual problems necessitate different prognoses and therapies. Two management strategies that have a psychodynamic, life history, focus, rather than an exclusively biological one have been developed in the last decade.

The first, referred to as the *Perspectives* model considers sexual problems from four different but often overlapping perspectives – *Disease, Dimension, Behavior, and Life Story.* This model, described in Peter J. Fagan's *Sexual Disorders: Perspectives on Diagnosis and Treatment,* developed from his experiences in directing the Sexual Behaviors Consultation Unit at Johns Hopkins University, and uses the method of perspectives as applied to psychiatric disorders (McHugh and Slavney,

The Perspectives of Psychiatry, 1998) as the basis for classifying sexual problems. Simply put – the four perspectives are what a patient has (Disease), what the patient is (Dimension), what the patient does (Behavior), and what the patient encounters (Life Story). Examples of this approach appear in the section below.

The second more radical approach in that it dispenses with the *DSM* diagnostic categories (see Appendix 4) altogether, was proposed in the year 2000 by feminist clinicians and social scientists seeking a new framework and classification system for women's sexual problems. The original proposal focused on women's sexual problems because it was felt that the *DSM* diagnostic categories ignored the differences between the male and female personal experiences of sex and the inequalities related to women's social, political, and economic conditions. More recently, however, the New View approach has been extended to men's sexual problems as well. From a therapeutic point of view the New View considers that sexual problems can be separated into four categories of causes. No 'normal' format for women's or men's sexual response or experience exists, and sexual problems may arise from many areas of life, although they likely arise in order of likely prevalence as follows:

• Sexual problems due to sociocultural, political, or economic factors

• Sexual problems due to partner and relationship

• Sexual problems due to psychological factors

• Sexual problems due to physiological or medical factors

They are listed in this order also to suggest that interventions be considered in this order as well. This will ensure that educational interventions are always considered. As many researchers and clinicians have discovered, factual information about human sexuality that integrates social, psychological and biological material is largely unavailable to all but the well-educated and welltrained. Unfortunately, we have found, even the well educated and well-trained often magnify the role of biological variables and interventions and underestimate the role of social context and norms. (48)

Despite appearing formally different, the Perspectives and New

View methodologies are similar in that both require that the clinician/ psychotherapist try to understand the unique circumstances of the individual seeking counsel, while being aware of the many different conditions, including multiple sclerosis, major depression, chronic disease, alcoholism, and endometriosis, as well. A few examples: a man with a colostomy would almost invariably feel that the abdominal sac would be difficult for his partner to accept; a woman who has had a bilateral mastectomy will be concerned that the absence of her breasts or the scars would be unattractive to her partner; a man might be unsettled by what he regards as a very sexually aggressive female partner; a woman whose husband has been disabled may resent his inability to perform sexually as he did before; adult survivors of childhood sexual abuse may find it difficult to accept and enjoy sexual intimacy

Sexual discontent – personal vignettes

It is much more important to know what sort of a patient has a disease than what sort of a disease a patient has. *(Sir William Osler, Canadian Physician, 1849-1919)*

Our sexual tribulations, to paraphrase Tolstoy, are each unique and troubling in their own way. We shouldn't be too surprised, for we know that each life history is unpredictability unique. The sources and causes of our 'Love Melancholy' are many and diverse. We can get a sense of this complexity from the following personal vignettes, taken from case studies of three different sets of psychotherapists specializing in sexual problems. The guiding principle the therapists in these cases used are variations of the biopsychosocial model, that is, incorporating personal, familial, cultural and biological factors in addressing the problems presented by each patient. You will understand why William Osler's admonition to focus on the patient is particularly relevant when you read them.

Vignettes 1 – 9 are taken from case studies collected in (31)

Vignette 1: *Low sexual desire*

Patrick left the Roman Catholic priesthood and married several years later. During courtship and in the early months of marriage, he and Colleen had satisfying sexual activity weekly. They gradually settled into a pattern of monthly and, thereafter, less frequent sex. He explained eventually, "it was one thing to abandon my commitment to celibacy and another thing to have frequent sexual behavior. I still vaguely feel it is wrong for me, even thought I know it is not." (p. 165)

Comment: For men who choose celibacy for religious reasons, sexual desire is incompatible with moral purity. In Patrick's case, even after having left the priesthood, his moral reservations about sexual desire remain. Resolution of this inner conflict may not always be possible.

Vignette 2: *Low sexual drive*

Whitney worked in therapy individually and conjointly for over two years trying to understand and reverse his acquired HSDD (low sex drive). He consistently reported a complete absence of sexual drive manifestations and a marked aversion for sex with his wife or "anyone". One day, he casually reported that he had been masturbating once or twice a week for years while thinking about other women. Shocked, I said to Whitney, "Gee, I thought you said that you had no inclination to masturbate and felt that you could live the rest of your life without any sexual expression." "Did I say that?" Whitney asked. "Many times," his stunned wife quickly added. He replied, "Well, I am not dead. I don't have any desire to have sex with other women. That is morally wrong. I still can't bring my self to have any kind of sex with you. Maybe I just did not want to hurt you more than I have already done. I don't know." (p. 168)

Comment: In Whitney's case, it took some time for him to acknowledge the internal prohibitions in the manifestation of his desire. Resolution of this conflict may be very difficult.

Vignette 3: Low sexual drive

Ben and Betty were referred for marital and sexual therapy by their respective individual therapists. Both patients were being treated for depression with medication and individual psychotherapy. Betty's frequent jealous questioning Ben about his life outside of the marriage depressed and angered him. He explained his HSDD (low sexual desire) as being due to consistently low testosterone levels and his continued need for an SSRI (anti-depressant). After 2 years of infrequent marital therapy sessions, Betty discovered that Ben had been having an active sexual relationship with a associate at work. His desire for the associate was intense, and its frequency was whenever they could be together. Ben lied to his wife, individual and conjoint therapists, internist and endocrinologist before his wife's discovery of his ongoing sharing of genital photos with the other woman ended their marriage. To maintain the façade, Ben had allowed himself to undergo a liver biopsy to investigate his idiopathic hypogonadism (low testosterone of unknown origin). (p.165)

Comment: Not all men who complain of low sexual drive have low sexual drive.

Vignette 4: *Secret desires*

Amy and Adam had individual sessions and two conjoint ones before the reasons for his 3-year pattern of sexual avoidance and unreliable erections became clearer. In response to the clinician's failure to understand something that was said, the couple exchanged a long permissiongiving look at each other. Amy eventually said, "The problem began when I refused to continue to indulge his wish to have us both dress up in fulllength slips as a prelude to foreplay . . . I want to be with a man who wants to *be* a man, not one who wants to pretend that he is a woman!" (p.171)

Comment: Amy's displeasure in acquiescing to Adam's secret desire was their undoing.

Vignette 5: *Secret desires*

Ten years after being diagnosed and treated for a prolactin-secreting pituitary tumor, Charles, now in his mid-30s, returned to talk about entering psychotherapy. Bromocriptine returned his sexual drive manifestations to him, but his sexual life was not improved. He revealed that he had been too embarrassed a decade ago to reveal that he had long struggled with masochistic erotic imagery. He routinely thinks of being humiliated through bondage and domination by a woman. "I know where this comes from: my mother was an extremely impulsive, demeaning, critical woman who abused me until I was well into high school. I need to get beyond this because I am ashamed, and my new best–of–my-life partner wants nothing to do with this behavior. I don't want to spend my life masturbating to my imagery, occasionally sneaking off to a dominatrix, and lying to my partner about my low level of sexual interest. Can you help me?"

The clinician replied, " I usually try to help this problem by arranging individual psychotherapy." After discussing the patient's ability to pay, the doctor arranged a referral to low-fee psychotherapy with an experienced therapist who had in interest in sexual abuse and its consequences. The patient never called. (p.179)

Vignette 6: *Erectile problems*

George was 70 years old when he presented to his family doctor with a 4-year history of inability to attain his erection during lovemaking with his wife Carol, age 64. They had been married for 48 years. They had no relationship conflicts. His family doctor prescribed sildenafil (Viagra) with instructions on usage. . . He returned to his doctor 6 weeks later, reporting that no improvement had occurred in his erectile ability. He was referred to a urologist and underwent a thorough medical examination and extensive investigations. Penile arterial insufficiency was not evident. The urologist advised him to continue persevering with the sildenafil. After a further 3 months of using sildenafil, George still saw no improvement and returned to his family doctor, who referred him to our clinic.

Summary of marital history: no sexual experimentation; sexual intercourse on Saturday evening in the dark; George had never seen his wife's vulva; intercourse in missionary position which lasted no longer than 5 min; Carol never had orgasm, and often went immediately to the bathroom, and unknown to George, masturbated to orgasm. She mentioned this only when George was not present.

Comment: George and Carol were advised to learn to explore each other's bodies, find the pleasure points, see each other naked, and experiment. After 3 months: they were enjoying frequent sexual caressing and intercourse. Carol continued to be orgasmic in their sexual interactions. (p.234)

Vignette 7: *Delayed ejaculation*

Arthur is a 31-year-old plumber who has been married for 4 years to Angela, who accompanied him to his appointment. Arthur is a mentally and physically healthy man who enjoys life and has many friends. However, Arthur is convinced that he has delayed ejaculation and feels unhappy about it. Angela confirmed her husband's story, adding that she is not satisfied with their sex life because intercourse takes too much time. Angela reported that she always had difficulty achieving orgasms by self-stimulation of the clitoris and has rarely reached orgasm by coitus. She does not like self-stimulation. After being asked for more details about the way the couple is making love, Arthur reported that he usually has an ejaculation after about 15 min. In his previous relationship, a delay was never a problem, but Angela has repeatedly told him that she does not like his penile thrusting for such a long time. (p.275)

Comment: Ejaculation time of 15 minutes is statistically quite normal, but Angela who did not like such a long duration, convinced Arthur that he suffered from delayed ejaculation.

Vignette 9:

Bob, a 41-year-old clergyman, has been married for about 12 years. Bob reported his complaint in a very clear and technical way. Whatever he does while make love, he rarely ejaculates. Sometimes, with great effort, he has been able to ejaculate after a long period of masturbation, but he has never been able to ejaculate during coitus, even after 1 hour of frequent and vigorous thrusting. His wife, who accompanied Bob to his appointment, confirmed his story and added that she is very sorry for Bob that he cannot experience the pleasurable feelings of an ejaculation and associated orgasm. She has told Bob that she suffers from 2-3 days of vaginal pain after they sex and she asked him to seek medical treatment to be able to ejaculate sooner. (p.276)

Comment: In contrast to Arthur in **Vignette 8,** Bob suffers from a real and very severe ejaculatory disorder. The causes of the Bob's ejaculatory disorder are unknown, and effective drug treatment is not yet available.

Vignettes 10 – 17 are taken from (40)

Vignette 10: *Disease perspective*

Frank consulted the clinician for an evaluation of his premature ejaculation. His marriage of 12 years was stable, and the premature ejaculation had developed over the past 6 months. During the evaluation, he sweated profusely and seemed to be physically agitated. He was referred for a long overdue physical examination and was found to have hyperthyroidism. As the thyroid function was normalized with medication, the premature ejaculation resolved. (p.20)

Comment: The cause of the hyperthyroidism remains unknown, but its treatment led to resolution of Frank's sexual problem.

Vignette 11: *Disease perspective*

Ralph was a 45-year-old man who had enjoyed a 20-year marriage with his wife. Their 3 children, now in their teens, added no more that the usual amount of Sturm and Drang of adolescence to the household. Ralph had been in sales throughout his career and presently was making another shift in employment – this time to assume major responsibility for a national product line.

Ralph was in apparent good health, although slightly overweight. He drank one beer daily with his main meal and exercised infrequently. In their sexual life, Ralph and his wife had usually had intercourse about 3 times a month and neither had experienced sexual dysfunction – until recently. For the past several months, Ralph had noticed himself becoming less and less interested in sex. The frequency of intercourse had decreased, and he had not wanted to have sex for the past 2 months. Sexual thoughts and fantasies were absent. While he had masturbated on occasion in the past, this behavior was absent in the past 6 months. He noticed the he and his wife were not getting along as well as usual, and more frequently than in the past were "getting on each other's nerves".

Consultation with a physician: serum testosterone level test ordered because of suspicion of too much alcohol. Result: very low testosterone (explained the low sexual desire), but more remarkably, very high prolactin levels – hyperprolactinenmia due to benign pituitary tumor.

Bromocriptine and testosterone prescribed. After several months therapy, Ralph's problems resolved. (p.22)

Comment: Although Ralph's low sex desire might have been attributed to a combination of circumstances – aging, alcohol consumption, stress and work pressure – it was in fact due to low testosterone and high prolactin levels.

Vignette 12: *Dimension perspective*

The Dimension perspective does not focus on understanding the cause of the problem, but rather focuses on ways to change the behaviors that are problematic George and Millie had been happily married for 43 years when Millie was diagnosed with cancer. She was ill both with the cancer and with the effects of the chemotherapy for the next 2 years. During the last 2 months of her life, Millie was bed-bound, and George, having retired from his position as sales manager with a large industrial firm, was available to care for her 24 hours a day. Their love was a great support to them both, although they did not express it sexually during the last year because of the effects of the illness.

One year after Millie's death, George began to date. 6 months later he began a relationship with Grace, a woman who was a widow and with her husband, had been social friends with George and Millie. When they first began to express themselves sexually, George suffered from erectile problems. George sought therapy immediately, because he did not want anything to interfere with the new relationship with Grace An initial evaluation, he completed the NEO-PI-R, a personality inventory – this indicated that among other traits that George was high in Extraversion, Agreeableness (very high Altruism scale), and Conscientiousness. In therapy, he professed no guilt about "being unfaithful" to his deceased wife, and spoke gently about his relationship with Grace. Within 2 months, George was no longer experiencing erectile problems.

Comment: The curative factor appeared largely to have been the opportunity to talk about the new relationship in an accepting, non-judgmental environment. At last contact, George and Grace were thinking about marriage. (p.45)

Vignette 13: *Behavior perspective*

The Behavior perspective focuses on conditions that maintain the problematic behavior rather than on what may have started the behavior initially.

Andrew was a very successful stockbroker who had had a series of extramarital affairs with his female staff members. The most recent employee to become a target of his attention probably had a borderline personality structure that decompensated (al la Fatal Attraction) when Andrew could not meet all her demands for attention. Her phone call to his wife, informing her of their relationship, precipitated the consultation.

In talking about his family of origin, Andrew non-defensively described how he and his sibs engaged in sexual play and during adolescence had girlfriends and boyfriends in the home for sex. Both parents seemed to tolerate this behavior. Alcoholics, they were preoccupied with other matters. Andrew said his mother complaining to him about her poor sexual relationship with his father – clearly an emotional boundary violation of the mother-son relationship. The home had an atmosphere of his "free-floating' sexuality, quite in contrast to his cultural peers.

Comment: As Andrew made no emotional connection between his present pattern of sexual behavior with employees and his developmental influences. As therapy progressed, he became aware of these factors, but they remained of 'intellectual' interest only. Other more behavioral interventions were necessary to stop the behaviors. (p.82)

Vignette 14: *Behavior perspective*

Allan sought help for what he felt was a serious problem: his penis was too small to give his girlfriend adequate sexual pleasure. He added that this was her complaint also. Allan was quite insistent that he wanted a referral to a surgeon who specialized in penile augmentation. The treatment for Allan's 'small penis' consisted largely in not colluding with his speculation about augmentation surgery. This was accomplished by reinforcing every trace of ambivalence he had about the procedure. He was not referred to a urologist for the purpose of "proving' to him that his penis was not too small. Such authoritative decree is seldom curative.

Instead the therapist helped Allan critically observe the relationship with his girlfriend: her practice of attributing all sexual problems to his small penis; his inability to assert himself with her in all aspects of their relationship.

Comment: Allan and his girlfriend decided to end relationship. (p.82)

Vignette 15: *Life story perspective*

Harriet recalled that when she was 6 years old, her mother slapped her hands severely when she found her masturbating as she went to sleep. In response, Harriet had to promise to sleep with her hands outside the covers and was disciplined in the middle of the night should she be found with her hands under the covers. Now married, she came to the clinic to report persistent and recurrent genital pain whenever she attempted to have intercourse with her husband. (p.71)

Comment: The harsh punishment that Harriet suffered as a child made it difficult for her as an adult to integrate sexual pleasure into expressions of intimacy with her husband.

Vignette 16: *Life story perspective*

Megan was physically abused by both parents and by her stepfather when her mother remarried. To protect herself from these beatings, she would withdraw socially and attempt to become "invisible." At the time, the strategy was adaptive and reduced the number of times she was physically abused. Megan 'learned" that to avoid physical and emotional trauma, she would be quiet, obedient, and best of all, invisible. While this pattern of behavior was protective of her as a child, when she married a rather domineering man, Ronald, whom she thought would protect her, she continued to practice becoming invisible in times of potential disagreement. Her invisibility extended to her sexual intimacy with Ronald. She had no sexual desire for him; she wished to be left alone – and safe.

Comment: Megan "wanted to desire,' to be sexual with Ronald, but she just did not know how. Her adaptive learning how to avoid physical abuse by her parents was the same maladaptive learning that made her ignorant of how to be intimate with her husband. (p73)

Vignette 17: *Life story perspective*

Regina, single and 29 years old, was in therapy because of a pattern of casual sexual encounters that she knew was harmful to her. Because of the pattern, she was at risk for contracting a sexually transmitted disease, and she was unable to develop a lasting relationship with a man. She said she wanted marriage and children; but it was clear to her that her behaviors was saying the opposite.

Regina's life story: sexually abused by stepfather between ages of 11 and 14; abuse included sexual intercourse, she was so ashamed that she never told her mother or anyone else; abuse stopped when mother divorced stepfather. Teen year marked by several sexual relationships with young men; most were brief affairs; most were depersonalized and casual; two abortions, and she now had Herpes

Comment: In therapy, Regina came to understand that her present behavior in the light of her past experiences. The task of therapy was to construct with her the basis of a new narrative of what she as a woman could be with a man as a potential life partner. (p.109)

Vignettes 18 – 21 are taken from (41)

Vignette 18: *A woman beset by multiple life problems*

A 32-year-old Salvadoran married woman, a documented immigrant, works 40 hours cleaning houses, looks after her 2 children and her husband's aging mother, cares for the house, and does all the housework and cooking. She tells her family physician she has an urgent concern about sex. She reports that for the last few months, she has not been interested in having sexual relations and worries that her husband will seek sex elsewhere. Family history reveals that her mother died when she was young. She was raised by an older brother in whose home she was a servant. She was never sexually abused but felt neglected and poorly treated by her brother and sister-in-law. Further inquiry reveals that communication between her and her husband about sex or the relationship is minimal and he is not affectionate. Nevertheless, she finds him to be a good provider and good father. She has no interest in other partners or in divorce. She reports that although she used to become sexually aroused, she has never had orgasm. She takes oral contraceptives and wonders if they are the cause of her lack of interest. She does not feel depressed although sometimes she is tired for days on end, but she wonders if her husband could be depressed.

Comment: This patient is typical of the women from the multicultural population at the urban community health center where Dr. Lucy M. Candib, University of Massachusetts Medical School, Worcester, practices. Under a DSM-IV classification of women's sexual dysfunctions, this patient can be viewed as suffering from disorders of sexual desire, arousal, and orgasmic dysfunction. Oral contraceptives or depression may be contributing factors. Under the New View approach, her problems can be dissected in the following ways.

This woman faces many challenges that would negatively affect her sexual function. Her financial status alone will constrain her access to some therapeutic options. For example, sexual therapy or psychotherapy may not be covered by her medical insurance plan if she has one. She needs to be asked about her reading abilities, and hopefully she can obtain and read a copy of Nuestros Cuerpos, Nuestras Vidas (the Spanish version of Our Bodies, Ourselves) to give her some basic sexuality education. In addition, if she can read English well enough, the clinician might also recommend Latina Realities: Essays on Healing, Migration and Sexuality. Given what she has said about the long working hours that she cannot cut back on, she may not be able to regularly attend organized meetings or leave her employment to go to lengthy therapy appointments, it could be recommended to her that she join a relevant community support group to work on personal issues as a vehicle for gaining more awareness of dynamics that constrain her life and have a negative impact on her relationship with her husband. She will probably not know of any, so it would be useful for her clinician to have on hand a list of active community groups in the area. If she attends an urban community health center, it is possible that the center has programs on adult sexuality, and if so she should be encouraged to participate in one. It would be ideal if she could be involved in culturally relevant couples relationship therapy. The clinician should also ask her whether she thinks that her husband would be amenable to participating in such therapy. At a minimum, a community organization with a support group environment is indicated. She should be evaluated for depression and, if present, a treatment plan is indicated. She should be asked whether she thinks it might be realistically feasible for her to consider changing her contraceptive to something other than the pill to see if that makes a difference in her sexual response and affect.

Vignette 19: A Young Woman Unable to Achieve Orgasm During Intercourse

Melissa is a 21-year-old college senior from a liberal family who thinks she has a problem because she "can't come with penis-in-vagina sex", although she has no problem having orgasm with external stimulation, oral sex, or masturbation. She has been with the same partner for a year and had hopes that he would be "the one," but her partner feels dissatisfied that he can't "satisfy" her. She is worried that this will jeopardize their long-term relationship.

Comment: This young woman has described her problem clearly. However, she does lack information about human biology. She believes that because she cannot achieve orgasm through sexual intercourse there may be something wrong with her. She also seems to lack information about how gender roles influence men's and women's sexual expectations, beliefs, and behaviors. She is worried that her partner will reject her because she is unable to achieve orgasm through intercourse. This young couple seems to believe that an enduring relationship must be based on mutual satisfaction through sexual intercourse. They seem not to have been able to effectively discuss their sexual relationship. The patient needs to learn that many women are unable to achieve orgasm with intercourse and that there is nothing wrong with her. Her partner needs to know that he is not failing her by not being able to bring her to orgasm with intercourse. The clinician should ask this young woman whether she feels pressure from her boyfriend. Does she feel that she is a reasonably assertive person? Can she assert herself in this situation? Does she feel shame? Does she believe that her inability to achieve orgasm through intercourse is a "defect"? These are important questions for her to explore, perhaps with a therapist, as simple education about the facts are insufficient to address pressure, assertiveness, and feelings of shame.

The clinician can also recommend informative reading material.

Vignette 20: A Perimenopausal Woman Experiencing Pain With Intercourse

Alice is a 45-year-old woman who has recently been having pain during sex. Previously she had no pain but only enjoyed sex occasionally. She wonders if it is menopause, as she has been having hot flashes, although her periods are still regular. She denies problems with lubrication, but she does say that it hurts more if her husband enters her before she is ready. Further inquiry reveals that her husband has been laid off for a year and has been drinking excessively. They fight about his drinking, and sometimes when he comes back from the bar he makes her have sex when she does not want to. She denies "abuse" but admits that he calls her fat and ugly when he is drunk. Alice is not familiar with non-physically violent forms of sexual abuse, i.e., emotional and psychological abuse. She is being emotionally abused by her husband. She is bearing the brunt of his personal problems with unemployment and probably depression/anxiety about his job situation. As a couple, they are not confronting the reality of their present situation in a healthy manner. They are not able to communicate honestly with each other and therefore find it hard to work on a resolution that respects both of their present needs.

Comment: The clinician should ask Alice to describe a recent sexual episode and go through it step by step, pointing out how the situation, her feelings, and the interaction all preclude her arousal and result in pain. The clinician should ask her to brainstorm her options for dealing with the situation, and should also suggest she consider seeking counseling, preferably jointly with her husband. It would be helpful also to suggest that the patient's past history of limited enjoyment may have contributed to the present problem, and that this would be a good time for her to take some time to have a deeper and greater understanding of her sexual life. The clinician should be able to refer the patient to a therapist who has experience treating women in abusive relationships.

Vignette 21: A Busy Executive With Low Desire

Crystal is a 35-year-old married software engineer who is a team leader in a highly competitive company. She works 12-hour days and says she has no time for exercise or relaxation. Her husband is also an engineer. She has been trying to get pregnant for the past 8 months. They have been having scheduled intercourse on the 13th and 15th days of her regular cycle without success. She states that sex seems like work and she just wants to get it over with. When she married 5 years ago, her sex life was satisfying and she had no difficulty with interest or orgasm. She has heard that testosterone will increase her desire and asks for a prescription.

Comment: Top of Form

Bottom of Form

The couple needs to combine sex for pregnancy with sex for intimacy. They need to discuss their priorities in life and realize that trying to get pregnant is a high priority but that scheduled sex will have negative consequences on their intimacy. Testosterone is not approved for the treatment of low desire, and there is no information on its impact on fertility or pregnancy, so it is probably not a good idea to prescribe it. The clinician should make it clear that this is not just Crystal's problem. Couples therapy might be helpful, although if they can work together it might not be necessary. An infertility workup might be appropriate in several months.

Vignettes 22 – 25 taken from (42)

Vignette 22: A 59-Year-Old Man Diagnosed With Prostate Cancer at an Early Stage

Jerry is a 59-year-old gym teacher who was recently diagnosed with prostate cancer at an early stage. The urologists have presented the various options to Jerry and his wife Barbara, including surgery, radiation, or brachytherapy, along with information about the various risks of incontinence and loss of erections. Barbara thinks he should have the surgery and that a cure is the most important thing. Jerry can't imagine life with incontinence or impotence. He is sorry he agreed to have the prostate screening test, because he finds the choices intolerable. Barbara thinks he is afraid of the surgery and can't see why he doesn't want to go for the radical cure. She doesn't think sex is such a big thing and would rather have him alive. He doesn't think life will be worth living if he can't have sex, or if he needs to wear a diaper.

Comment: Barbara's attitude is common; studies show that men are more concerned about the sexual losses associated with aggressive treatment than their partners. Studies also show that incontinence can be a major and independent obstacle for sexual relations. Partners' lives are profoundly affected by the consequences of treatment decisions, so in addition to respecting issues of patient autonomy and disparate wishes for full information and collaboration, it is wise to help the couple to come to a mutual decision. An interview study on the effects of prostatism on wives for example, showed that men's urinary problems had extensive effects on wives' daily routines, travel, recreation, and social life. Matching patients and couples to "buddies" who have faced similar diagnostic and treatment situations can add knowledge of real-life coping strategies to the "facts" of diagnosis and treatment choice. Men with prostate cancer who resist attending larger groups may accept "buddy" referrals. In the New View approach, discussions with this couple would incorporate issues of sex education, cultural norms, relationship obligations, and psychological factors.

Vignette 23: A 45-Year-Old Married Man With Sexual Secrets and a Possible Alcohol Problem

Murray is a 45-year-old senior executive in an international firm who works 80 hours a week. He likes to come home to a couple of martinis. He sometimes has a few drinks at lunchtime over business deals. He travels a lot for business and has occasionally had casual sex on a business trip. He has never told his wife, Margaret, about these one-night stands, and she has never questioned him. He feels a bit guilty but maintains that he feels loyalty to his marriage and that these events don't matter. On the return from a particularly long trip, he loses his erection during sex with Margaret. He attributes it to fatigue, but the problem also occurs a couple of nights later. Margaret wonders if perhaps he is drinking "a bit too much"? He wonders if it is the routine of marital sex. On his next trip, he makes a point of picking up a young woman in a bar to test out his theory. He loses his erection again. He goes to his doctor looking for a sexuopharmaceutical.

Comment: The doctor should see this consultation as an opportunity to facilitate discussion and education about the effects of fatigue, alcohol, guilt, marital routines, and apprehension on erectile function. Murray has had a lot going on in his sex life, and this sexual "crisis" offers an opportunity to reflect on his sexual habits and their consequences. Murray's is a typical example of the ubiquity of sexual secrets in marriage. Margaret probably has some sexual concerns herself, and sexual counseling, while not betraying the couple's secrets, may be able to facilitate some substantial improvement in this couple's intimate relations. As to the efficacy of sildenafil or the other sexuopharmaceuticals -- if this patient's workup is negative (eg, normal morning erections and masturbatory function and no medical or medicinal risk factors), a prescription would not seem indicated. Margaret may not know about Murray's infidelity, but her suspicions may be aroused if he starts using sildenafil without her involvement in decision-making. With the New View approach, discussions with Murray would incorporate issues of gender roles, family obligations, quality of relationship, guilt and shame, and psychological perspectives on agerelated life changes.

Vignette 24: A 21-Year-Old College Junior's First Experience With Sexual Intercourse

Kent is a 21-year-old college junior who has been dating Marla seriously for 6 months. They have been moving more toward having intercourse, and the opportunity happens when Kent's roommate is away for the weekend. Kent has been concerned about whether he could have sex with a woman because he had several homosexual experiences in high school. When Marla and Kent start making out and removing their clothes, Kent is initially excited but then loses his erection. He comes to school health service for help, saying his friends have tried sexuopharmaceuticals and he thinks it might help him.

Comment: Since the FDA approved sildenafil in 1998 to treat erectile problems, there have been many news stories about its popularity as sexual "insurance" for men without medical problems, especially young single men. Most recently, a long *Washington Post* story focused on "impotence on campus" resulting from stress and the use of recreational drugs and alcohol. Prescriptions for men 18 to 45 years of age are the fastest-growing sildenafil segment. Apparently, many clinicians feel dispensing sexuopharmaceuticals is harmless, although one might wonder whether the issue is that they are fearful of "opening Pandora's box" if they refuse to write a prescription and instead insist on a discussion.

Kent might respond well to reassurance and the opportunity to briefly discuss his worries. If his morning and masturbatory erections are normal, the implications of this should be pointed out. Limited information might also include some statistics on the prevalence of adolescent sexual experimentation and the commonality of "beginners'" erectile insecurities. If Kent's sexual identity questions seem troubling, he certainly should be referred to the college counseling center where issues of sexual orientation are a common topic. A prescription for sildenafil does not seem indicated. With the New View approach, discussions with this young man would also incorporate issues of sex education, gender role norms and expectations, feelings about the body, concerns about sexual orientation and past experiences, and beliefs about self-worth and desirability.

Vignette 25: A 65-Year-Old Man With Diabetes and Hypertension and a New Relationship

Ronald is a 65-year-old man with dietcontrolled diabetes and hypertension controlled on medications. He is overweight. He has a strong family history of heart disease. He quit smoking a few years ago. He has been divorced for 15 years but has recently taken up with a new lady friend. He found on several occasions that he was unable to maintain an erection. He wonders if a *sexuopharmaceutical* would help.

Comment: Ronald needs a full medical workup to assess his cardiac and vascular function. He seems a good candidate for the PDE5 inhibitor erectogenic drugs. However, because of his potential for heart disease he might be given a nitrate drug in an emergency, thus the clinician must provide information about the dangers of this in combination with these sexuopharmaceuticals.

At the same time, Ronald is a good candidate for resources explaining that erectile function is not all there is to dating, intimacy, and sexual pleasure with his "new lady friend." Her questions, wishes and capacities need to be considered, and if she isn't present in this consultation, a referral for 1 or 2 sessions of sexual counseling might be in order. Ronald could benefit from reading a patientoriented sexuality books that emphasize pleasure and communication.

Because Ronald could easily have obtained sildenafil over the Internet, I would also want to know whether there is a "hidden" agenda for this medical consultation -- that is, that the consultation would give him permission to express worries and concerns that might not be apparent from his simple presenting question. With the New View approach, discussions with Ronald (and perhaps also with Ronald and his partner) would incorporate sex education and sexual enhancement issues, discussion of cultural norms about relationships and sexual activity, and any relevant psychological factors.

Vignette 26: *A Type 1 Diabetic Considering an Implant*

Tom and Harry are a gay couple married in Massachusetts. They have been together for 15 years and are committed to each other. Tom has type 1diabetes and has had retrograde ejaculation for many years. He now has almost complete loss of erection. He is thinking about a penile implant, but Harry is worried about the possible complications. He doesn't want Tom to do it to please him -- he loves him the way he is. Tom thinks Harry deserves a better sex life and thinks that a penile prosthesis would offer that to him.

Comment: This case requires that the practitioner know something about gay sexual mores, or at the very least, be comfortable exploring issues in some depth. Discussing the situation with both partners would be essential, beginning with background about how the couple's sexual relationship has evolved over the years. How have they been dealing with Tom's changing sexual function? If they've disengaged, then suddenly starting up again might be fraught with difficulty. What has their monogamy -nonmonogamy history been, and how would this implant affect this arrangement? Do they have desire for sex with each other now? The implant would only give Tom an erection and not affect sexual desire. Penile implants can be satisfactory, but they also can have mechanical and psychological consequences, so the motivation and flexibility of the couple has to be strong. In terms of the New View approach, discussions with this couple would incorporate issues of norms and expectations, individual differences, sex enhancement, and relationship obligations.

Complete List of Citations and Readings

Chapter 1   What is Sex Anyway?

(1) Margaret Atwood (1994) *The female body* In *Minding the Body*, ed. Patricia Foster. Anchor Books: New York

(2) G. Bell (1982) *The Masterpiece of Nature The evolution and genetics of sexuality.* University of California Press, Berkeley, CA

(3) Denis Roze (2012) Disentangling the benefits of sex *PLoS Biology* 10(5), 1-4

(4) Plato *Symposium The Dialogues of Plato* Tr. Benjamin Jowett. Encyclopedia Britannica, Inc.: Chicago, 1952

(5) J.F. Crow (2006) Age and sex effects on the human mutation rates: an old problem with new complexities *Journal of Radiation Research* 47, Suppl. B75 – B82

(6) Richard E. Michod (1995) *Eros and Evolution A Natural Philosophy of Sex* Helix Books: Reading, MA

R. Bellig and G. Stevens, Eds *The Evolution of Sex* Nobel Conference XXIII. (1988) Harper and Row, Publishers: San Francisco

J.F. Crow (1994) Advantages of sexual reproduction *Developmental Genetics* 15(3), 205- 213

J.F. Crow (1997) The high spontaneous mutation rate: Is it a health risk? *Proceedings of the National Academy of Sciences* (USA) **94(16)**, 8380-8386

Lynn Margulies and D. Sagan (1997). *What is Sex?* Simon and Schuster

Editions: New York.

Sarah P. Otto (2009) The evolutionary enigma of sex *The American Naturalist* 174, Suppl. S1 – S14

J. Maynard-Smith (1978) *The Evolution of Sex* Cambridge University Press: London

M. Ridley (1993) *The Red Queen. Sex and the Evolution of Human Nature* Macmillan Publishing Co.: New York

Joan Roughgarden (2004) *Evolution's Rainbow Diversity, Gender, and Sexuality in Nature and People.* University of California Press: Berkeley

Chapter 2   Rumination on Sex and Love

Citations and Readings

(1) Jean de la Fontaine, *L'Amour et la folie* (Cited in Jean-Claude Kaufman (2011) *The Curious History of Love* Polity Press: Cambridge, UK)

Tela Incantata

(2) Alexander Beckam (ca. 1200) The Secret History of Virgil, said to be based on a History by Gaius Asineous Pollo. Manuscript in Old Royal Library in the British Museum, edited and translated by Joannes Opsopeoeus Brettanus, 1996

(3) Robert Burton (1621) Anatomy of Melancholy, Partition 3, the Preface Published by the Exclassics Project, 2009 http://www.exclassics.com

An unbounded fabrication

(4) Marcus Aurelius *Meditations* 6.13, Cited in Garry Wills (2011) *Augustine's Confessions – The Biography of a Book,* p.60 Princeton University Press: Princeton, NJ

(5) James Joyce (1914) *Ulysses* The Modern Library: New York. p.717

(6) Wallace Shawn (2009) Is Sex Interesting? *Harper's Magazine,* August

2009

William Simon (2002) *Desire is a fuzzy matrix.* Invited lecture entitled "Human Sexuality – the Future of an Illusion, presented at the 25th Annual Meeting of the Academy of Sex Research in Stony Brook, NY in June 1999

Jean-Claude Kaufman (2011) The Curious History of Love Polity Press: Cambridge, UK

Sexual fantasy

(7) Pliny the Younger

(8) Helen S. Kaplan (1974 October) Friction and fantasy – no-nonsense therapy for sex malfunctions *Psychology* Today, p. 77-86

(9) Sigmund Freud (1962) *Creative writers and daydreaming* In J. Strachy *Sigmund Freud* (Vol. 9, pp 142-152) London: Hogarth. (Original work published 1908)

(10) Nancy Friday (1975) Forbidden Flowers Pocket Books: New York

(11) Nancy Friday (1973) My Secret Garden. Pocket Books, New York

(12) Jonathan Ames (2004) Wake up Sir! Scribner: New York

(13) Brett Kahr (2008) *Who's been sleeping in your head? The secret world of sexual fantasies* Basic Books: New York, p.21

(14) Eileen L. Zurbriggen and Megan R. Yost (2004) Power, desire, and pleasure in sexual fantasies *Journal of Sex Research* 41(3), 288-300

Jenny Bivona and Joseph Critelli (2009) 'The Nature of Women's Rape Fantasies: An Analysis of Prevalence, Frequency, and Contents', *Journal of Sex Research,* 46: 1, 33 — 45

S. Brownmiller (1975). *Against our will: Men, women, and rape.* Simon & Schuster: New York

Claire D. Coles and JoHanna Sharp (1984) Some sexual, personality, and demographic characteristics of women's readers of erotic romances *Archives of Sexual Behavior* 13(3), 187- 209

Joseph W. Critelli and Jenny M. Bivona (2008) Women's erotic rape fantasies: an evaluation of theory and research. *Journal of Sex Research* 45(1), 57-70

Sigmund Freud (1962) *Creative writers and daydreaming* In J. Strachy *Sigmund Freud* (Vol. 9, pp 142-152). London: Hogarth. (Original work published 1908)

E. B. Hariton (1973, March) The sexual fantasies of women *Psychology Today,* pp. 39-44

P.H. Hawley and William A. Hensley IV (2009) Social dominance and forceful submission fantasies: feminine pathology or power? *Journal of Sex Research* 46(6), 568-585

H. Hazen (1983) Endless Rapture. Scribner: New York

Harold Leitenberg and Kris Henning (1995) Sexual Fantasy *Psychological Bulletin* 117(3), 469-494

Why we have sex

(15) C. M. Meston and D. M. Buss (2007) Why humans have sex *Archives of Sexual Behavior* 36, 477-507

(16) F. A. Beach (1976) Cross-species comparisons and the human heritage *Archives of Sexual Behavior* 5, 469-485

(17) St. Augustine, *Confessions* 5:66, cited in Garry Wills (2011) *Augustine's Confessions: the Biography of a Book* Princeton University Press: Princeton, NJ

(18) Cited in Peter Brown (1988) *The Body and Society, Men, women and sexual renunciation in early Christianity* Columbia University Press: New York

(19) Cited in Thomas Cahill (1995) How the Irish Saved Civilization Nan A. Talese: New York. p.65

(20) Cited in Carl N. Degler (1974) What ought to be and what was: women's sexuality in the 19th century The American Historical Review 79(5), 1467-1490.

(21) Clelia Mosher Hygiene and Physiology of Women Mosher Papers, Stanford University Archives, cited in Degler

(22) Cited in Alan Soble (2009) A history of erotic philosophy *Journal of Sex Research* 46(2-3), 104- 120

(23) W. Shakespeare, *A Midsummer Night's Dream*

(24) Dante, *La Vita Nuova*

(25) William Shakespeare, *Romeo and Juliet,* 1.5

(26) Richard Burton

(27) Marcel Proust (1923) *Remembrance of Things Past II* p. 1075

(28) W.B. Yeats (1924) *Later Poems* MacMillan and Co.: London.

(29) Walter Benton (1943) *This Is My Beloved* Alfred A. Knopf: New York.

(30) Ossip Madelstam, *The Necklace,* tr Christian Wiman

(31) William Simon (2002). *Desire is a fuzzy matrix.* Invited lecture entitled "Human Sexuality – the Future of an Illusion", presented at the 25th Annual Meeting of the Academy of Sex Research in Stony Brook, NY in June 1999

(32) William Shakespeare, *Love Poems Let Me Not to the Marriage of True Minds*

(33) Claire Rayner (1977) The meaning of sex: a view from the agony column *Journal of Medical Ethics* 3, 157-159

E. Abbott (2000) *A History of Celibacy Scribner:* New York

Anders Ågmo (2007) *Functional and Dysfunctional Sexual Behavior A Synthesis of Neuroscience and Comparative Psychology* Academic Press: San Diego, C

Peter Brown (1988) *The Body and Society, Men, women and sexual renunciation in early Christianity* Columbia University Press: New York

V. L Bullough (1994) *Science in the Bedroom A history of sex research* Basic Books: New York

Vern L. Bullough and Bonnie Bullough (1991) Should Sex Have A Different Meaning For Humanists? *Humanism Today,* 140-160

Carl N. Degler (1974) What ought to be and what was: women's sexuality in the 19th century *The American Historical Review* 79(5), 1467-1490

L. Kipnis (2006) *The Female Thing Dirt, Sex, Envy, Vulnerability.* Pantheon Books: New York

C. M. Meston and D. M. Buss (2007) Why humans have sex. *Archives of Sexual Behavior* 36, 477-507

National Survey of Sexual Health and Behavior, Center for Sexual Health Promotion, Indiana University, (www.nationalsexstudy.indiana.edu/)

William Simon (2002) *Desire is a fuzzy matrix* Invited lecture entitled "Human Sexuality – the Future of an Illusion, presented at the 25th Annual Meeting of the Academy of Sex Research in Stony Brook, NY in June 1999

Alan Soble (2009) A history of erotic philosophy *Journal of Sex Research* 46(2-3), 104-120

Does sex have meaning?

(34) The Electronic Text Corpus of Sumerian Literature http://etcsl.orinst.ox.ac.uk. ETCSL translation: t.4.08.16

(35) ETCSL translation: t.4.08.04

(36) ETCSL translation: t.4.08.30

(37) cited in C. Miles and J. J. Norwich (1977) *Love in the Ancient World* Weidenfield and Nicolson: London.

(38) Vern L. Bullough and Bonnie Bullough (1991) Should Sex Have A Different

Meaning For Humanists? *Humanism Today,* p. 149

(39) St Jerome *On marriage and virginity,* from letter XXII (20) to Eustochium and from the treatise against Jovinian www.fordham.edu/halsall/source/jeromemarriage.asp

(40) Stephen Mitchell (2004) *Gilgamesh A new English version* Free Press: New York

(41) Bertrand Russell quotes: http://en.thinkexist.com/quotation199968.html

Alex Kucznski (2007) *Sweet Chastity* New York Times, March 25

Ancient Greece Mythology www.ancientgreece.com/s/mythology

Hanne Blank (2007) *Virgin The Untouched History.* Bloomsbery, NY

Catholic Encyclopedia *Nuns* www.catholic.org

D. Hanke (2004) Teleology: the explanation that bedevils biology In *Explanation: Styles of Explanation in Science.* J. Cornwell, edit. Oxford Press, pp 143-155

C. Miles and J. J. Norwich (1977) *Love in the Ancient World* Weidenfield and Nicolson: London

William Ramsay (1875) *Vestales* In William Smith *A Dictionary of Greek and Roman Antiquities,* pp 1189-1191 John Murray, London http://penelope.uchicago.edu/Thayer/E/home.html

Claire Rayner (1977) The meaning of sex: a view from the agony column *Journal of Medical Ethics* 3, 157-159

Alan Soble (2009) A history of erotic philosophy *Journal of Sex Research* 46(2-3), 104-120

Chapter 3   **Anatomy of Sex**

The iconic tissues

(1) John Moir (1620) *Anatomical Education in a Scottish University An Annotated Translation of the Lecture Notes of John Moir* (1975) ed. and trans. R. K. French, Equipress: Aberdeen

(2) Baldasar Heseler *Andreas Vesalius' First Public Anatomy at Bologna 1540: An Eyewitness Report (1959)* ed. and trans. Ruben Eriksson, Almqvist & Wiksells: Uppsala

(3) *Aristotle's Masterpiece or The Secrets of Generation* Author unknown, published in England around 1680, erroneously attributed to Aristotle. Banned in Britain until 1960

(4) Shalom Auslander (2007) *Foreskin's Lament: a Memoir* Riverhead Books: New York

(5) A. Frank (1997) *The Diary of a Young Girl:* the definitive edition; new translation. Ed. Otto A. Frank & Mirjan Pressler. Puffin: London

(6) Renaldo Colombo (1559) *De re anatomica.* Cited in T. Laqueur (1990) *Making Sex: Body and Gender from the Greeks to Freud* Harvard University Press: Cambridge, MA

(7) J. Sharp (1671) *A Midwives Guide* Cited in T. Laqueur (1990). *Making Sex: Body and Gender from the Greeks to Freud* Harvard University Press: Cambridge, MA

(8) N. Culpepper (1675) *A dictionary for midwives.* Cited in T. Laqueur (1990). *Making Sex: Body and Gender from the Greeks to Freud* Harvard University Press: Cambridge, MA

(9) Catherine Blackledge (2003) *The Story of V: Opening Pandora's Box* Weidenfeld & Nicholson: London

(10) Erica Jong (1973) *At the edge of the body* Holt, Rinehardt, & Winston: New York

(11) Robert Burton (1671) *The Anatomy of Melancholy,* Partition 2 Published by the Exclassics Project, 2009 http://www.exclassics.com

(12) M. Yalom (1997) A History of the Breast Alfred A. Knopf: New York

D.M. Friedman (2001) *A Mind of its Own A Cultural History of the Penis* The Free Press: New York

Michael P. Goodman (2011) Female genital cosmetic and plastic surgery – a review *Journal of Sexual Medicine* 8, 1813-1825

W.J.G. Hellstrom (2008) Clinical applications of centrally acting agents in male sexual dysfunction *International Journal of Impotence Research* 20, S17-S23

Max Hirshkowitz and Markus H. Schmidt (2005) Sleep-related erections: clinical perspectives and neural mechanisms *Sleep Medicine Reviews* 9, 311-29

B. Kelly and C. Foster (2011) Should female genital cosmetic surgery and genital piercing be regarded ethically and legally as female genital mutilation? *BJOG* 119, 389-392

M. Koraim & R. Ammar (1965) *Female Circumcision and Sexual Desire* (Part I)

Complications of Female Circumcision (Part 2) Ein Shams University Press: Cairo.

E.O. Laumann (1999) The circumcision dilemma *Scientific American*, 68-73

H. Lightfoot-Klein (1989) The sexual experience and marital adjustment of genitally circumcised and infibulated females *Journal of Sex Research* 26, 375-392

U. Megafu (1983) Female ritual circumcision in Africa: an investigation of the presumed benefits among the Ibo of Nigeria *East African Medical Journal* 60, 793-800

Sarah W. Rodriquez (2007). Rethinking the history of female circumcision and clitoridectomy: American medicine and female sexuality in the late nineteenth century *Journal of the History of Medicine and Allied Sciences* 63(3), 323-347.

The sexual sensory apparatus

(13) W. Shakespeare *The Merchant of Venice, III, ii, 63*

(14) David J. Linden (2007) *The accidental mind. How brain evolution has given us love, memory, dreams, and god* Belknap Press: Harvard University, Cambridge, MA

(15) The Brain (#632) T*he poems of Emily Dickinson* (1955) edit. T.H. Johnson, Belknap: Cambridge, MA

(16) Cited in Heidi Ledford (2008) 'Monogamous' vole in love-rat shock Nature 451 (7 February), p617

(17) Mac E. Hadley (2005) Discovery that a melanocortin regulates sexual functions in male and female humans *Peptides* 26, 1687-89

(18) Leonardo da Vinci. K.S. Keele and C. Pedretti (eds) (1979) *Leonardo da Vinci: Corpus of the anatomical studies in the collection of Her Majesty the Queen at Windsor Castle* 72r, 3 vol Johnson Reprint/ Harcourt Brace Jovanovich: New York

(19) Cited in the Philadelphia Inquirer (2005) *Carnal Knowledge / Paralyzed women rediscover orgasms.* 11/07

V.L. Bullough (1994) *Science in the Bedroom A History of Sex Research* Basic Books: New York

W. H. Masters and V. E. Johnson (1966) *Human Sexual Response* Little, Brown & Company: Boston

C. Miles & J.J. Norwich (1997) *Love in the Ancient World* Weidenfield & Nicholson: London

The brain – does sex matter?

(20) Lise Eliot (2011) The trouble with sex differences *Neuron* 72, 895-898.

(21) L. Brizendine (2006) *The Female Brain* Morgan Road Books: New York, p. 8.

(22) T. M. Wizemann (2001) *Exploring the biological contributions to human health: does sex matter?* (ed. M. L. Pardue). National Academy,

Washington, D.C.

S. Baron-Cohen *et al.* (2005) Sex differences in the brain: implications for explaining autism Science 310, 819-823

Larry Cahill (2012) A half-truth is a whole lie: on the ncecessity of investigating sex influences in the brain *Endocrinology* 153(6), 2541-2543

C. Dennis (2004) The most important sexual organ Nature **427,** 390-392

P. A. Lawrence (2006) Men, women, and ghosts in science *PLoS Biology* **4(1),** 13-15

Margaret M. McCarthy et al. (2012) Sex differences in the brain: the not so inconvenient truth *The Journal of Neuroscience* 32(7), 2241- 2247

Chapter 4　　　　**Our Sexual Theater**

(1) Philip Larkin (1963) *Annus Mirabilis*

The coital drama

(2) J. Milne Chapman (1883) On masturbation as an etiological factor in the production of gynic diseases *American Journal of Obstetrics* 16, 454

(Cited in Carl N. Degler (1974) What ought to be and what was: women's sexuality in the 19th century *The American Historical Review* 79(5), 1467-1490)

(3) T. H. van de Velde (1965) originally published 1926 *Ideal Marriage Its physiology and technique* William Heinemann Medical Books: Westport

Anders Ågmo (2007) *Functional and Dysfunctional Sexual Behavior: A Synthesis of Neuroscience and Comparative Psychology* Academic Press: San Diego, CA.

Helen Kaplan (1979) *Disorders of Sexual Desire and other New Concepts and Techniques in Sex Therapy* Brunner/Hazel Publications: New York.

W.H Masters and V.E. Johnson (1966) Human Sexual Response Little, Brown, Lippincott Williams and Wilkins Publishers: Boston.

Desire / Arousal

(4) William Blake The Question Answer'd (1793) In Northrop Frye (ed) (1953) *Selected Poetry and Prose of William Blake* Random House: New York

(5) S. B. Levine (2003) The nature of sexual desire: a clinician's perspective *Archives of Sexual Behavior* 32, 279-285

(6) Cited in P. C. Regan and E. Berscheid (1999) *Lust: What we know about human sexual desire* Sage: Thousand Oaks, CA

(7) *DSM-IV-TR*, 2004

(8) Helen Kaplan (1979) *Disorders of Sexual Desire and other new concepts and techniques in sex therapy* Brunner/Hazel Publications: New York

(9) R. Basson *et* al (2004) Revised definitions of women's sexual dysfunction *Journal of Sexual Medicine* 1(1), 40-48

(10) Cited in Daniel Bergner (2009) What do women want? The New York Times Magazine, February 8, 2009

(11) Anders Ågmo (2011) On the intricate relationships between sexual motivation and arousal *Hormones & Behavior* 59, 681-688

(12) Walter Benton (1943) *This Is My Beloved* Alfred A. Knopf: New York

(13) Cited in Deborah Lutz (2011) *Pleasure Bound Victorian Sex Rebels and the New Eroticism* W. W. Norton & Co.: New York

(14) Robert Burton, *Anatomy of Melancholy*

(15) Cited in Tim Parks (2011) Dying Laughter *New York Review of Books,* November 24

(16) Cited in Amy Muise (2011) Women's Sex Blogs: Challenging Dominant Discourses of Heterosexual Desire *Feminism & Psychology* 21(3), 411-419

(17) William Shakespeare, *Venus and Adonis*

Anders Ågmo (2007) On the concept of sexual arousal: a simpler alternative *Hormones & Behavior* 53(2), 312-314

Anders Ågmo (2007) *Functional and Dysfunctional Sexual Behavior: A Synthesis of Neuroscience and Comparative Psychology* Academic Press: San Diego, CA

Stephanie Both, E. Everaerd, and E. Laan (2007) Desire emerges from excitement: a psychophysiological perspective on sexual motivation, in E. Janssen (ed) The Psychophysiology of Sex, pp. 327-39. Indiana University Press: Bloomington, IN Lori A. Brotto, Julia R. Heiman, and Deborah L. Tolman (2009) Narratives of desire in mid-age woman with and without arousal difficulties Journal of Sex Research 46(5), 387-398

John H. Gagnon (2004) *An Interpretation of Desire: Essays in the Study of Sexuality* University of Chicago Press: Chicago

C. Groneman (2000) *Nymphomania: A History.* W. W. Norton: New York.

Erick Janssen (2011) Sexual arousal in men: a review and conceptual analysis *Hormones & Behavior* 59, 708-716

Ellen Laan and Stephanie Both (2008) What makes women experience desire *Feminism & Psychology* 18(4), 505-514

R. J. Levin (2004) Sexual arousal and orgasm in subjects who experience forced or non-consensual sexual stimulation – a review *Journal of Clinical Forensic Medicine* 11, 82-88

S. B. Levine (2003) The nature of sexual desire: a clinician's perspective Archives of Sexual Behavior 32, 279-285

M. Meana (2010) Elucidating Women's (hetero)Sexual Desire: Definitional Challenges and Content Expansion *Journal of Sex Research* 47(2-3), 104-22

Amy Muise (2011) Women's Sex Blogs: Challenging Dominant Discourses of Heterosexual Desire *Feminism & Psychology* 21(3), 411-419

Paula Nicolson and Jennifer Burt (2003) What is 'normal' about women's (hetero)sexual desire and orgasm?: a report of an in-depth interview study *Social Science and Medicine* 57, 1735-1745

William Simon (2002) Desire is a fuzzy matrix Invited lecture entitled "Human Sexuality – the Future of an Illusion, presented at the 25th Annual Meeting of the Academy of Sex Research in Stony Brook, NY in June 1999

Kelly D. Suschinsky, Martin L. Lalumiere, and Meredith L. Chivers (2009) Sex differences in patterns of genital sexual arousal: measurement artifacts or true phenomena Archives of Sexual Behavior 38, 559-573.

Jill M. Wood, Patricia B. Koch, and Phyllis K. Mansfield (2006) Women's Sexual Desire: a feminist critique *The Journal of Sex Research* 43(3), 236-244

M. L. Chivers and J. M. Bailey (2005) A sex difference in features that elicit genital response *Biological Psychology* 79, 115-120

Orgasm

(18) D. F. Barber (1972) *Pornography and Society* Charles Skilton: London

(19) Thomas W. Laqueur (2003) *Solitary Sex: A Cultural History of Masturbation* Zone Books: New York

(20) Catharine Gallagher and Thomas Laqueur, edit. (1987) Orgasm, generation, and the politics of reproductive biology, *in The Making of the Modern Body:* Sex and Society in the 19th century University of California Press: Berkeley, CA

(21) Appollodorus, The Library 3.6.7

(22) Peter van Foreest (1653) *Observationem et Curationem ac Chirurgicarum Opera Omnia* Cited in Rachel P. Maines (1999) *The technology of orgasms: Hysteria, the vibrator, and women's sexual satisfaction* Johns Hopkins University Press: Baltimore

(23) Sigmund Freud (1905) Fragment of an analysis of a case of hysteria *Standard Edition* 7, 7-122

(24) Wilhelm Reich (1960) Selected Writings *An Introduction to Orgonomy* Farrar, Straus, and Giroux: New York

(25) Cited in Ariel Levy, Novelty Acts, *The New Yorker,* September 19, 2011

(26) Donald Hall After Love The New Yorker, December 11, 2006)

(27) Donald Symons (1979) *Evolution of Human Sexuality* Oxford University Press: New York

(28) Sharon Block (2006) *Rape and Sexual Power in Early America* University of North Carolina Press: Chapel Hill, NC

(29) Huntington Willard, cited by Maureen Dowd, *New York Times,* March 20, 2005

(30) C. M. Meston et al (2004) Women's orgasm *Annual Reviews of Sex Research* 15, 173-257.

(31) Cited in Paula Nicolson and Jennifer Burt (2003) What is 'normal' about women's (hetero)sexual desire and orgasm? a report of an in-depth interview study *Social Science and Medicine* 57, 1735-1745

(32) Cited in a book review P. W. Barlow (2005) in *Archives of Sexual Behavior* 34(3), 357-369 of 'O': *The Intimate History of the Orgasm* (2004) Jonathan Margolis. Century: London

(33) *The Poems of Emily Dickinson* (1983) Thomas H. Johnson (Ed) Harvard University Press: Cambridge, MA

Anders Ågmo (2007) *Functional and Dysfunctional Sexual Behavior: A Synthesis of Neuroscience and Comparative Psychology* Academic Press: San Diego, CA

M. Chia and M. Winn (1984) *Taoist secrets of love: cultivating male sexual energy.* Aurora Press: Santa Fe, NM

J.R. Georgidis and G. Holstege (2005) Human brain activation during sexual stimulation of the penis *Journal of Comparative Neurology* 493(1), 33-38

Robert King, Jay Belsky, Kenneth Mah and Yitzchak Binik (2010) Are there different types of female orgasm *Archives of Sexual Behavior,* published online 10 Aug. 2010

L. Kipnis (2006) The Female Thing. Dirt, Sex, Envy, Vulnerability Pantheon Books: New York Barry R. Komisaruk, Carlos Beyer-Flores, and Beverly Whipple (2006) *The Sceince of Orgasm* Johns Hopkins University Press: Baltimore, MD

Roy J. Levin (2009) Revisiting post-ejaculation refractory time – what we know and what we do not know in males and females *Journal of Sexual Medicine* 6, 2376-2389

Ariel Levy, Novelty Acts, *The New Yorker,* September 19, 2011

Elisabeth a. Lloyd (2005) *The Case of the Female Orgasm: Bias in the Science of Evolution* Harvard University Press: Cambridge, MA

K. Mah and Y. M. Binik (2001 The nature of human orgasm: a critical review of major trends *Clinical Psychology Review* 21(6), 823-856

C. M. Meston *et al* (2004) Women's orgasm *Annual Reviews of Sex Research* 15, 173-257

Jonathan Margolis (2004) *'O': The Intimate History of the Orgasm* Century: London Martin Portner (2009) The orgasmic mind *Scientific American*

V.S. Ramachandran and Sandra Blakeslee (1998) Phantoms of the Brain: Probing the Mysteries of the Human Mind Quill/William Morrow: New York.

Christopher Turner (2011) Adventures in the Orgasmatron How the Sexual Revolution Came to America Farrar, Straus & Giroux: New York

Madeline Vann (2011). Faking orgasms? Why do women do it www.everydayhealth.com.

Marlene Zuk (2006) The case of the female orgasm *Perspectives in Biology and Medicine* 49(2), 294-298

The one character play

(34) Cited in Alan Soble (2009) A history of erotic philosophy *Journal of Sex Research* 46(2-3), 104- 120

(35) Silverstein, C. (1984) The ethical and moral implications of sexual classification: A commentary *Journal of Homosexuality* 9(4), 29– 38

(36) Thomas W. Laqueur (2003) *Solitary Sex: A Cultural History of Masturbation* Zone Books: New York

(37) Daniel Mendelsohn (2008) 'As good as great poetry gets' *The New York Review of Books* 55(18), November 20

(38) Shalom Auslander (2007) *Foreskin's Lament: a memoir* Riverhead Books: New York

(39) Cited in John Studd (2007) A comparison of 19th century and current attitudes to female sexuality *Gynecological Endocrinology* 23(12), 673-681

(40) Krisha McCoy (2010) Self-stimulation isn't just for pleasure as women gel older. http://www.everydayhealth.com

Aniruddha Das (2007) Masturbation in the United States *Journal of Sex & Marital Therapy* 33, 301- 317

Frederick M. Hodges (2005) The antimasturbation crusade in antebellum American medicine *Journal of Sexual Medicine* 2, 722-731

Charita Mallants and Kristina Casteels (2008) Practical approach to childhood masturbation *European Journal of Pediatrics* 167, 1111-1117

Krisha McCoy (2010) Self-stimulation isn't just for pleasure as women gel older http://www.everydayhealth.com

Tiffany L. Meyer and Tina L. Cheng (2002) Unveiling the secrecy behind masturbation *Pediatrics Review* 23, 148-153.

Patrick Singy (2004) The history of masturbation: an essay review *Journal of the History of Medicine and Allied Sciences* 59(1), 112-121

Patrick Singy (2003) Friction of the genitals and secularization of morality *Journal of the History of Sexuality* 12(3), 345-364

Chapter 5   Erotic Preference and Gender Diversity

(1) John Milton (1667) *Paradise Lost* (ed. J. Leonard, 2000). Penguin Books: London.

What is normal?

(2) Jeremy Benthan (1789) *Introduction of the Principles of Morals and Legislation* (Cited in Amy Bloom (2002) Normal: *transsexual* CEOs, *cross-dressing cops, and hermaphrodites with attitude* Random House: New York

Amy Bloom (2002) *Normal: transsexual CEOs, cross-dressing cops, and hermaphrodites with attitude* Random House: New York

Vern L. Bullough (1976) *Sex, Society and History* Science History Publications: New York

Defining 'natural' (2008) *Nature* 452 (7188), April 10

Bert C Verstraete & Vernon Provencal (Ed) (2006) *Same-Sex Desire and Love in Greco-Roman Antiquity and in the Classical Tradition of the West* Huntington Park Press: New York

Claudia Lang and Ursula Kuhnle (2008) Intersexuality and Alternative Gender Categories in Non-Western *Cultures Hormone Research* 69, 240-250

C. Miles and J. J. Norwich (1977) *Love in the ancient world* Weidenfield and Nicolson: London.

Perceptions of ourselves

(3) J. N. Katz (1995) *The invention of heterosexuality* Dutton: New York

Anders Ågmo (2007) *Functional and Dysfunctional Sexual Behavior: A Synthesis of Neuroscience and Comparative Psychology* Academic Press: San Diego, CA.

M. Castells (1997) *The power of identity* Blackwell Publishers: Oxford.

J. N. Katz (1995) *The invention of heterosexuality* Dutton: New York

Laumann, E.O., *et al* (1994) *The social organization of sexuality: Sexual practices in the United States* University of Chicago Press: Chicago

Garret Keizer (2008) Turning away from Jesus: Gay rights and the war for the Episcopal Church *Harper's Magazine,* June, p39-50

Walter Bockting, Autumn Bemmer, Eli Coleman (2009) Gay and bisexuality identity development among female-to-male transsexuals in North America: emergence of a transgender sexuality *Archives of Sexual Behavior* 38, 688-701

John Boswell (1980) *Christianity, Social Tolerance, and Homosexuality.* University of Chicago Press: Chicago

Beatrice C. Green (2005) Homosexual signification: a moral construct in social contexts *Journal of Homosexuality* 49(2), 119-135

Juliet Richerts (2009) Bodies, pleasure and displeasure *Culture, Health & Sexuality* 11(3), 225-236

Sexual orientation/identity

(4) Claude Levi-Strauss, (1986) Parenthood Revisited, reprinted in *Harpers Magazine,* April 2013, pp 17-29, from lecture at Ishizaka Foundation Tokyo in *Anthropology Confronts the Problems of the Modern World Harvard University* Press: Cambridge, MA

(5) John Maynard Keynes (Cited in Tony Judt (2009) What is living and what is dead in social democracy *The New York Review of Books,* 56(20), p. 86

(6) David F. Greenberg (1988) *The Construction of Homosexuality* The University of Chicago Press, Chicago

(7) Summa Theologia, cited in John Boswell (1980) *Christianity, Social Tolerance,* and *Homosexuality* University of Chicago Press: Chicago.

(8) St. Augustine *Confessions* 4.6

(9) St. Augustine *Confessions* 3.5

(10) H. Longino (1990) *Science as Social Knowledge* Princeton University

Press: Princeton, NJ.

(11) Margaret Nichols (2008) Dreger on the Bailey controversy: Lost in the drama, missing the big picture *Archives of Sexual Behavior* 37, 476-480.

(12) (Robert DiGiacomo in "PhiladelphiaGay News" on December 12, 2005, cited in Madeline H Wyndzen (2008) A social psychology of a history of a snippet in the psychology of transgenderism *Archives of Sexual Behavior* 37, 498-502

(13) John H. Gagnon (2008) Is this a work of science? *Archives of Sexual Behavior* 37, 444-447

(14) 2009 Report of the American Psychological Association Task Force on Appropriate Therapeutic Responses to Sexual Orientation. www.apa.org/pi/lgbc/publications.

(15) Benedict Carey (2012) Psychiatry giant sorry for backing gay 'cure' *New York Times*, May 18

(16) 2012 Position Statement from the World Health Organization 'Cures' for an illness that does not exist, 17 May

(17) S.L. Jones and M.A. Yarhouse (2000) *Homosexuality: The use of scientific research in the church's moral debate* InterVarsity Press: Downers Grove, IL

(18) Moritz Goldstein, *Deutsch-Judischer Parnass* Anders Ågmo (2007) *Functional and Dysfunctional Sexual Behavior: A Synthesis of Neuroscience and Comparative Psychology* Academic Press: San Diego, CA

John Boswell (1980) *Christianity, Social Tolerance, and Homosexuality* University of Chicago Press: Chicago

Linda D. Garnets (2002) Sexual orientations in perspective *Cultural Diversity and Ethnic Minority* Psychology 8(2), 115-129

Kenneth A. Locke (2004) The Bible on homosexuality: exploring its meaning and authority *Journal of Homosexuality* 48(2), 125- 136

John Boswell (1994) *Same-sex unions in premodern Europe* Villard

Books: New York.

David F. Greenberg (1988) *The Construction of Homosexuality* The University of Chicago Press, Chicago

Vern L. Bullough (2002) (Ed) *Before Stonewall: Activists for Gay and Lesbian Rights in Historical Context* Harrington Park Press: New York.

William Armstrong Percy III (2005) Reconsiderations about Greek homosexualities *Journal of Homosexuality* 49(3/4), 13-61

J. Edgar Bauer (2005) On the nameless love and infinite sexualities: John Henry Mackay, Magnus Hirschfeld and the origins of the sexual emancipation movement *Journal of Homosexuality* 50(1), 1-26.

The search for causes

Louis Gooren (2006) Biology of human psychosexual differentiation *Hormones and Behavior* 50, 589-601

Melissa Hines (2006) Prenatal testosterone and gender-related behavior *European Journal of Endocrinology* 155, S115-S121.

Robert Epstein (2009) Do gays have a choice? *Scientific American* 63-69.

Peter A. Lee and Christopher P. Houk (2006) Lack of differences between males with or without perceived same sex attraction *Journal of Pediatric Endocrinology & Metabolism* 19, 115-119

Jane P. Sheldon, et al (2007) Beliefs about the etiology of homosexuality and about the ramifications of discovering its possible genetic origins *Journal of Homosexuality* 52(3/4), 111-151

Glenn Wilson and Qazi Rahman (2005) *Born Gay: the Psychobiology of Sex Orientation* Peter Owen Publishers, London

Reparative therapy

Christopher W. Blackwell (2008) Nursing implications in the application of conversion therapies on gay, lesbian, bisexual, and transgender clients *Issues in Mental Health Nursing* 29, 651-665

André P. Grace (2008) The charisma and deception of reparative therapies: science beds religion *Journal of Homosexuality* 55(4), 545-580

R.L Spitzer (2003) Can some gay men and lesbians change their sexual orientation? 200 participants reporting a change from homosexual to heterosexual orientation *Archives of Sexual Behavior*, 32(5), 403–417

Kenneth J. Zucker (2003) The politics and science of "reparative therapy" *Archives of Sexual Behavior* 32(5), 399-402

Report of the American Psychological Association Task Force on Appropriate Therapeutic Responses to Sexual Orientation www.apa.org/pi/lgbc/publications.

Exodus Global Alliance

www.exodusglobalalliance.org

Transgender

(19) Wislawa Szymborska, excerpt from poem HERE, cited in *Harper's*, July 2010, p.22 J. Meyerowitz (2002) *How Sex Changed: A History of Transsexuality in the U.S.* Harvard University Press: Cambridge, MA

Amy Bloom (2002) Normal: *transsexual CEOs, cross-dressing cops, and hermaphrodites with attitude* Random House: New York

Vern L. Bulllough (1975) Transsexualism in History *Archives of Sexual Behavior* 4, 561-511

G. Herdt (1996) (Ed) *Third Sex, Third Gender: Beyond Sexual Dimorphism in Culture and History* Zone Books: New York.

M. Wiesner-Hanks (2001) *Gender in History: New Perspectives on the Past.* Wiley-Blackwell: Malden, MA.

Vern L. Bullough (2007) Legitimizing Transsexualism *International Journal of Transgenderism* 10, 3-13.

Claudia Lang and Ursula Kuhnle (2008) Intersexuality and Alternative Gender Categories in Non-Western Cultures Hormone Research 69, 240-250

A perspective

(120) Vern L. Bullough (1987) A nineteenth century transsexual *Archives of Sexual Behavior* 16(1), 81-85.

(21) Walter Bockting, Autumn Benner, and Eli Coleman (2009) Gay and bisexual identity development among female-to-male transsexuals in North America: emergence of a transgender sexuality *Archives of Sexual Behavior* 38, 688-701

(22) Madeline H. Wyndzen (1998) Gender identity disorder case study or an autobiography of a transsexual psychology graduate student? All mixed up: A transgendered psychology professor's perspective on life, the psychology of gender, & "gender identity disorder". *Available: http://www.GenderPsychology.org/gid_case_study/*

The Transgender Spectrum

(23) Joanne M. Hall (2008) Tomboys: meanings, marginalization, and misunderstandings *Issues in Mental Health Nursing* 29, 555-565

(24) National Public Radio All Things Considered (2008) Two Families Grapple with Son's Gender Preferences NPR.org, May 7, 2008

(25) National Public Radio Alix Speigel (2008) Therapists on Gender Identity Issues in Kids NPR.org, May 7, 2008

(26) Holly Devor (1997) *FTM: Female-to-Male Transsexuals in Society* Indiana University Press: Bloominton & Indianapolis.

(27) National Public Radio Alix Spiegel (2008) Doctors on Puberty-Delaying Treatments NPR.org, May 8, 2008

(28) Vern L. Bullough (1975) Transsexualism in History *Archives of Sexual Behavior* 4(5), 561-571

(29) Vern L. Bullough (2007) Legitimizing Transsexualism *International Journal of Transgenderism* 10(1), 3-12

(30) P.R. McHugh (1995) Witches, multiple personalities and other psychiatric artifacts *Nature Medicine* 1, 110-114

S. Brill and R. Pepper (2008) *The transgender child: A handbook for families and professionals* Cleis Press: San Francisco, CA

Peggy T. Cohen-Kettenis and Friedemann Pfäfflin (2009) The *DSM* Diagnostic Criteria for Gender Identity Disorder in Adolescents and Adults *Archives of Sexual Behavior,* published on-line 17 September, 2009

Peggy T. Cohen-Kettenis, Henriette A. Delemarrevan de Waal, and Louis J. G. Gooren (2008) The treatment of adolescent transsexuals: changing insights *Journal of Sexual Medicine* 5, 1892-1897.

Arnold H Grossman & Anthony R. D'Augeilli (2006) Transgender youth: invisible and vulnerable http://www.haworthpress.com/web/JH

Kenneth J. Zucker (2008) On the "Natural History" of Gender Identity Disorder in Children *Journal of the Academy of Child Adolescent Psychiatry* 47, 1361-1362

NPR.org. Alix Spiegel (2008) Doctors on PubertyDelaying Treatments May 8, 2008

L. Feinberg (1996) *Transgender warriors:* Making History from Joan of Arc to RuPaul Beacon Press: Boston

Holly Devor (1997) *FTM: Female-to-Male Transsexuals in Society* Indiana University Press: Bloominton & Indianapolis

S. S. Ware (1998) *Seven women who shaped the American century* W. W. Norton: New York

Walter Bockting, Autumn Bemmer, Eli Coleman (2009) Gay and bisexuality identity development among female-to-male transsexuals in North America: emergence of a transgender sexuality *Archives of Sexual Behavior 38,* 688-701

W.O. Bockting (2008) Psychotherapy and the reallife experience: From gender dichotomy to gender diversity *Sexologies* 17, 211-224

S. Stone (1991) The empire strikes back: a posttranssexual manifesto In J. Epstein & K. Straub (Eds), *Body guards: The cultural politics of gender ambiguity* Routledge: New York

Femke Olyslager and Lynn Conway (2007) On the calculation of the prevalence of transsexualism Paper presented at the WPATH 20th international Symposium, Chicago, IL September, 2007

SRS

Griet De Cuypere and Herman Vercruysse Jr. (2009) Eligibility and readiness criteria for sex reassignment surgery: recommendations for revision on the WPATH *Standards of Care International Journal of Transgenderism* 11, 194- 205.

Michael Sohn and Hartmut A. G. Bosinski (2007) Gender identity disorders: diagnostic and surgical aspects *Journal of Sexual Medicine* 4, 1193-1208.

S. Winter (2009) Cultural considerations for the WPATH *Standards of Care:* the Asian perspective *International Journal of Transgenderism* 11, 19-41

Chapter 6   Our Disturbing Sexual Corridors

(1) **Emily Dickinson** #570 *The poems of Emily Dickinson* (1955) edit. T.H. Johnson, Belknap: Cambridge, MA

Our sexual corridors

(2) John H. Gagnon and William Simon (1967, edit). *Sexual Deviance.* Harper and Row: New York

Arousal in the margins

Less traveled byways

(3) Brett Kahr (2008) *Who's Been Sleeping in Your Head? The Secret World of Sexual Fantasies.* Basic Books: New York

(4) Vladimir Nabokov *Lolita*

(5) Cited in J. M. Coetzee (2006) Sleeping Beauty *The New York Review*

of Books 53(3), February 23, p.6

(6) Cited in Richard Tuch (2010) Murder on the mind: tyrannical power and other points along the perverse spectrum *International Journal of Psychoanalysis* 91, 141-162

Daniel Bergner (2009) *The Other Side of Desire.* HarperCollins: New York

Dinesh Bhugra, Dmitri Popelyuk, and Isabel McMullen (2010) Paraphilias across cultures: contexts and controversies *Journal of Sex Research* 47(2/3), 242-256

Anil Aggrawal (2009) Forsenic and Medico-legal Aspects of Sexual Crimes and Unusual Sexual Practices CRC Press: Boca Raton, LA

The paraphilias – the DSM classification

(7) M. Khan (1979) *Alienation in perversions* International UP: New York

(8) Cited in Kate Robertson (2009) Medical classics British *Medical Journal* 338;b140

(9) Cited in C. Moser and P.J. Kleinplatz (2005) *DSM*-IV-TR and the paraphilias: An argument for removal *Journal of Psychology and Human Sexuality* 17(3/4), 91-109

(10) Patricia A. Cross and Kim Matheson (2006) Understanding sadomasochism: an empirical examination of four perspectives *Journal of Homosexuality* 50(2/3), 133-156

Anil Aggrawal (2009) References to the paraphilias and sexual crimes in the Bible *Journal of Forensic and Legal Medicine* 16, 109-114

C. Scorolli et al. (2007) Relative prevalence of different fetishes *International Journal of Impotence Research* 19, 432-437

Sexual violence – an ancient scourge

(11) Emily Dickinson, #556 *The poems of Emily Dickinson* (1955) edit. T.H. Johnson, Belknap: Cambridge, MA

What price sex?

(12) World Health Organization (2002) World report on violence and health, Chapter 6. Sexual Violence 149-181 www.who.int/violenceinjury.../violenceworld

K.C. Basile *et al* (2007) Prevalence and characteristics of sexual violence victimization Violence and Victims 22(4), 43-448

P. Tjaden and N. Thoennnes (2006) Extent, nature, and consequences of rape victimization: Findings from the National Violence Against Women Survey Washington: US Department of Justice, Publication No. NCJ210346

Mary P. Koss et al (1994) The global health burden of rape *Psychology of Women's Quarterly* 18, 509-527

Rape

A moral injury

(13) Jean Hampton (1999) Defining wrong and defining rape In *A Most Detestable Crime New Philosophical Essays on Rape* K. Burgess-Jackson (edit) (2001) Oxford University Press: New York

(14) Susan Brownmiller (1975) *Against Our Will: Men, Women and Rape* Simon and Schuster: New York

(15) Sharon Block (2006) *Rape and Sexual Power in Early America* University of North Carolina Press: Chapel Hill, NC

(16) Kathleen Barry (1979) Female Sexual Slavery Prentice-Hall: Englewood Cliffs, NJ.

(17) Catharine A. MacKinnon (1989) *Towards a Feminist Theory of the State* Harvard University Press: Cambridge

Keith Burgess-Jackson, edit (2001) A Most Detestable Crime: New Philosophical Essays on Rape *The Philosophical Quarterly* 51(204)

Diane Johnson (1975) The War Between Men and Women *The New York Review of Books.* www.nybooks.com/articles/archives/1975/dec/11

The past is always with us

(18) Kathryn Gravdal (1992) *Chretien de Troyes, Gratian,* and *the Medieval Romance of Sexual Violence Signs* 17(3) (Spring, 1992), pp. 558-585

(19) Jennifer J. Thompson (2004) Accept this twofold consolation, you faint-hearted creatures": St. Augustine and contemporary definitions of rape *Studies in Media and Information Literacy Education* 4(3).http://www.utpress.utoronto.ca/journal/ejourn al/simile

(20) Corinne J. Saunders (1997) Classical Paradigms of Rape in the Middle Ages In *Rape in Antiquity*. Susan Deacy and Karen F. Pierce (edit) Duckworth: London

(21) Geoffrey Chaucer *The Legend of Good Women* Gerard NeCastro (ed and trans). eChaucer:http://www.umm.maine.edu/faculty/neca stro/chaucer

(22) Ovid, *Metamorphoses* 6. 574-78

(23) D. Wolfthal (1999) *Images of Rape: The 'Heroic' Tradition and Its Alternatives* Cambridge University Press: Cambridge, UK

Susan Deacy and Karen F. Pierce (edit, 1987) *Rape in Antiquity* Duckworth: London.

Germaine Greer (2001) Let's forget the rape shall we? *The Guardian* (1 June) .www.guardian.co.uk/books/2001/jun01/classics.ar ts

James C. Harris (2008) The suicide of Lucretia *Archives of General Psychiatry* 65(4), 374-375 Samantha Anne Banbury (2010) How Ignorance Perpetuates Sexual Assault Myths, Abuse, and Injustice *Journal of Sex Research* 47(5), 511 — 512

Can rape be understood?

(24) Louise du Toit (2009) *A Philosophical Investigation of Rape.* Routledge: New York

(25) S. Freud (1962) *Three contributions to the theory of sex.* E.P. Dutton: New York

(26) C. Paglia (1992) *Sex, Art, and American Culture.* Vintage Books: New York

(27) J. Bivona and J. Critelli (2009) The nature of women's rape fantasies: an analysis of prevalence, frequency, and content *Journal of Sex Research* 46(1), 33-45

(28) Steven Rose (1995) The rise of neurogenetic determinism *Nature* 373, 380-382

(29) D.D. Gilmore (1990) *Manhood in the Making:Cultural Concepts of Masculinity.* Yale University Press: New Haven, CT

(30) J. Stolenberg (1989) *Refusing to Be a Man: Essays on Sex and Justice.* Breiten Bush Books: Portland, OR

(31) H. Olsson (1984) The woman, the love, and the power, in K. Barry et al. (eds) *International Feminism:* Networking Against Female Sexual Slavery. International Tribune Center: New York

(32) Lawrence Kramer (1997). After the Love Death. Sexual Violence and the Making of Culture. University of California Press: Berkeley, CA

(33) Martha McCaughey (2008). *The Cavemen Mystique. Pop-Darwinism and the Debates over Sex, Violence, and Science.* Routledge: New York; p. 1

(34) Andrea Dworkin (1987) *Intercourse* The Free Press: New York

(35) W. H. Auden (1937) O *who can ever gaze his fill?*

(36) T. S. Eliot *Sweeney Agonistes*

(37) William Shakespeare *King Lear*

Barbara Ehrenreich (2000) How natural if rape? *Time* (31 January

Richard Parker and Peter Aggleton (edit. 2007) *Culture, Society and Sexuality,* second edition). Routledge: London and New York

Adrienne Rich (1982/1986) Compulsory heterosexuality and lesbian existence. In Richard Parker and Peter Aggleton (edit. 2007). *Culture, Society and Sexuality,* second edition). Routledge: London and New

York

P. Sanday (1981) The socio-cultural context of rape: a cross-cultural study. *Journal of Social Issues* 37(4), p. 5-27

D. Counts, J. Brown, and J. Campbell (eds) (1992) *Sanctions and Sanctuary.* Westwiew Press: Boulder, CO

Lori L. Heise (1995) Violence, sexuality, and women's lives. In Richard Parker and Peter Aggleton (edit. 2007). *Culture, Society and Sexuality,* second edition). Routledge: London and New York

D. Levinson (1989) *Violence in Cross-Cultural Perspective.* Sage Publishers: Newbury Park, CA

Hayden Herrera (1983) Frida: a biography of Frida Kahlo Harper & Row: New York

C. MacKinnon (1991) Does sexuality have a history. *Michigan Quarterly Review* 30(1), p. 1-11

Corinne J. Saunders (1997) Classical paradigms of rape in the Middle Ages. In *Rape in Antiquity,* Susan Deacy and Karen F. Pierce (edits,), Duckworth: London

Jean Hampton (1999) Defining Wrong and Defining Rape In *A Most Detestable Crime.* Keith Burgess-Jackson (edit) Oxford University Press: New York and Oxford

(38) Dante Alighieri *The Divine Comedy,* translator Clive James (2013) Liveright: New York

What then?

(39) W. B. Yeats, *What then?*

Child Sexual Abuse

Definition

(40) American Psychological Association (2001) 'Understanding Child Sexual Abuse: Education, Prevention, and Recovery: What is Child Sexual Abuse?' www.apa.org/releases/sexabuse/

Richard Green (2002) Is pedophilia a mental disorder? *Archives of Sexual Behavior* 31(6), 467- 471

(41) Sarah D. Goode (2009) *Understanding and Addressing Adult Sexual Attraction to Children. A Study of Paedophiles in Contemporary Society* Routledge: London and New York

(42) J. Levine (2002) *Harmful to minors: The perils of Protecting Children from Sex.* University of Minnesota Press: London and Minneapolis, MN

(43) Susan A. Clancy (2009) *The Trauma Myth* Basic Books: New York

R. Kempe and C. H. Kempe (1978) *Child Abuse.* Harvard University Press: Cambridge, MA

Historical perspective

(44) E. Olafson, D.L. Corwin, and R. S. Summit (1993) Modern History of Child Sexual Abuse Awareness: cycles of discovery and suppression *Child Abuse & Neglect* 17, 7-24

L. Bender and A. Blau (1937) The reaction of children sexual relations with adults. *American Journal of Orthopsychiatry* 7, 500-18, p. 514

Fercnczi, S. (1955) Confusion of tongues between adults and the child: The language of tenderness and passion. In M. Balint (ed) *Child sexual abuse awareness: Final contributions to the problems and methods of psychoanalysis.* The Hogarth Press: London

Kate Robertson (2009) Medical classics *British Medical Journal:* 338; b140

Florence Rush (1977) *Freud and the Sexual Abuse of Children*

Lynn Sacco (2009) Unspeakable: Father-daughter incest in American History The Johns Hopkins University Press: Baltimore, MD

Pedophilia

(45) Peer Briken, Andreas Hill, and Wolfgang Berner (2009) Abnormal attraction. *Scientific American.* www.SciAmMind.com. 76-81

(46) L. Berliner and J. Conte (1990) The process of victimization: the

victim's perspective. *Child Abuse and Neglect* 14, 29-40

Sarah D. Goode (2009) *Understanding and Addressing Adult Sexual Attraction to Children A Study of Paedophiles in Contemporary Society.* Routledge: London and New York

Pedophilia (2010) http://www.DSM5.or/ProposedRevisions/Pages/pr oposedrevisions

Stephen J. Clark (2006) Gay priests and other bogeymen *Journal of Homosexuality* 51(4), 1-13

David Finkelhor (2003) The legacy of the clergy abuse scandal *Child Abuse and Neglect* 27, 1225- 1229

Pessimism about Pedophilia (2010) *Harvard Mental Health Letter* 27(1), 1-4

Peter J. Fagan *et al* (2009) Pedophilia *Journal of the American Medical Association* 288 (19), 2458- 2465

E. Olafson, D.L. Corwin, and R. S. Summit (1993) Modern History of Child Sexual Abuse Awareness: cycles of discovery and suppression Child Abuse & Neglect 17, 7-24

Susan A. Clancy (2009) *The Trauma Myth Basic* Books: New York

Scope of CSA

(47) D. Spiegel (200) Suffer the children: long term effects of sexual abuse *Society* 4, 18-20

(48) D. Finkelhor (2009) The Prevention of Childhood Sexual Abuse *Future Child* 19(2), 169- 194

Jennifer J. Freyd, *et al* (2005) The science of child sexual abuse *Science* 308 (22 April), 501

George B. Palermo (2007) The mind of the sexual predator. *Current Opinion in Psychiatry* 20, 497- 500

Charles F. Johnson (2004) Child sexual abuse *The Lancet* 364, 462-470

Denis A. Hines and David Finkelhor (2007) Statutory sex crime relationships between juveniles and adults: a review of social scientific research *Aggression and Violent Behavior* 12, 300- 314

Karl Abraham (1927) The experiencing of sexual traumas as a form of sexual activity. In *Selected Papers of Karl Abraham* Hogarth Press: London

Susan A. Clancy (2009) *The Trauma Myth* Basic Books: New York

Debra Rose Wilson (2010) Health consequences of child sexual abuse *Perspectives in Psychiatric Care* 46(1), 56-64

Paul Bouvier (2003) Child sexual abuse: vicious circles of fate or paths to resilience? *The Lancet* 361 (8 February), 446-447

Kate Walsh, Michelle A. Fortier and David DiLillo (2010) Adult coping with child sexual abuse: a theoretical and empirical review *Aggression and Violent Behavior* 15, 1-13

Sandy K. Wertele (2009) Preventing Sexual abuse of children in the 21st century: preparing for challenges and opportunities *Journal of Child Sexual Abuse* 18, 1-18

George A. Bonnano (2005) Resilience in the face of potential trauma *Current Directions in Psychological Sciences* 14, 135-140

Chapter 7   **Sexual Discontent and its Origins**

The tragedy of the bedroom

(1) Leo Tolstoy, *Anna Karenina*

Richard Balon & Robert T. Segraves, edit. *Clinical Manual of Sexual Disorders* (2009). American Psychiatric Publishing Inc., Washington, D.C

E. O. Laumann *et al.* (2005) Sexual problems among women and men aged 40-80 yr: prevalence and correlates identified in the Global Study of Sexual Attitudes and Behaviors *International Journal of Impotence Research* 17, 39-57

Sexual discontent - a perspective

(2) Robert Burton (1621) *The Anatomy of Melancholy, Partition 2, Passions and Perturbations of the Mind* Published by the Exclassics Project, 2009 http://www.exclassics.com

Masculinity and its discontents

(3) Michel de Montaigne *Essays* Penguin Books 1993, p.42

(4) Paula Nicolson and Jennifer Burt (2003) What is 'normal' about woman's (hetero)sexual desire and orgasm?: a report of an in-depth interview study. *Social Science and Medicine* 57, 1735-45.

(5) Martial, Epigrams 11.46

(6) Angus McLaren (2007) *Impotence A Cultural History* University of Chicago Press: Chicago, p.97

(7) Ovid Amores 3.7- 6, p. 67 Edit A. D. Melville, 1999, Oxford, UK

(8) Cited in Emily Wentzell (2008) Imagining Impotence in America: From Men's Deeds to Men's Minds to *Viagra*. Michigan Discussions in Anthropology Midwest Junto for the History of Science New Directions in Medical Anthropology 17(1)

(9) Ernest Hemingway (1954) The Sun Also Rises

(10) Howard L. Harrod (2003) *An essay on desire Journal of the American Medical Association* 289(7), 813-814

(11) Mark Twain (1938) *Letters from the Earth,* edited by B. Devoto, p.40. Harper & Row, Publishers, New York

(12) Meika Loe (2004) Sex & the Senior Woman: Pleasure & Danger in the Viagra Era *Sexualities* 7(3), 303-326

(13) Kurt Vonnegut

Kamran Ahmed & Dinesh Bhugra (2004) The role of culture in sexual dysfunction

John Bancroft (2007) Sex and Aging *The New England Journal of*

Medicine 357, 8-10

Zoë L. Barnett, Sofia Robleda-Gomez & Nancy A. Pachana (2011) Viagra: *The little blue pill with big repercussions, Aging & Mental Health,* http://dx.doi.org/10.1080/13607863.2011.583622

Dinesh Bhugra and Padmal de Silva (1995) Sexual dysfunction and sex therapy: an historical perspective *International Journal of Psychiatry* 7, 159-166

Toni Colasanti and Neal King (2005) Firming the floppy penis: age, class, and gender relations in the lives of old men Men & Masculinities 8, 3-22

Scott Mendelson (2011) The Great Singapore Penis Panic: And the Future of American Mass Hysteria CreateSpace

The female also rises

(14) Elaine Pagels (2012) *Revelations: Visions, Prophecy, and Politics in the Book of Revelations*

(15) St Augustine Letters, #243

(16) Cited in Carl N. Degler (1974) What ought to be and what was: women's sexuality in the 19th century *The American Historical Review* 79(5), 1467-1490

(17) Shoshana Felman (1993). *What does a woman want? Reading and Sexual Difference* The Johns Hopkins University Press: Baltimore

(18) Rachel Mesch (2009) Housewife or Harlot? Sex and the Married Woman in Nineteenth Century France *Journal of the History of Sexuality* 18(1), 65-83

(19) H. Wright (1955, first published 1930). *The sex factor in marriage.* Williams and Norgate: London. Cited in Angel

(20) Cited in P. Cryle (2009) 'A terrible ordeal from every point of view': (not)managing female sexuality on the wedding night. *Journal of the History of Sexuality* 18, 44-64

(21) Sigmund Freud Letter to Marie Bonaparte, as quoted in Sigmund Freud: Life and Work (1955) by Ernest Jones, Vol.2, Pt.3, Chap 16

(22) Thomas Cahill (1995) *How the Irish Saved Civilization* Nan A. Talese: New York

(23) www.curemyanxiety.com/Husband-DoesntWant-Sex.htm

(24) Lisa Diamond (2009) *Sexual Fluidity: Understanding Women's Love and Desire*

(25) Ana A. Cavalheira, Lori A. Brotto, Isabel Leal

(2010) Women's motivations for sex: exploring the *DSM-IV* test revision criteria for hypoactive sexual disorder and female sexual arousal disorder *Journal of Sexual Medicine* 7, 1454-63

(26) Marta Meana (2010) Elucidating Women's (hetero)Sexual Desire: Definitional Challenges and Content Expansion Journal of Sex Research 47(2), 104-122

(27) Karen E. Sims and Marta Meana (2010) 'Why Did Passion Wane? A Qualitative Study of Married Women's Attributions for Declines in Sexual Desire', *Journal of Sex & Marital Therapy*, 36: 4, 360 - 380

(28) Cited in Daniel Bergner (2009) What do women want? *The New York Times,* 22 January

(29) Joyce Carol Oates, All She Knows, *The New Yorker*, May 16, 2011, p. 126; from Margaret Drabble, *A Success Story*

(30) Daniel Mendelsohn, *The New Yorker,* March 7, 2011, p.79. quotation taken from Theodore Fontane's novel *On Tangled Paths*

Katherine Angel (2010). The history of 'Female Sexual Dysfunction' as a mental disorder in the 20th century. *Current Opinion in Psychiatry* 23(6), 536-541.

Jill L. Bean (2002) Expressions of female sexuality *Journal of Sex & Marital Therapy* 28(2), 29-38

Jody R. Godfrey (2006) Toward optimal health: Sandra R. Leiblum,

Ph.D. discusses sexual dysfunction in women *Journal of Women's Health* 18(7), 815-817

C. A. Graham (2004) Turning on and turning off: A focus group study of the factors that affect women's sexual arousal *Archives of Sexual Behavior,* 33, 527-538

Erwin J. Haeberle (2007) A brief history of female sexuality Invited keynote lecture at the third conference of the Society for Scientific Study of Sexuality in Taiwan, Nov 11, 2007. (www2.huberlin.de/sexology/BIB/HistFemSEx.htm)

Graham Hart and Kaye Wellings (2002) Sexual behavior and its medicalization: in sickness and in health *British Medical Journal* 326 (15 April), 896-900

Meika Loe (2004) Sex & the Senior Woman: Pleasure & Danger in the Viagra Era *Sexualities* 7(3), 303-326

Kyle R. Stephenson and Cindy M. Meston (2010) When are sexual difficulties distressing for women? The selective protective value of intimate relationships *Journal of Sexual Medicine* 7, 3683- 3694

M. Stopes (1918) *Married love: a new contribution to the solution of sex difficulties.* AC Fifield: London

John Studd (2006) History of Female Sexuality A Comparison of 19th century and Current Attitudes to Female Sexuality A lecture to the London Medical Society in 2006 (www.studd.co.uk/sexuality.php)

John Studd and Anneliese Schwenkhagen (2009) The historical response to female sexuality Maturitas 63, 107-111

Leonore Tiefer (2006) Female sexual dysfunction: a case study of disease mongering and activist resistance *PLoS Medicine* 3(4), 0436-0440

Leonore Tiefer, Marny Hall, and Carol Tavris (2002) Beyond dysfunction: a new view of women's sexual problems *Journal of Sex & Marital Therapy* 28(s), 225-232

Leonore Tiefer (2007) Beneath the veneer: the troubled past and future of sexual medicine. Journal of Sex & Marital Therapy 33, 437-477

H. Wright (1955, first published 1930) *The sex factor in marriage.* Williams and Norgate: London Cited in Angel

Sexual discontent - origins

Biological causes

(40) Richard Balon & Robert T. Segraves, edit *Clinical Manual of Sexual Disorders* (2009) American Psychiatric Publishing Inc., Washington, D.C.

(41) Richard Balon (2008) The *DSM* criteria of sexual dysfunction: need for a change. *Journal of Sex & Marital Therapy* 34, 186-197

(42) Canadian Society for the Study of the Aging Male (2007) 'Failure to treat sexual dysfunction can pose a serious risk for aging males' (press release, 5 February, 2007)

(43) P Bracken and P Thomas (2005) Postpsychiatry: Mental Health in the Postmodern World Oxford University Press: Oxford, p. 179

(44) R.C. Rosen and M. P. O'Leary (1997) Proceedings of The Cape Cod Conference: Sexual Function Assessment in Clinical Trials. Hyannis, MA, 30-31 May 1997. *International Journal of Impotence Research* 10 (Supple 2), p.S1

(45) Cited in S. Mayor (2004) Pfizer will not apply for a licnese for sildenafil for women British Medical Journal 328, p.542

(46) William Shakespeare, *A Midsummer Night's Dream*

John Bancroft (2007) Sex and Aging *New England Journal of Medicine* 357, 820-822.

Toni Colasanti and Neal King (2005) Firming the floppy penis: age, class, and gender relations in the lives of old men Men & Masculinities 8, 3-22

M. Enserink (2005) Let's talk about sex – and drugs, Science 308,1578–80

Allen Frances (2011) Drug companies peddle female sexual dysfunction.

Psychiatric Times, 14 February

Irwin Goldstein (2010) In the end, "Sex is complicated" Journal of Sexual Medicine 4, 523- 525

J. Lexchin (2006) Bigger and better: How Pfizer redefined erectile dysfunction PloS Med 3 Barbara l. Marshall (2010) Science, medicine and virility: Surveillance 'sexy seniors' in the pharmaceutical imagination *Society of Health and Illness* 32(2), 211-224

S, Mayor (2004) Pfizer will not apply for a license for sildenafil for women British Medical Journal 328, 542-543

Ray Moynihan (2010) Drug for low sexual desire carries significant harms, FDA advisers find *British Medical Journal* 34(1), 341

R. Moynihan (2005) The marketing of a disease: female sexual dysfunction *British Medical journal* 330, 192-194

Ronald Swedloff and Christina Wang (2011) Testosterone treatment of older men – why are controversies created? *Journal of Clinical Endocrinology and Metabolism* 96(1), 62-65

John E. Morley (2007) The politics of testosterone Journal of Sexual Medicine 4, 554-557.

Leonore Tiefer (1999) The medicalization of sexuality: conceptual, normative and profession issues Annual Review Se Research 7, 252-282

L. Tiefer (2006) Female Sexual Dysfunction: a case study of disease mongering and activitst resistance *PLoS Medicine* 3(4), 0436-0440

Leonore Tiefer (2006) Female sexual dysfunction: a case study of disease mongering and activist resistance *PLoS Medicine* 3(4), 0436-0440

Leonore Tiefer (2006) The Viagra phenomenon *Sexualities* 9, 273-294

Viagra and erections: Do the benefits persist? (2003) Harvard Men's Health Watch, January (www.health.harvard.edu)

T. Zwillich (2004) FDDA rejects libido drug for women (www.webmd.com/content/article/97/104342.htm)

Social causes

(47) Patrik Ourednik (2005). *Europeana: a brief history of the 20th century.* Tr. Gerald Turner. Dalley Archive Press, p.48

(48) Medscape Urology 2006

Richard Balon & Robert T. Segraves, edit. *Clinical Manual of Sexual Disorders* (2009) American Psychiatric Publishing Inc., Washington, D.C.

Richard Balon (2008) The *DSM* criteria of sexual dysfunction: need for a change *Journal of Sex & Marital Therapy* 34, 186-197

Toni Colasanti and Neal King (2005) Firming the floppy penis: age, class, and gender relations in the lives of old men *Men & Masculinities* 8, 3-22

Peter J. Fagan (2004) *Sexual Disorders Perspectives on Diagnosis and Treatment* The Johns Hopkins University Press: Baltimore, p. 134

Paul H. McHugh (2005) Striving for Coherence Psychiatry's efforts over classification *Journal of the American Medical Association* 293, 2526-2528

P. R. McHugh and P. R. Slavney (1998) *The Perspectives in Psychiatry*, 2d ed. Johns Hopkins Unviersity Press: Baltimore

E. Kaschak and L. Tiefer (eds) *A New View of Women's Sexual Problems* The Haworth Press: New York

'New View' Approach to Men's Sexual Problems **(medscape.org/viewarticle/541364_15)**

Leonore Tiefer (2007) Beneath the veneer: the troubled past and future of sexual medicine *Journal of Sex & Maritcal Therapy* 33, 473-477

Leonore Tiefer, Marny Hall, and Carol Tavris (2002) Beyond dysfunction: a new view of women's sexual problems *Journal of Sex & Marital Therapy* 28(s), 225-232

Sexual discontent – personal vignettes

(49) Peter J. Fagan (2004) Sexual Disorders Perspectives on Diagnosis and Treatment The Johns Hopkins University Press: Baltimore, p. 134

(50) The *New View of Women's Sexual Problems*. Cases originally published in Lucy M. *Candib "A New View of Sexual Problems - A Family Physician's Response." Kaschak E, Tiefer L (eds). A New View of Women's Sexual Problems New York, NY: The Haworth Press; 2001:9-15. Reproduced with permission from Haworth Press*

(51) 'New View' Approach to Men's Sexual Problems (**medscape.org/ viewarticle/541364_15**)

L. Tiefer, M. Hall, & C. Travis (2002) Beyond dysfunction: a new view of women's sexual problems *Journal of Sex and Marital Therapy* 28(s) 225-232

www.ingramcontent.com/pod-product-compliance
Lightning Source LLC
Chambersburg PA
CBHW060858120626
46553CB00001B/132